Publication of this book was assisted by a grant from the McKnight Foundation to the University of Minnesota Press's program in the health sciences.

Anorexia Nervosa & Bulimia

Publications in the health sciences.

Anorexia Nervosa & Bulimia

DIAGNOSIS AND TREATMENT

JAMES E. MITCHELL, M.D., Editor

University of Minnesota
Continuing Medical Education
Volume 3

University of Minnesota Press
Minneapolis

Published by the University of Minnesota Press,
2037 University Avenue Southeast, Minneapolis, MN 55414
Printed in the United States of America

Library of Congress Cataloging in Publication Data
Main entry under title:

Anorexia nervosa and bulimia.
    (University of Minnesota continuing medical education;
v. 3) (Publications in the health sciences)
    Includes index.
    1. Anorexia nervosa.   2. Bulimarexia.   I. Mitchell,
James E. (James Edward), 1947–   II. Series.
III. Series: Publications in the health sciences. [DNLM:
1. Anorexia Nervosa—diagnosis.   2. Anorexia Nervosa—
therapy.   3. Appetite Disorders—diagnosis.   4. Appetite
Disorders—therapy.   W1 UN944T v.3 / WM 175 A61515]
RC552.A5A5754   1985   616.85'2   84-26933
ISBN 0-8166-1388-5

The University of Minnesota
is an equal-opportunity
educator and employer.

Contents

Preface

When I joined the faculty at the University of Minnesota in the late 1970s, Dr. Elke Eckert solicited my help in treating outpatients with eating disorders. For several years, she had been working with patients who had anorexia nervosa; but the clinic also began to see many patients with bulimia, who were binge-eating and inducing vomiting. Our search of the medical literature for information on this problem uncovered very little, despite the large number of patients we were seeing. Since that time, several groups of investigators, including our group at the University of Minnesota, began to study bulimia. Besides Dr. Eckert and myself, our group includes Dr. Dorothy Hatsukami and Dr. Richard Pyle.

We developed an eating disorders program with both clinical and research components. The program provides several services, including evaluation, inpatient and outpatient treatment, psychotherapy (group, individual, and family), pharmacotherapy, and dietary counseling. The separate parts of the program have been developed specifically for use with eating disorder patients. This clinical program now evaluates 8-10 patients each week, experiences about 500 patient visits each month, and coordinates the inpatient treatment of 8-15 eating disorder patients at any given time.

This book reflects the interests of this group of investigators. Our concern about the medical aspects of eating disorders is reflected in the emphasis on medical evaluation and treatment. We have been interested in pharmacological strategies for the treatment of eating disorders, as reflected in a separate chapter detailing this area of research. We have also increasingly utilized behavioral approaches—particularly cognitive behavioral approaches—in our treatment programs, and these strategies are stressed.

We have attempted two tasks that are not easily integrated: to present a thorough, scientifically rigorous review of the literature on eating disorders and to offer a readable book that will offer practical help to clinicians who work with these patients. The text was developed for a professional audience, and the language assumes some basic knowledge concerning medical science, behavioral psychology, and pharmacology.

Part 1 concerns diagnosis and clinical characteristics. The first two chapters provide an introduction to the topic. Since much more has been published about anorexia nervosa than bulimia, the anorexia nervosa review emphasizes recent publications. The introductory chapter about bulimia, on the other hand, surveys much of the available literature. Chapter 3 reviews medical considerations in anorexia nervosa and bulimia and details both the common and uncommon problems that can cause or result from these eating behaviors. Chapter 4 offers an overview of the relevant psychodynamic literature, as well as the clinical observations of the author; the emphasis is practical rather than theoretical.

Part 2 of the book is devoted to treatment. Chapter 5 deals with the behavioral aspects of therapy, and chapter 6 reviews the available psychopharmacological research. Chapters 7 and 8 offer comprehensive treatment models for these two disorders. Our experiences with our treatment programs are perhaps most obvious here.

Part 3 presents original research data. To understand anorexia nervosa and bulimia, we need first to understand what constitutes normal eating behavior—particularly in adolescence, when eating disorders usually originate. This research section reports the findings of a large, well-designed study of eating patterns that represents an important contribution to our knowledge in this area.

Several people deserve special thanks. The first is Kris Servin, who typed the numerous drafts of the chapters and whose skills with a word processor are paralleled by her consistent cooperation and patience. I would especially like to thank Sue Wickham, who served as an editorial assistant on the project and whose gifts with the English language and tenaciousness as an editor smoothed much of the jargon and abruptness from this work. Lastly, I would like to thank Dr. Johnson and Dr. Stuckey, who agreed to join our Minnesota group on the project and contribute to this book.

Minneapolis   James E. Mitchell, M.D.

Part 1

Diagnosis

tell what is

1

Characteristics of Anorexia Nervosa

Elke D. Eckert, M.D.

Anorexia nervosa is primarily a disorder of young women. The cardinal feature is a relentless pursuit of thinness, often leading to life-threatening weight loss. This pursuit of thinness becomes associated with intense fears about eating, gaining weight, and getting fat and with fear of loss of control over food intake. Typically, the disorder begins innocently: a young girl goes on a simple diet, but before long the diet is out of control.

Several methods are used to lose weight. First, high-calorie foods are eliminated from the diet; then other foods are systematically curtailed. Finally, only a few low-calorie food items remain in the diet. The girl may begin binge-eating and thereby validate her fear of loss of control over food intake, creating tremendous anxiety. She may immediately try to rid herself of this food by self-induced vomiting, by taking large doses of laxatives, or by exercising excessively. Often she learns all these behaviors. Before long she begins to look emaciated. Whereas at first she may have received praise for her weight loss, friends and family soon criticize her looks and try to get her to eat. The anorectic shuns advice—usually thinking others are trying to make her fat—and becomes more determined in her desire to lose weight. She is usually unaware of her extreme thinness; even if she recognizes it, however, her intense fears about getting fat prevent her from changing the anorectic behavior that has become dominant in her life.

This chapter considers the diagnostic criteria, clinical characteristics, demographics and epidemiology, etiological considerations, associated psychiatric problems, and outcome in anorexia nervosa. Physical symptoms and medical complications of the disorder are discussed in chapter 3.

3

Diagnostic Criteria

Preoccupation with dieting and weight control has become endemic among young women in Western culture. In 1971, Nylander[1] proposed that the classical cases of anorexia nervosa occur at an extreme point in a continuum of eating problems associated with this cultural preoccupation. Controversy continues about the point on this continuum where anorexia nervosa begins and normal weight preoccupation ends. There is as yet no agreement about the essential features of anorexia nervosa.

Although a variety of characteristics typify the disorder, a 1975 report by the Pathology of Eating group[2] identified three central features: 1) Severe self-inflicted weight loss behaviors: avoidance of foods considered to be fattening, excessive exercise, self-induced vomiting or laxative abuse; bouts of binge-eating may occur. 2) An endocrine disorder that manifests itself clinically in the female as amenorrhea. 3) A morbid fear of getting fat associated with a fear of being unable to control eating. These features are useful in trying to identify a patient with anorexia nervosa. Because they do not include a definition of the degree of weight loss, however, they make it difficult to assure comparability of cases, especially for research purposes. They also do not differentiate clearly between anorexia nervosa and the bulimic syndrome as recently described by DSM-III criteria.[3]

Another set of features are the Feighner diagnostic criteria for anorexia nervosa (table 1).[4] These criteria provide a useful summary of many of the chief characteristics of the disorder, but they are misleading and may be no more useful as diagnostic criteria than those of the Pathology of Eating group. For example, although they offer a definition of degree of weight loss, this definition presents its own difficulties. The criterion calls for 25% of weight loss from original weight, thus including persons who were markedly overweight at onset and who are still above normal weight after the loss. This criterion also excludes persons who are thin or still growing in height at illness onset who lose less than 25% of their original body weight, yet are still markedly underweight.

The use of Feighner criteria poses other problems. Because it is not uncommon to develop the disorder after age 25 or even 30,[5-10] the criterion of age onset prior to age 25 is too restrictive. Few investigators are currently using age as an exclusion criterion. The identification of anorexia (loss of appetite) as a criterion, with the accompanying weight loss, is also a problem. Although about 50% of anorexia nervosa patients at first claim to have no appetite,[11] under close questioning many will admit to having an appetite, except perhaps late in the illness when they are severely cachectic.[12] The anorectic's preoccupation with food and the frequent development of cooking as a hobby also suggest that hunger must be present.

Table 1. Feighner Diagnostic Criteria for Anorexia Nervosa

A. Age of onset prior to 25

B. Anorexia with accompanying loss of at least 25% of original body weight

C. Distorted, implacable attitude toward eating, food, or weight that overrides hunger, admonitions, reassurance, and threats, e.g.:

Denial of illness with failure to recognize nutritional needs
Apparent enjoyment in losing weight with overt manifestation that food refusal is a pleasurable indulgence
Desired body image of extreme thinness with overt evidence that it is rewarding to the patient to achieve and maintain this state
Unusual hoarding or handling of food

D. No known medical illness that could account for the anorexia and weight loss

E. No other known psychiatric disorder with particular reference to primary affective disorders, schizophrenia, obsessive-compulsive, and phobic neurosis (although it may appear phobic or obsessional, food refusal alone is assumed not to be sufficient to qualify for obsessive-compulsive or phobic disorder)

F. At least two of the following manifestations:

Amenorrhea
Lanugo
Bradycardia (persistent resting pulse of 60 or less)
Periods of overactivity
Episodes of bulimia
Vomiting (may be self-induced)

Source: Feighner, et al. Diagnostic criteria for use in psychiatric research. *Archives of General Psychiatry,* 26, p. 61.
For a diagnosis of anorexia nervosa, A through E are required.

The inclusion of amenorrhea as a diagnostic criterion raises other questions. Virtually all anorexia nervosa patients have amenorrhea. This finding may be attributable to the practice of many investigators of requiring its presence for a diagnosis. The Pathology of Eating group included it as an essential feature, but the Feighner criteria did not. Since amenorrhea occurs in up to one-third of anorexia nervosa patients before there is significant weight loss,[13,14] many people believe that it reflects early hypothalamic impairment and that amenorrhea should thus be included as a criterion. Others, however, believe that amenorrhea merely reflects the dieting and physical state of starvation[15] and (like other starvation effects) should not be included. Currently, the consensus of most investigators is that amenorrhea should be included in the diagnostic criteria.

The DSM-III diagnostic criteria[3] for anorexia nervosa (table 2), correct for several of the deficiencies in the other diagnostic schemes. They do not specify an age of onset, and the weight loss requirement takes growth in children into account. One major objection to these criteria, however, is

Table 2. DSM-III Diagnostic Criteria for Anorexia Nervosa

A. Intense fear of becoming obese, which does not diminish as weight loss progresses

B. Disturbance of body image, e.g., claiming to "feel fat" even when emaciated

C. Weight loss of at least 25% of original body weight or, if under 18 years of age, weight loss from original body weight plus projected weight gain expected from growth charts may be combined to make the 25%

D. Refusal to maintain body weight over a minimal normal weight for age and height

E. No known physical illness that would account for the weight loss

Source: American Psychiatric Association, *Diagnostic and statistical manual of mental disorders,* 3rd ed. (Washington, D.C.), p. 69.

the 25% weight loss requirement, which most investigators find too restrictive. Other signs of illness may be quite clear even without a 25% weight loss. The criterion "refusal to maintain body weight over a minimal normal weight for age and height" is sufficient for ensuring that the patient is below normal weight. Another objection to the DSM-III criteria is the omission of amenorrhea.

Researchers continue to disagree about adding psychological signs and symptoms to the existing diagnostic criteria. Bruch identified an "all-pervasive sense of ineffectiveness," body image disturbance of delusional proportions, and disturbance in the accuracy of perception or cognitive interpretation of stimuli arising within the body as three fundamental diagnostic signs.[16] Evidence to support her position is emerging. A recent study found that anorexia nervosa patients were distinguished from weight-preoccupied college and ballet students by significantly greater pathology on scales of the Eating Disorder Inventory assessing "ineffectiveness" and "lack of interoceptive awareness."[17]

Common Clinical Features

Denial or Failure to Acknowledge Illness

The failure of some patients to acknowledge their anorectic illness—their denial of illness—can be a stumbling block during the diagnosis and assessment of patients. They may fail to acknowledge their thinness, hunger, and fatigue and to recognize their nutritional needs. Because they don't perceive themselves as abnormal, they refuse help. This denial, which is considered a typical characteristic with diagnostic significance,[18] is included in the Feighner diagnostic criteria for anorexia nervosa. Failure to acknowledge illness is considered by some to be an early sign of the disorder.[19,20]

There is evidence that denial may be associated with greater severity of illness. For example, more denial of illness was associated with less weight gain during a 35-day treatment study of hospital anorectics.[21] In the same study, denial was associated with body size overestimation[22] and depression.[23]

Failure to acknowledge illness sometimes extends beyond the strictly anorectic issues to include psychological changes. Anorectic "deniers" rated themselves in a recent study as having significantly less neurotic and somatic complaints, being more self-defensive and socially extroverted, and being less psychologically disturbed when compared with anorectics who admitted their anorectic illness.[24]

Body Image Disturbance

One of the fundamental characteristics of anorexia nervosa is a disturbance in body image. Laseque[25] described this over a century ago in 1873:

> The patient when told that she cannot live upon an amount of food that would not support a young infant replies that it furnishes enough nourishment for her adding that *she is neither changed nor thinner.*

Bruch first recognized that body image disturbance was an essential characteristic of anorexia nervosa.[26] It is a DSM-III diagnostic criterion for anorexia nervosa, specifically described as "claiming to feel fat even when emaciated." Clinically, the anorectic patient claims that her body is larger than it really is. She seems unaware of her changed body proportions even though her body may appear totally starved. She may insist she looks just right, or "still fat." She may stubbornly insist she is not as thin as another anorectic who is as thin as or thinner than she; yet she will recognize the other anorectic as too thin. This misperception of the actual dimensions of her body may appear of delusional proportions.

In addition to this body size estimation disturbance, body image disturbance involves the anorectic's attitude toward her body. Self-loathing of her developing female body parts, such as the normal slight curve of stomach or rounding of hips or buttocks, is not necessarily the same as body size overestimation and should be carefully differentiated. The DSM-III criterion of disturbance of body image does not establish this difference clearly.

The manner of assessing body image disturbance, and the results of studies using various methods, have been controversial. Most experimental data have been obtained in an attempt to assess only one of the aspects of body image disturbance—the size estimation disturbance. Using various measurement devices (movable caliper technique, image marking methods, distorting photograph technique), anorectic patients have been found to vary in the amount of overestimation of the width of various parts (usually face, chest, waist, hips) and of body depth. In various studies, the mean overestimation has been between 12% and 59%.[22,27-29] In some patients, the overestimation is restricted to a particular part of the body such as the stomach or thighs; in others, it is a more general phenomenon. Some patients do not overestimate at all, and some even underestimate.[22,30]

It remains controversial whether this disturbance in body size estimation is limited to anorexia or whether a similar disturbance is seen in control populations. Some studies found that anorectics overestimate when compared with normal controls;[27,31,32] but many studies failed to find a difference between anorectics and control groups,[22,28,29,33,34] thus indicating that the tendency to overestimate cannot be considered a feature unique to anorexia nervosa.

Body size overestimation is significant in anorexia nervosa even though it is not unique to this population. In anorectics, it may indicate a greater severity of illness, may have value in predicting outcome, may relate to psychopathology, or may relate to specific subgroups of anorectics. In most studies where it predicted outcome, size overestimation was related to poor prognosis and less weight gain.[22,27,28,32,34,35] Patients who overestimated the most were also those that were the most malnourished,[22] were previous treatment failures,[22] professed a more pronounced loss of appetite,[22] had a greater tendency to deny their illness,[22] vomited,[34] showed greater psychosexual immaturity,[22] were more depressed,[23] and had more symptoms of anorexia nervosa as measured by the Eating Attitude Test.[36]

Hyperactivity

In contrast to starving normals who generally attempt to conserve energy and reduce their activities, anorectics are often inappropriately hyperactive in the face of emaciation. This hyperactivity was vividly described by Sir William Gull in 1874:[37]

> The patient complained of no pain, but was restless and active. This was in fact a striking expression of the nervous state, for it seemed hardly possible that a body so wasted could undergo the exercise which seemed agreeable.

Anorectic patients express this hyperactivity in various ways. They may intensify an already existing interest in a sport by pursuing it with a driven, almost obsessive quality. They may develop exercise programs with highly structured and ritualized routines. They may seem constantly busy, moving about restlessly until late into the night, almost never sitting down.

Although this hyperactivity is reported in variable frequency from 10% to 38% of patients during the acute illness,[38-41] it probably occurs more frequently. Many investigators may fail to note hyperactivity because patients and families rarely identify it as a problem. However, it is not generally present before the onset of the anorectic illness.[11]

Hyperactivity has been comparatively neglected in the literature. Perhaps because it is difficult to measure objectively, there are almost no systematic studies of it. Stunkard, using a pedometer, was able to show that anorectics walked an average of 6.9 miles per day compared with normal controls who walked 4.9 miles.[42] One study involving hospitalized anorectics found greater hyperactivity to be associated with greater weight gain,[43] a finding that seems paradoxical.

Fear of Becoming Obese

Crisp has described anorectics as suffering from a "weight phobia."[19] Regardless of the initial stimulus for dieting, weight gain begins to generate severe anxiety, whereas weight loss serves to reduce anxiety. Not only does the anorectic appear to have a phobia about her normal body weight, this fear appears to intensify as she becomes thinner. The anorectic often weighs herself daily or more frequently, becoming severely anxious if the scales read in excess of the previous weight.

In addition to this phobic attitude toward weight, the anorectic becomes secondarily phobic toward food. At first, high-carbohydrate foods are feared and hence deleted from the diet. Soon, more foods are systematically curtailed until only a few low-calorie foods such as vegetables, fruits, and salads remain in the diet. Food portions are also rigidly controlled, with a daily allotment of food that must not be exceeded. If it is, the anorectic suffers severe anxiety and imposes more rigorous control of food intake.

There is some controversy about whether anorexia nervosa can be considered a phobic illness. Salkind, Fincham, and Silverstone have argued against a precise association and have demonstrated minimal skin conductance changes in anorectic patients in response to the presentation of a series of stimuli related to food and weight.[44] The appropriateness of the phobic illness model requires further study.

Behavior Related to Eating

Anorectic patients are often reluctant to describe their symptoms, and they may minimize the anorectic behavior. They often become experts in devious food-related behavior. Because of family pressure to eat, they may slip food to the dog under the table or hide food in their napkins, which they later flush down the toilet or throw in the garbage. Many of the pathological behaviors occur in secret: hiding food, self-induced vomiting, laxative abuse, and binge-eating. Self-induced vomiting occurs in 28%-43%,[10,11,38,39,45-47] binge-eating in 10%-47%[10,11,38,39,46,47] and laxative abuse in very few to 58% of anorectic patients.[10,11,38,39,46,47]

Subgroups in Anorexia Nervosa

Attempts to delineate subgroups within the diagnosis of anorexia nervosa date back to 1919 when Janet[48] recognized two different anorectic personality types: obsessional and hysterical. Dally, in 1969,[5] again focusing on personality, described hysterical, obsessional, and mixed personality types within the anorectic population. Clinicians continue to be aware of the heterogeneity of personality disorders in anorectic patients, but as yet no meaningful classification and relationship of personality to treatment response and prognosis have been determined. One reason is the absence of valid or reliable personality assessment instruments.

Perhaps a more productive approach has been to base subgroups on behavioral characteristics. Clinical differences have been found between anorectic patients who restrict their food intake ("dieters") and those who lose weight through vomiting, laxative abuse, or diuretic abuse ("vomiters and purgers").[49,50] Several interesting differences have been shown. The dieters were more introverted on the Eysenck Personality Inventory. Both groups rated as highly obsessional on the Leighton Obsessional Inventory. The vomiters and purgers were believed to be more histrionic, and they were also more likely to have been overweight premorbidly and to have been sexually active. Another study, however, found no substantial personality or symptomatic differences between these two anorectic groups.[51]

Much recent interest has been focused on the subgroup of anorectics who binge-eat. In two large surveys of 105[46] and 141[47] anorectic patients, about half periodically resorted to binge-eating. These bulimic anorectic patients were characterized by self-induced vomiting and by abuse of laxatives and diuretics. They displayed various impulsive behaviors, such as alcohol abuse, stealing, and suicide attempts. They were more extroverted, but they manifested greater anxiety, guilt, depression, and interpersonal sensitivity and had more somatic complaints than anorectic patients who exclusively dieted to lose weight. In one of the studies,[47] a high frequency of obesity occurred in mothers of the bulimic anorectics. Bulimia has also been shown to be an indicator of poor prognosis in anorexia nervosa.[52] In a 1-year follow-up study of 40 anorectics,[53] those with bulimia were found to be a chaotic group with personality features of lying, "psychotic tendencies," and difficult interpersonal relationships.

They were also more preoccupied with somatic complaints than their counterparts who were exclusively dieters.

Starvation and Anorexia Nervosa

Starvation itself, whatever the cause, can lead to many of the symptoms regularly seen in anorexia nervosa, including changes in cognition, emotion, and physiology. A thorough understanding of starvation is therefore important.

The results of the Minnesota Study of Starvation done during World War II are instructive.[54,55] In this study, conscientious objectors were placed on a semistarvation diet for 6 months in order to study the psychological and biological effects of starvation. The results of this study provide particularly apt comparisons with the findings in anorexia nervosa because the subjects voluntarily "starved in the midst of plenty." Like anorexia nervosa patients, they became intensely preoccupied with food while losing interest in other things: they collected recipes, read cookbooks, dawdled over food, invented unusual food mixtures, spent an inordinate amount of time planning meals, and made food the chief topic of their conversations. They drank more tea, coffee, and other liquids and increased the frequency of such behaviors as smoking and gum chewing. They had colorful dreams of food. During subsequent weight gain, some individuals reported extreme hunger after completing a normal meal and some subjects developed binge-eating.

In the Minnesota study, psychological and personality changes appeared: irritability, anxiety, difficulty with concentration, social introversion, self-preoccupation, depression, mood lability, indecisiveness, obsessive thinking, and compulsive behavior. Food and other items were hoarded. Sleep became disturbed, and there was a loss of sexual interest.

These effects in starving normals make it obvious that the same characteristics in anorectics can be attributed to starvation alone. However, intense fears of food and weight gain, restless hyperactivity, body image distortion, and the ability to suppress hunger appear only in anorexia nervosa, not in starving normals.[56]

Anorexia nervosa patients with weight loss have a variety of physical and biological abnormalities, including a disturbance in hypothalamic-pituitary function.[57,58] For example, they have an "immature" 24-hour secretory pattern of serum gonadotropins resembling that found in normal pubertal or prepubertal girls.[59] This immature biological pattern is interesting when viewed in the context of one prevalent etiological theory: that anorexia nervosa results from fear of the responsibility and consequences of sexual maturation with consequent avoidance of a normal adolescent weight. Anorectic patients often appear quite regressed and immature psychologically. Perhaps this immature biological mechanism contributes in a complex interaction to the reinforcement of the immature psychological patterns.

Other symptoms of starvation reinforce anorectic illness and perpetuate it. For example, malnourished anorectics suffer from constipation and have been shown to have decreased gastric emptying.[60] This may be felt as "bloating" and a feeling of fullness after eating only small amounts of food. Anorectics interpret this as a signal that they are "fat," and they reinforce their dietary intentions.

Demographics and Epidemiology

Sex Distribution

Anorexia nervosa occurs predominantly in females.[19,20,61] Most authors indicate that between 4% and 10% of cases are males.[5,38,62-64] There is no definitive answer about the relative frequency of anorexia nervosa in males and females, however, because no direct population study has been done that includes both sexes. Many studies also exclude male patients because the relative infrequency of male anorectics would unnecessarily complicate statistical assessment.

Although earlier studies suggested that male anorectics are more often prepubertal than females,[20,65] most recent studies do not bear this out.[66-68] A recent study comparing anorexia nervosa in males and females indicated that male patients display the classical syndrome of anorexia nervosa.[68] The dietary pattern displayed by these males is remarkably similar to that of females. They show carbohydrate avoidance; and although binge-eating, vomiting, laxative abuse, and anxiety about eating in company are found marginally less often than in females, the frequencies in males lie within the range found in other studies of female patients. The male patients, however, may be more often hyperactive.[68]

Epidemiology

Although there is growing evidence that anorexia nervosa is increasing in frequency,[10,16,38,64,69-72] the true incidence and prevalence are still not known because of a lack of good epidemiological research in this area.[73] It appears that anorexia nervosa has become more common, although the greater public and medical awareness, caused in part by reports in the popular press and news media, may have increased case-finding. Most of the reports of increased frequency have been based on series of cases assembled by investigators interested in the disorder[10,16,38] or on psychiatric case registers[64,71] and are thus subject to bias.

The following data should be considered in the context of these restrictions. In 1970, Theander[10] described and followed 94 female anorectic patients in southern Sweden who had been diagnosed over a 30-year period. Using the total population of that region, he estimated the incidence of anorexia nervosa patients referred for psychiatric help at 0.24 per 100,000 population per year. Over the 30-year period, he found an increase from 1.1 to 5.8 new cases per year. In 1973, Kendall et al.[71] analyzed data from three psychiatric registers in northeast Scotland, England (southeast London), and the United States (Monroe County, New York). The average incidence varied from 0.37 per 100,000 population per year in Monroe County to 1.6 per 100,000 in northeast Scotland. In all three areas, the number of cases reported per year was increasing. The significance of the differences is hard to determine. Differences in diagnostic practices, referral patterns, and reporting could account for some of the discrepancy. In 1980, Jones et al.[64] used the Monroe County psychiatric case registry to investigate the incidence of anorexia nervosa over two time periods, 1960-69 and 1970-76. The results indicated that the number of cases almost doubled between the two periods, from 0.35 to 0.64 per 100,000. This increase was accounted for by the sharp increase in the number of females (but not males) with the disorder, particularly those aged 15 to 24.

Two studies have recently addressed the prevalence of anorexia nervosa in school populations. In 1971, Nylander[1] reported a prevalence of one severe case of anorexia nervosa per 155 school females surveyed. He also found that 10% of the females could be considered "mild" cases of anorexia nervosa. In 1976, Crisp, Palmer and Kalucy[74] surveyed nine populations of high school girls in England, including both public and private schools. They found anorexia nervosa to be more prevalent in the private than in the public schools, implying a social class factor. In the private schools, the prevalence was one severe case in every 200 girls. In those aged 16 and over, the prevalence was even higher—one severe case in every 100 girls. Although these figures are repeatedly cited, it must be remembered that they are based on a selected group of students (higher socioeconomic, high school age group) and cannot necessarily be applied to other populations.

Age of Onset

Anorexia nervosa is primarily an illness of adolescence. Mean age of onset has been reported between 16.6 and 18.3 years[10,38,39,75] In a recent large series of 105 anorectics, a bimodal distribution with ages of onset at 14.5 and 18 years was found.[76] Although the usual range of age of onset is 12 to 25 years, the disorder may begin in younger and in older ages. Theander[10] reported that 5.3% of his 94 female anorectic patients fell ill at age 12 or earlier. Frequency of onset after age 25 has been reported at 14%[38] and 30%.[77] There are also case reports of women developing the disorder after menopause[78,79] but in those cases one must be sure that the weight loss is not related to other disorders or that the anorectic illness does not represent an exacerbation of a previously missed eating disorder.

Etiological Considerations

The etiology of anorexia nervosa remains unknown, but most of the evidence suggests that the disorder is determined by relationships among various predisposing, precipitating, and perpetuating factors. Individual characteristics, familial factors, sociocultural patterns, stress factors, the starvation syndrome itself, and other physiological factors must be considered in each case.

Genetic Aspects

The role of heredity in anorexia nervosa is not at all clear. Theander[10] found an increased incidence of anorexia nervosa in the families of his 94 female patients. He calculated the morbidity risk of anorexia nervosa among sisters of the probands to be 6.6%. Studies of other large series of patients have also found an increased incidence of anorexia nervosa in family members.[9,11,39,66]

Twin studies in anorexia nervosa have largely been limited to case reports.[80-82] A recent review of this literature indicated that about 50% of 24 sets of monozygotic twins reported were concordant for the disorder.[83] Only a few dizygotic pairs have been reported, but the question of zygosity in many of the cases is in question. Moreover, it is thought that there may be underreporting of discordant cases. Adoptive studies are needed to tease out environmental from genetic factors, especially since it has been suggested that the process of "induction"[10] or "anorexia a deux"[84] may operate in families: the disorder in one family member may help precipitate the illness in another.

The largest study of twins with eating disorders to date involved 34 twin pairs and one set of triplets.[85] The study indicated that anorexia nervosa is more likely to affect both members of a twin pair if they are monozygotic. In discordant pairs, there is a trend toward the affected twin being disadvantaged from birth and having more perinatal complications. The affected twin in a discordant pair is also more likely to have been second to reach menarche and to be the less dominant. These interesting findings need further confirmation.

Family Pathology

There is great diversity of opinion about the effects of the family on anorexia nervosa. As early as 1873, Laseque[86] described striking family enmeshment and an adverse effect of the family on the patient. Several authors have described what they believe to be typical family interactional pathology. Bruch[20] found the parents of anorectics to be overprotective, overambitious, and preoccupied with outward appearances and success. They failed to establish a sense of autonomy in the anorectic child. Palazzoli[87] also found the parents to be overprotective and described the families as characteristically showing covert alliances, blame shifting, impaired communication, and poor conflict resolution. Minuchin et al.[88] have described anorectic families as "dysfunctional" and supportive of the somatic expression of emotional distress. The dysfunctional characteristics identified were enmeshment, overprotectiveness, lack of conflict resolution, and rigidity. They saw the anorectic's symptoms as a detour to avoid family or parental conflicts. In the absence of controlled studies investigating family interactional patterns, these reports must be considered speculative. Many of the family relationships described may merely reflect changes engendered by the starving anorectic child.

Some studies have reported "typical" personalities among parents of anorectics, with high frequencies of neurotic disturbances.[39,89,90] The mothers are often described as overcontrolling, intrusive, and domineering, and the fathers are described as passive and ineffectual.[90] Many studies failed to find any consistent pattern of personalities or neurotic traits, concluding that the level of emotional disturbance was the same as in families with other types of neurotic disorders.[5,10,63,77]

Recent attempts to delineate characteristics in the families of patients with anorexia nervosa using systematic assessments and control groups have been reported. Strober,[91] using a series of psychometric tests, found that parents of bulimic anorectics reported significantly higher levels of marital discord than did parents of nonbulimic anorectics. The family environment of bulimic anorectics was also characterized by significantly greater conflict and less cohesion. Garfinkel et al.,[92] using another series of psychometric tests, found that parents of anorectics were similar to a normal control group in their psychological functioning, with little parental psychopathology evident. On the Family Assessment Measure, the anorectic families reported increased pathology on several subscales (task accomplishment, role performance, communication, and affective expression). It was not possible to say whether these disturbances were part of the pathogenesis or resulted from the illness.

Much attention has recently been focused on findings that affective disorder may be increased in relatives of anorectics compared with controls and that the relatives of the bulimic subgroup may have a higher prevalence of psychopathology—specifically affective disorder and alcoholism—than the relatives of the nonbulimic subgroup. These findings are discussed later in this chapter.

The question of the importance of the family in the onset and perpetuation of anorexia nervosa requires much further research. Yager has recently written a good review of this area.[93]

Social and Cultural Aspects

Anorexia nervosa has been reported to predominate in the upper social classes.[9,20,74,94] In recent years, however, a shift to more equal distribution among the social classes has been described.[10,30] This finding can be explained by the hypothesis that anorexia nervosa is the product of culturally determined attitudes or behavior patterns, probably concerning food or sexuality, that were originally found only in middle class families but now are spreading through society. Until recently no reports of black anorectic patients existed, but a few reports of the disorder in blacks are now beginning to appear.[64,71]

Although anorexia nervosa is prevalent in Western society, it is rare in the developing countries.[95] This finding has not yet been satisfactorily explained.

In Western society, there appears to have been a shift in our cultural standards for feminine beauty toward a preference for a thinner size. Garner et al.[96] reviewed the height and weight data for the contestants and winners of the Miss America Pageant and the centerfolds from Playboy magazine over the last 20 years. All measurements of Playboy centerfold girls, except for height and waist, decreased significantly. Although in 1959 the average Playmate weighed 91% of average, in 1978 she weighed only 83.5% of average. Miss America Pageant contestants and winners have shown an average yearly decline in weight of 0.13 kg and 0.17 kg, respectively, since 1959. Since 1970, the winners have weighed significantly less, at 82.5% of average, than the other contestants. Garner et al. pointed out, however, that this emphasis on thinness is occurring in a society that is actually becoming heavier. Actuarial statistics indicate that the average female under 30 has become heavier over the last 20 years.[96] These findings demonstrate that the cultural pressure on women to be slim conflicts with biological realities. Bruch[97] has suggested that the cultural ideal of thinness particularly affects vulnerable adolescents who believe that weight control and thinness will lead to beauty and success and that the ideal indirectly helps precipitate the development of anorexia nervosa. This idea finds confirmation in the finding that the anorectic disorder is more common in women who must rigorously control their body shapes, such as models and ballerinas.[96,98,99] Garner et al.[96] compared the prevalence of anorexia nervosa in two different ballet schools, one that was highly competitive and one with lower performance expectations. Since there were twice as many cases of anorexia nervosa in the highly competitive school (7.6% compared with 3.8%), they concluded that competitiveness or high expectation is an additional significant factor in the development of anorexia nervosa.

The argument that social and cultural pressures increase the likelihood of developing anorexia nervosa is convincing. But since only a few of those at risk develop the disorder, other factors must contribute.

Premorbid Characteristics

There is considerable debate about the premorbid characteristics of anorectics. Although many people believe that all anorectics have deep-seated psychological problems, others point to great variability in the amount and type of psychological disturbance before the onset of illness. Anorectics have been described as well behaved, somewhat introverted and shy, with more "neurotic" disturbances than other children.[77] Many, however, are believed to have had normal childhood adjustments.[9] As part of a large study of 105 patients,[11] family members and patients were interviewed to assess predominant premorbid personality characteristics: "very well behaved" typified 56%; perfectionistic, 61%; and competitive and achieving, 61%. Their school performance was commensurate with their premorbid personality. Two-thirds had above-average performance in grade school and high school. These findings confirm those of other studies.[38,39,100]

Bruch[20] and Palazzoli[87] suggested that these children fail to establish a sense of autonomy and control over their lives and that they suffer from a paralyzing sense of ineffectiveness. They come to interpret thinness and starvation as the way to self-respecting identity. Crisp[19] suggests that a fear of growing up and assuming adult responsibilities is highly characteristic of anorectics, with starvation representing an avoidance of adolescent maturational changes and adult body weight. This psychodynamic theory has yet to be tested empirically.

Associated Psychiatric Problems

Affective Disorder

Evidence for an association between affective disorder and eating disorders is accumulating. One model is to view anorexia nervosa as an atypical affective disorder occurring in an adolescent female at a time in her life when body image issues are important.[101,102] Anorectic patients are often reported as depressed before the onset of anorectic illness, and they may be at an increased risk for affective disorder after the anorectic illness.[101-105] The proportion of patients showing depression during the acute illness varies from 35% to 85% in various studies.[10,77,103,105,106] As a group, anorectics are not as overtly depressed during the acute illness as patients with affective disorder.[23,104,107] Two open-trial studies have suggested that the antidepressant amitriptyline is effective in inducing weight gain and relieving depression in these patients.[108,109]

One uncontrolled[101] and two controlled[110,111] family studies have shown an association of affective disorder with anorexia nervosa. In the first controlled study,[110] 22% of the relatives of the 25 anorectic probands had a history of primary affective disorder, whereas only 10% of the relatives of controls had such histories. In the second study,[111] both major and minor affective disorder was significantly more frequent in the first-degree relatives of the 24 anorectic probands than in relatives of controls.

Biological markers recently reported for primary affective disorders, such as high plasma cortisol levels,[112] dexamethasone nonsuppression,[113] and low urinary 3-methoxy-4-hydroxyphenylglycol[114] also occur in anorectics,[115-120] although the abnormalities appear to be reversible with weight gain. An impaired growth hormone response[115,121,122] and an abnormal thyroid-stimulating hormone (TSH) response to thyrotropin-releasing hormone (TRH)[123-126] also occur both in depressed patients and in anorectics.

Alcoholism

Little attention has been given to alcoholism in anorectics and their relatives. Through the 1960s, only sporadic case reports of anorectics with alcoholism appeared.[66,77] In 1977, Cantwell et al. reported 23% of 26 anorectics used or abused alcohol at follow-up.[101] In 1979, in a large collaborative hospital study of 105 female anorectics, Eckert et al. found that 6.7% had well-documented alcoholism.[127] This is a high frequency considering the youth of this population and the fact that the lifelong expectancy for alcoholism in women has been reported to be 1%.[128] Another interesting finding in this study was the association of particular anorectic characteristics with alcohol problems. Anorectics with alcohol problems were more likely to self-induce vomiting, have a greater frequency of bulimia, exhibit kleptomania, have a higher number of previous hospitalizations for the anorectic illness, and have a family history of depression and alcoholism. The authors concluded that anorectics with alcohol problems probably belong to a poor prognostic subgroup of anorexia nervosa.

Several studies have been done examining the frequency of alcoholism in the families of anorectics. Halmi and Loney found that 13% of the fathers and 2% of the mothers of their 94 anorectics had well-documented alcoholism.[129] Cantwell et al.[101] reported that 15% of the fathers and 12% of the mothers had alcohol abuse in a follow-up study of 26 anorectics. Eckert et al.[127] found that 17% of the fathers and 2% of the mothers of the 105 patient sample had well-documented alcoholism. There also appears to be an association between bulimia in anorectic patients and alcoholism in their families. Strober et al.[130] demonstrated this association by their finding that familial alcoholism and drug abuse disorders were significantly higher in bulimic anorectics than in nonbulimic anorectics. Alcoholism was three times more prevalent in fathers of bulimic anorectics than of nonbulimics (29% versus 9%) This suggests a strong association between bulimia in anorectics and familial risk for impulse disturbance.

Outcome and Prognosis

Outcome

Anorexia nervosa has a variable course and outcome. The course varies from spontaneous recovery without treatment to gradual deterioration resulting in death despite treatment. There may be recovery after one episode or a fluctuating pattern of weight gain followed by relapses. There are no consistent data concerning the effect of treatment on long-term outcome.

None of the follow-up studies reported to date has been free of methodological problems. Ideally, a follow-up study should include all cases in a given region, including all ages and both sexes, followed over a specific, long period of time. It should include cases that are not treated and cases treated by professionals in various settings. Data should be collected not only on anorectic outcome, but also on nonanorectic psychiatric outcome and life adjustment. Data should be collected using standardized instruments and procedures.

Given the existing methodological limitations, follow-up studies have varied in outcome.[4-7,9,10,20,38,40,41,52,70,77,90,94,100,101,131-144] Follow-up time varies considerably from 1[20,100,133-135,137] to 22[139] years. Despite treatment, the illness carries a considerable mortality. From 0%[101,132-134] to 21%[6] of anorectic patients die from the disorder—usually from complications of inanition or electrolyte disturbance, but also from suicide. Although most studies report a mortality rate below 10%,[5,7,9,20,41,100,131-135,138,142-144] several report a rate greater than 15%.[6,136,137,139] Two studies with the longest follow-up time reported the highest death rates.[6,139] Theander's study of 94 patients followed over 22 years is noteworthy because it indicates an increase in mortality rate over a longer period of follow-up (6.4% at 5 years after onset of illness, 11.7% at 10 years, and 18.1% by 30 years after onset of illness).[139] Suicide rates vary from 0% to 5.3%.[5,6,9,20,88,100,101,131-135,139] Theander found an increasing suicide rate over a longer period of follow-up, with the rate of suicide at 5 years after onset of illness being 1.1% and by 20 years after onset reaching 5.3%.[139] These findings suggest that many chronic anorectics do not live full-term lives but may succumb to their illness or to related problems.

Nutritional outcome varies, with 40%-80% recovering normal weight at follow-up.[7,9,10,40,94,131,132] The best results are often observed in patients whose illness began at an early age.[40,133,134,142,144] Body weight is still persistently below 75% of normal in 15%-25% of anorectics.[7,9,131,132] Obesity is uncommon, with 2%-7% being overweight by 15% or more at follow-up.[7,9,131,132] Although weight may be normal at follow-up, abnormal eating behavior may persist: only 33%-48% of patients eat normally at follow-up, while one-half still practice dietary restriction and avoid high-calorie foods.[7,9,132] Bulimia or compulsive overeating is present in 14%-50%,[5,7,94,101,131,133] while vomiting occurs in 10%-28%.[7,9,10,94,131,132] Laxative abuse for the purpose of losing weight is also common, occurring in 10%-33%.[7,9,131,132]

Normalization of menstrual periods is reported in 33%-66% at follow-up,[5,7,9,10,40,77,94,131,132,135,137] but menstrual irregularity is common.[7,9,40,77,94,131,137] Between 13% and 39% are still reported to be amenorrheic despite, in some cases, a return to normal weight.[7,9,10,40,135,138]

Psychiatric impairment, aside from purely anorectic symptoms, is also common at follow-up. Depressive symptoms were seen in 29%-45%.[7,9,10,101] Cantwell et al.[101] were the only investigators to use diagnostic criteria for depression. They found that 44% were diagnosed as having an affective disorder, based on Feighner criteria applied to patient self-reports and 46% based on reports by parents. Other common psychiatric problems at follow-up were obsessive-compulsive symptoms and personality traits (6%-44%)[5,7,9,10,101,137,142,144] and social phobias (24%-45%).[7,9,10] Drug dependence[94,101] and shoplifting[94,101] were also reported. Several studies indicated that psychiatric symptoms are more common and severe in anorectics who still have a low weight, have abnormal eating behavior, or are preoccupied with food and weight.[5,7,9,10,137]

Although sexual attitudes have been reported to be abnormal in anorectics, it has been difficult to assess these in follow-up studies. Two studies reported that 20% of patients clearly had abnormal sexual attitudes and behavior at follow-up.[7,9] Abnormal sexual attitudes and behavior have been related to chronic anorexia nervosa by several authors.[5,7,9,137] Marriage and childbearing are more common among recovered anorectics.[5,7,9,20,40,137,138]

Many anorectic patients remain poorly adjusted in the psychosocial area. Surprisingly, a high proportion (67%-100%) are employed fulltime,[7,9,10,40,77,101,137] and studies suggest that patients can maintain good work attendance despite low weight.[9,10,77] Some have a poor vocational adjustment, however.[131,135] Social relationships are more impaired if the patient remains anorectic.[5,7,9] Social phobia, or anxiety in meeting people, may be a problem even in patients who have recovered weight and menstrual function.[7] Family relationships are often impaired, especially if the patient remains anorectic.[5,7,9,94]

Three good reviews of follow-up studies in anorexia nervosa have recently been published by Hsu, Crisp, and Harding,[7] Schwartz and Thompson,[145] and Steinhausen and Glanville.[146]

Prognostic Indicators

Studies have consistently shown that certain characteristics of the anorectic illness can predict outcome. Most researchers associate a favorable prognosis with an early age of onset of illness and a less favorable outcome with a higher age of onset.[6,7,9,10,38,41,144] Poor outcome has also been associated with a longer duration of illness or with many previous hospitalizations;[7,9,41,131,137,140] a very low weight during illness;[5,7,9] and the presence of symptoms such as bulimia, vomiting, and laxative abuse.[6,7,10,38,131] Other less frequently mentioned factors predicting poor outcome are overestimation of one's body size,[70,131] premorbid difficulties in personality and family relations,[5,7,9] depressive and obsessive-compulsive symptoms,[52] high rates of physical complaints,[52] neuroticism,[5,41] psychological tests suggesting psychosis,[41] and lower social class.[7,52,131,140]

These prognostic factors are usually associated with long-term outcome. One systematic collaborative hospital study found that a variety of factors were related to weight change while anorectic patients were hospitalized during a 35-day treatment program.[43] Greater weight gain was associated with a greater degree of hyperactivity and exercising, less denial of illness, a greater expressed hunger or appetite, less psychosexual immaturity, less tendency to overestimate actual body size, and less sleep disturbance.

Conclusion

Many questions about the characteristics of anorexia nervosa remain unanswered, and clear diagnostic criteria are not yet agreed upon. Anorexia nervosa has yet to be differentiated from other eating disorders, particularly the bulimic syndrome and atypical eating disorders. Some of the common clinical features—denial or failure to acknowledge illness, hyperactivity, and body distortion—remain perplexing phenomena. The identification of subgroups within anorexia nervosa shows promise. Common factors appear to associate the bulimic subgroup of anorexia nervosa with the bulimia syndrome that will be described in chapter 2.

The true incidence and prevalence of anorexia nervosa are still unknown, but there is evidence that the disorder is increasing in frequency. The etiology of the disorder is probably a combination of predisposing, precipitating, and perpetuating factors. Of the associated psychiatric problems, the relationship between affective disorder and anorexia nervosa has received the most attention, although it needs further clarification. Finally, many questions remain concerning outcome and prognosis. Lacking a good outcome study that meets sound criteria, we are left with the crucial question: Are the treatments that we are using today really effective?

REFERENCES

1. Nylander, I. 1971. The feeling of being fat and dieting in a school population: Epidemiologic, interview investigation. *Acta Sociomed. Scand.* 3:17-26.
2. Garrow, J. S., A. H. Crisp, H. A. Jordan, J. E. Meyer, G. F. M. Russell, T. Silverstone, A. J. Stunkard, and T. B. Van Itallie. 1975. Pathology of eating, group report. In *Dahlem Konferenzen, Life Sciences Research Report 2,* ed. T. Silverstone. Berlin.
3. American Psychiatric Association. 1980. *Diagnostic and statistical manual of mental disorders* 3rd ed. Washington, D.C.
4. Feighner, J. P., E. Robins, S. B. Guze, R. A. Woodruff, Jr., G. Winokur, and R. Munoz. 1972. Diagnostic criteria for use in psychiatric research. *Arch. Gen. Psychiatry* 26:57-63.
5. Dally, P. J. 1969. *Anorexia nervosa.* New York: Grune and Stratton.
6. Halmi, K. A., G. Brodland and C. Rigas. 1975. A follow-up study of 79 patients with anorexia nervosa: An evaluation of prognostic factors and diagnostic criteria. *Life Hist. Res. Psychopathol.* 4:290-98.
7. Hsu, L. K., A. H. Crisp and B. Harding. 1979. Outcome of anorexia nervosa. *Lancet* 1:65-73.
8. Kellett, J., M. Trimble, and A. Thorley. 1976. Anorexia nervosa after menopause. *Br. J. Psychiatry* 128:555-58.
9. Morgan, H. G., and G. F. Russell. 1975. Value of family background in clinical features as predictors of long-term outcome in anorexia nervosa. *Psychol. Med.* 5:355-71.
10. Theander, S. 1970. Anorexia nervosa. *Acta Psychiat. Scand. Suppl.* 214.
11. Halmi, K. A., S. C. Goldberg, E. D. Eckert, R. Casper and J. M. Davis. 1977. Pretreatment evaluation in anorexia nervosa. In *Anorexia nervosa,* ed. R. A. Vigersky. New York: Raven Press.

12. Garfinkel, P. E. 1974. The perception of hunger and satiety in anorexia nervosa. *Psychol. Med.* 4:309-15.
13. Falk, J. R., and K. A. Halmi. 1982. Amenorrhea in anorexia nervosa: Examination of the critical body weight hypothesis. *J. Biol. Psychiatry* 17:799-806.
14. Russell, G. F., and C. J. Beardwood. 1970. Amenorrhea in the feeding disorders: Anorexia nervosa and obesity. *J. Psychother. Psychosom.* 18:358:64.
15. Frisch, R. E. 1977. Food intake, fitness, and reproductive ability. In *Anorexia nervosa,* ed. R. A. Vigersky. New York: Raven Press.
16. Bruch, H. 1965. Anorexia nervosa and its differential diagnosis. *J. Nerv. Ment. Dis.* 141:555-66.
17. Garner, D. M., M. P. Olmstead, P. E. Garfinkel. Does anorexia nervosa occur on a continuum? Subgroups of weight-preoccupied women and their relationship to anorexia nervosa. *Int. J. Eating Disorders* 2:11-20.
18. Crisp, A. H. 1967. The relationship of denial to the differential diagnosis of anorexia nervosa. In *Proceedings of the 7th European conference on psychosomatic research* ed. F. Antonelli and I. Ancoma, pp. 432-36. *Acta Medica Psychosomatica,* Rome.
19. Crisp , A. H. 1970. Anorexia nervosa: "Feeding disorder," "nervous malnutrition," or "weight phobia?" *World Rev. Nutr. Diet.* 12:452-504.
20. Bruch, H., 1973. *Eating disorders: Obesity, anorexia nervosa, and the person within.* New York: Basic Books.
21. Goldberg, S. C., K. A., Halmi, E. D. Eckert, R. C. Casper, J. M. Davis, and M. Roper. 1980. Attitudinal dimensions in anorexia nervosa. *J. Psychiatric Res.* 15:239-51.
22. Casper, R. C., K. A. Halmi, S. C. Goldberg, E. D. Eckert, and J. M. Davis. 1979. Disturbances in body image estimation as related to other characteristics and outcome in anorexia nervosa. *Br. J. Psychiatry* 134:60-66.
23. Eckert, E. D., S. C. Goldberg, K. A. Halmi, R. C. Casper, and J. M. Davis. 1982. Depression in anorexia nervosa. *Psychol. Med.* 12:115-22.
24. Vandereycken, W. and J. Vanderlinden. 1983. Denial of illness and the use of self-reporting measures in anorexia nervosa patients. *Int. J. Eating Disorders* 2:101-7.
25. Laseque, C. [1873] 1964. De l'anorexie hysterique. *Arch. Gen. Med.* 385. Reprinted in *Evaluation of psychosomatic concepts. Anorexia nervosa: A paradigm,* ed. R. M. Kaufman and M. Heiman. New York: International Universities Press.
26. Bruch, H. 1962. Perceptual and conceptual disturbances in anorexia nervosa. *Psychosom. Med.* 24:187-94.
27. Slade, P. D. and G. F. M. Russell. 1973. Experimental investigations of bodily perception in anorexia nervosa and obesity. *Psychother. Psychosom.* 22:259-363.
28. Crisp, A. H., and R. S. Kalucy. 1974. Aspects of the perceptual disorder in anorexia nervosa. *Br. J. Med. Psychol.* 47:349-61.
29. Garner, D. M., P. E. Garfinkel, H. C. Stancer, H. Moldofsky. 1976. Body image disturbances in anorexia and obesity. *Psychosom. Med.* 38:227-336.
30. Garfinkel, P. E., and D. M. Garner. 1982. *Anorexia nervosa: A multidimensional perspective.* New York: Brunner/Mazel.
31. Pierloot, R. A., and M. E. Houben. 1978. Estimation of body dimensions in anorexia nervosa. *Psychol. Med.* 8:317-24.
32. Russell, G. F. M., P. G. Campbell, and P. D. Slade. 1975. Experimental studies on the nature of the psychological disturbance in anorexia nervosa. *Psychoneuroendocrinology* 1:45-56.
33. Strober, M., I. Goldenberg, J. Green, and J. Saxon. 1979. Body image disturbance in anorexia nervosa during the acute and recuperative phase. *Psychol. Med.* 9:695-701.
34. Button, E. J., F. Fransella, and P. D. Slade. 1977. A reappraisal of body perception disturbance in anorexia nervosa. *Psychol. Med.* 7:235-43.

35. Garfinkel, P. E., H. Moldofsky and D. M. Garner. 1977. Prognosis in anorexia nervosa as influenced by clinical features, treatment and self-perception. *Can. Med. Assoc. J.* 117:1041-45.
36. Garner, D. M. and P. E. Garfinkel. 1979. The Eating Attitude Test: An index of the symptoms of anorexia nervosa. *Psychol. Med.* 9:1-7.
37. Gull, W. 1874. Anorexia nervosa. *Clin. Soc. Lond.* 7:22-28.
38. Halmi, K. A. 1974. Anorexia nervosa: Demographic and clinical features in 94 cases. *Psychosom. Med.* 36:18-26.
39. Crisp, A. H., L. K. G. Hsu, and B. Harding. 1980. Clinical features of anorexia nervosa: A study of a consecutive series of 102 female patients. *J. Psychosom. Res.* 24:179-91.
40. Warren, W. 1968. A study of anorexia nervosa in young girls. *J. Child Psychol. Psychiatry* 9:27-40.
41. Pierloot, R., W. Wellens, and M. Houben. 1975. Elements of resistance to a combined medical and psychotherapeutic program in anorexia nervosa. *Psychother., Psychosom.* 36:101-17.
42. Stunkard, A. 1972. New therapies for the eating disorders: Behavior modification of obesity and anorexia nervosa. *Arch. Gen. Psychiatry* 26:391-98.
43. Goldberg, S. C., K. A. Halmi, R. Casper, E. D. Eckert, and J. M. Davis. 1977. Pretreatment predictors of weight change in anorexia nervosa. In *Anorexia nervosa,* ed. R. A. Vigersky. New York: Raven Press.
44. Salkind, M. R., J. Fincham, and T. Silverstone. 1980. Is anorexia nervosa a phobic disorder? A psychophysiological enquiry. *Biol. Psychiatry* 15:803-8.
45. Frazier, S. H. 1965. Anorexia nervosa. *Dis. Nerv. Syst.* 26:155.
46. Casper, R. C., E. D. Eckert, K. A. Halmi, S. C. Goldberg, and J. M. Davis. 1980. Bulimia: Its incidence and clinical importance in patients with anorexia nervosa. *Arch. Gen. Psychiatry* 37:1030-35.
47. Garfinkel, P. E., H. Moldofsky, and D. M. Garner. 1980. The heterogeneity of anorexia nervosa: Bulimia as a distinct subgroup. *Arch. Gen. Psychiatry* 37:1036-40.
48. Janet, P. 1919. *Les obsessions et la psychasthenie.* Paris: Felix Alcan.
49. Beumont, P. J. V., G. C. W. George, and D. E. Smart. 1976. "Dieters" and "vomiters and purgers" in anorexia nervosa. *Psychol. Med.* 6:617-22.
50. Beumont, P. J. V. 1977. Further categorization of patients with anorexia nervosa. *Aust. N.Z. J. Psychiatry* 11:223-26.
51. Ben-Tovin, D. I., V. Marilov, and A. H. Crisp. 1979. Personality and mental state within anorexia nervosa. *J. Psychosom. Res.* 23:321-25.
52. Halmi, K. A., G. Brodland, and J. Loney. 1973. Prognosis in anorexia nervosa. *Ann. Intern. Med.* 78:907-9.
53. Halmi, K. A., and J. R. Falk. In press. Pretreatment and posttreatment correlates of outcome in anorexia nervosa. In *Proceedings of the Third World Congress of Biological Psychiatry.* New York: Elsevier/North Holland Medical Press.
54. Keys, A., J. Brozek, A. Henschel, O. Mickelson, and H. L. Taylor. 1950. *The biology of human starvation.* Minneapolis: University of Minnesota Press.
55. Schiele, B. C., and J. Brozek. 1948. "Experimental neurosis" resulting from semistarvation in man. *Psychosom. Med.* 10:31-50.
56. Casper, R. C., and J. M. Davis. 1977. On the course of anorexia nervosa. *Am. J. Psychiatry* 134:974-78.
57. Halmi, K. A., and J. R. Falk. 1981. Common physiological changes in anorexia nervosa. *Int. J. Eating Disorders* 1:16:27.
58. Halmi, K. A. 1978. Anorexia nervosa: Recent investigations. *Annu. Rev. Med.* 29:137-48.

59. Boyar, R. M., J. Katz, and J. W. Finkelstein. 1974. Anorexia nervosa: Immaturity of the 24-hour luteinizing hormone secretory pattern. *New Engl. J. Med.* 291:861.
60. Holt, S., M. J. Ford, S. Grant, and R. C. Heading. 1981. Abnormal gastric emptying in primary anorexia nervosa. *Br. J. Psychiatry* 139:550-52.
61. Bemis, K. M. 1978. Current approaches to the etiology and treatment of anorexia nervosa. *Psychol. Bull.* 85:593-617.
62. Decourt, J. 1964. Sur l'anorexie mentale de l'adolescence dans le sexe masculin. *Rev Neuropsychiatrie Infant.* 12:499.
63. Bliss, E. L. and C. H. H. Branch. 1960. *Anorexia nervosa: Its history, psychology, and biology.* New York: Paul B. Hoeber.
64. Jones, D. J., M. M. Fox, H. M. Babigian, and H. E. Hutton. 1980. Epidemiology of anorexia nervosa in Monroe County, New York: 1960-1976. *Psychosom. Med.* 42:551-58.
65. Falstein, E. I., S. C. Feinstein, and I. Judas. 1956. Anorexia nervosa in the male child. *Am. J. Orthopsychiatry* 26:751:72.
66. Crisp, A. H., and D. A. Tomas. 1972. Primary anorexia nervosa or weight phobia in the male. *Br. Med. J.* 1:334-38.
67. Hasan, M. K., and R. W. Tibbeth. 1977. Primary anorexia nervosa (weight phobia) in males. *Postgrad. Med. J.* 53:146-51.
68. Crisp, A. H., and T. Burns. 1983. The clinical presentation of anorexia nervosa in males. *Int. J. Eating Disorders* 2:5-10.
69. Duddle, M. 1973. An increase of anorexia nervosa in a university population. *Br. J. Psychiatry* 123:711-12.
70. Kalucy, R. S., A. H. Crisp, J. H. Lacey, and B. Harding. 1977. Prevalence and prognosis in anorexia nervosa. *Aust. N.Z. J. Psychiatry* 11:251-257.
71. Kendall, R. E., D. J. Hall, A. Hailey, and H. M. Babigian. 1973. The epidemiology of anorexia nervosa. *Psychol. Med.* 3:200-203.
72. Willi, J., and S. Grossman. 1983. Epidemiology of anorexia nervosa in a defined region of Switzerland. *Am. J. Psychiatry* 140:564-67.
73. Lucas, A. R., M. P. H. Beard, J. S. Kranz, and L. T. Kurland. 1983. Epidemiology of anorexia nervosa and bulimia: Background of the Rochester Project. *Int. J. Eating Disorders* 2:85-90.
74. Crisp, A. H., R. L. Palmer, and R. S. Kalucy. 1976. How common is anorexia nervosa? A prevalence study. *Br. J. Psychiatry* 128:549-54.
75. Nemiah, J. C. 1950. Anorexia nervosa: A clinical psychiatric study. *Medicine* 29:225.
76. Halmi, K. A., R. C. Casper, E. D. Eckert, S. C. Goldberg, and J. M. Davis. 1979. Unique features associated with age of onset of anorexia nervosa. *Psychiatry Res.* 1:209-15.
77. Kay, D. W. K., and D. Leigh. 1954. The natural history, treatment and prognosis of anorexia nervosa based on a study of 38 patients. *J. Ment. Sci.* 100:411-31.
78. Kellett, J., M. Trimble, and A. Thorley. 1976. Anorexia nervosa after the menopause. *Br. J. Psychiatry* 128:533-58.
79. Launer, M. A. 1978. Anorexia nervosa in late life. *Br. J. Med. Psychol.* 51:375-77.
80. Vandereycken, W., and R. Pierloot. 1981. Anorexia nervosa in twins. *Psychother. Psychosom.* 35:55-63.
81. Halmi, K., and G. Brodland. 1973. Monozygotic twins concordant and discordant for anorexia nervosa. *Psychol. Med.* 3:521-24.
82. Bruch, H. 1969. The insignificant difference: Discordant incidence of anorexia nervosa in monozygotic twins. *Am. J. Psychiatry* 126:123-28.
83. Nowlin, N. S. 1983. Anorexia nervosa in twins: Case report and review. *J. Clin. Psychiatry.* 44:101-5.

84. Shafii, M., C. Salguero, and S. M. Finch. 1975. Anorexia a deux: Psychopathology and treatment of anorexia nervosa in latency age siblings. *J. Am. Acad. Child Psychiatry* 14:633:45.
85. Holland, A. J., A. Hall, R. M. Murray, G. F. M. Russell, and A. H. Crisp. In press. Anorexia nervosa: A study of 34 twin pairs and one set of triplets. *Br. J. Psychiatry.*
86. Laseque, C. 1973. On hysterical anorexia. *Med. Times Gaz.* 2:265-67.
87. Palazzoli, M. 1974. *Self-starvation.* New York: Jason Aronson.
88. Minuchin, S., L. Baker, B. L. Rosman, R. Liebman, L. Milman, and T. Todd. 1975. A conceptual model of psychosomatic illness in children. *Arch. Gen. Psychiatry* 32:1031-38.
89. Crisp, A. H., B. Harding, and B. McGuinness. 1974. Anorexia nervosa: Psychoneurotic characteristics of parents: relationship to prognosis. *J. Psychosom. Res.* 18:167-73.
90. Rowland, C. V. 1970. Anorexia nervosa: A survey of the literature and review of 30 cases. *Int. Psychiatry Clin.* 7:37-137.
91. Strober, M. 1981. The significance of bulimia in juvenile anorexia nervosa: An exploration of possible etiological factors. *Int. J. Eating Disorders* 1:28-43.
92. Garfinkel, P. E., D. M. Garner, J. Rose, P. L. Darby, J. S. Brandes, J. O'Hanlon, and N. Walsh. 1983. A comparison of characteristics in the families of patients with anorexia nervosa and normal controls. *Psychol. Med.* 13:821-28.
93. Yager, J. 1982. Family issues in the pathogenesis of anorexia nervosa. *Psychosom. Med.* 44:43-60.
94. Crisp, A. H. 1965. Some aspects of evaluation, presentation and follow-up of anorexia nervosa. *Proc. Roy. Soc. Med.* 58:814-20.
95. Buhrich, N. 1981. Frequency of presentation of anorexia in Malaysia. *Aust. N.Z. J. Psychiatry* 15:153-55.
96. Garner, D. M., P. E. Garfinkel, D. Schwartz, and M. Thompson. 1980. Cultural expectation of thinness in women. *Psychol. Rep.* 47:483-91.
97. Bruch, H. 1978. *The golden cage.* Cambridge, Mass.: Harvard University Press.
98. Frisch, R. E., G. Wyskak, and L. Vincent. 1980. Delayed menarche and amenorrhea in ballet dancers. *New Engl. J. Med.* 303:17-19.
99. Druss, R. G., and J. A. Silverman 1979. Body image and perfectionism of ballerinas. *Gen. Hosp. Psychiatry* 2:115-21.
100. Crisp, A. H. 1965. Clinical and therapeutic aspects of anorexia nervosa—A study of 30 cases. *J. Psychosom. Res.* 9:67-78.
101. Cantwell, D. P., S. Sturzenberger, J. Borroughs, B. Salkin, and J. K. Green. 1977. Anorexia nervosa—An affective disorder? *Arch. Gen. Psychiatry* 34:1087-93.
102. Kay, D. W. K. 1953. Anorexia nervosa: A study in prognosis. *Proc. Roy. Soc. Med.* 46:699-74.
103. Hsu, L. K. G., A. H. Crisp, and B. Harding. 1979. Outcome in anorexia nervosa. *Lancet* 1:161-65.
104. Stonehill, E., and A. H. Crisp. 1977. Psychoneurotic characteristics of patients with anorexia nervosa before and after treatment and at follow-up 4-7 years later. *J. Psychosom. Res.* 21:187-93.
105. Warren, W. 1968. A study of anorexia nervosa in young girls. *J. Child Psychol. Psychiatry* 9:27-40.
106. Ben-Tovin, D. I., V. Marilov, and A. H. Crisp. 1979. Personality and mental state (P.S.E.) within anorexia nervosa. *J. Psychosom. Res.* 23:321-25.
107. Folstein, M. 1977. Studies of central subjective states with the analog scale in anorexia nervosa. In *Anorexia nervosa* ed. R. Vigersky. New York: Raven Press.
108. Mills, I. H. 1976. Amitriptyline therapy in anorexia nervosa. *Lancet* ii, 687.

109. Needleman, H., L., and D. Waker. 1977. The use of amitriptyline in anorexia nervosa. In *Anorexia nervosa,* ed. R. Vigersky. New York: Raven Press.
110. Winokur, A., V. March, J. Mendels. 1980. Primary affective disorder in relatives of patients with anorexia nervosa. *Am. J. Psychiatry* 130:695-98.
111. Gershon, E. S., J. R. Hamovit, J. L. Schreiber, E. D. Dibble, W. Kaye, J. I. Nurnberger, A. Andersen, and M. Ebert. 1983. Anorexia nervosa and major affective disorders associated in families: A preliminary report. In *Childhood psychopathology and development,* ed. S. B. Guze, F. J. Earls, and J. E. Barrett. New York: Raven Press.
112. Sachar, E. J., L. Hellman, D. K. Fukushima, and T. F. Gallagher. 1970. Cortisol production in depressive illness. *Arch. Gen. Psychiatry* 23:289-98.
113. Carroll, B. J. 1982. The dexamethasone suppression test for melancholia. *Br. J. Psychiatry* 140:292-304.
114. Schildrant, J. J., B. A. Keeler, and M. Papousek. 1973. MHPG excretion in depressive disorders. *Science* 181:762-64.
115. Halmi, K. A., and B. M. Sherman. 1979. Prediction of treatment response in anorexia nervosa. In *Biological psychiatry today,* pp. 609-14. Amsterdam: Elsevier/North Holland Biomedical Press.
116. Gerner, R. H., and H. E. Gwirtsman. 1981. Abnormalities of dexamethasone suppression test and urinary MHPG in anorexia nervosa. *Am. J. Psychiatry* 138:650-53.
117. Gross, H. A., C. R. Lake, M. H. Ebert, M. G. Hegler, and I. J. Kopin. 1979. Catecholamine metabolism in primary anorexia nervosa. *J. Clin. Endocrinol. Metabolism* 49:805-9.
118. Halmi, K. A., H. Dekinmanjian, J. M. Davis, R. Casper, and S. C. Goldberg. 1978. Catecholamine metabolism in anorexia nervosa. *Arch. Gen. Psychiatry* 35:458-60.
119. Walsh, B. T. 1982. Endocrine disturbances in anorexia nervosa and depression. *Psychosom. Med.* 44:85-91.
120. Walsh, B. T., J. L. Katz, J. Levin, J. Kream, D. K. Fukushima, H. Weiner, and B. Zumoff. 1981. The production rate of cortisol declines during recovery from anorexia nervosa. *J. Clin. Endocrinol. Metabolism* 53:203-5.
121. Gruen. P. H., E. J. Sachar, and N. Altman. 1975. Growth hormone response in depressed patients. *Arch. Gen. Psychiatry* 32:31-33.
122. Sachar, E. J., M. Mushrush, and M. Perlow. 1972. Endocrine changes in depression. *Science* 170:1304-5.
123. Loosen, P. T., and A. J. Prangue. 1982. Serum thyrotropin response to thyrotropin-releasing hormone in psychiatric patients: A review. *Am. J. Psychiatry* 139:405-16.
124. Casper, R. C., and L. A. Frohman. 1982. Delayed TSH response in anorexia nervosa following injection of thyrotropin-releasing hormone (TRH). *Psychoneuroendocrinology* 7:59-68.
125. Croxson, M. S., and H. K. Ibbertson. Low serum triiodothyronine (T3) and hypothyroidism in anorexia nervosa. *J. Clin. Endoctrinol. Metabolism* 44:167-174.
126. Macaron, C., J. F. Wilber, O. Green, et al. 1978. Studies of growth hormone (GH), thyrotropin (TSH) and prolactin (PRL) secretion in anorexia nervosa. *Psychoneuroendocrinology* 3:181-85.
127. Eckert, E. D., S. C. Goldberg, K. A. Halmi, R. C. Casper, and J. M. Davis. 1979. Alcoholism in anorexia nervosa. In *Psychiatric factors in drug abuse,* ed. R. W. Pickens and L. L. Heston. New York: Grune and Stratton.
128. Woodruff, R. A., D. W. Goodwin, and S. B. Guze. 1974. *Psychiatric diagnosis.* New York: Oxford University Press.
129. Halmi, K. A., and J. Loney. 1973. Familial alcoholism in anorexia nervosa. *Br. J. Psychiatry* 123:53-54.
130. Strober, M., B. Salkin, J. Burroughs, and W. Morrell. 1982. Validity of the bulimia-restricter distinction in anorexia nervosa. *J. Nerv. Ment. Dis.* 170:345-51.

131. Garfinkel, P. E., H. Moldofsky, and D. M. Garner. 1977. The outcome of anorexia nervosa, significance of clinical features, body image, and behavior modification. In *Anorexia nervosa*, ed. R. Vigersky. New York: Raven Press.
132. Pertschuck, M. 1977. Behavior therapy: Extended follow-up. In *Anorexia nervosa*, ed. R. Vigersky. New York: Raven Press.
133. Rosman, B., S. Minuchin, R. Liebman, et al. 1977. Input and outcome of family therapy in anorexia nervosa. In *Adolescent psychiatry: Developmental and clinical studies*, vol. 5, ed. S. Feinstein and P. Giovacchini. New York: Jason Aronson.
134. Rosman, B., S. Minuchin, L. Baker, et al. 1977. A family approach to anorexia nervosa: Study, treatment and outcome. In *Anorexia nervosa*, ed. R. Vigersky. New York: Raven Press.
135. Thoma, H. 1967. *Anorexia nervosa*. Trans. G. Brydone. New York: International Universities Press.
136. Williams, E. 1958. Anorexia nervosa—a somatic disorder. *Br. Med. J.* 2:190-95.
137. Kay, D. W. K., and K. Schapira. 1965. The prognosis in anorexia nervosa. In *Symposium on anorexia nervosa*, ed. J. E. Meyer and H. Feldman. Stuttgart: Thieme Verlag.
138. Beck, J. C., and K. Brochner-Mortensen. 1954. Observations on the prognosis in anorexia nervosa. *Acta. Med. Scand.* 149:409-30.
139. Theander, S. 1983. Research on outcome and prognosis of anorexia nervosa and some results from a Swedish long-term study. *Int. J. Eating Disorders* 2:167-74.
140. Seidensticher, J. F., and M. Tzagournis. 1968. Anorexia nervosa: Clinical features and long-term follow-up. *J. Chron. Dis.* 21:361-67.
141. Farquharson, R. F., and H. H. Hyland. 1966. Anorexia nervosa: The course of 15 patients treated from 20 to 30 years previously. *Can. Med. Assoc. J.* 94:411-419.
142. Goltz, P. L., R. A. Succop, J. B. Reinhart, and A. Miller. 1977. Anorexia nervosa in children: A follow-up study. *Am. J. Orthopsychiatry* 47:597-603.
143. Rollins, N., and E. Piazza. 1981. Anorexia nervosa: A qualitative approach to follow-up. *J. Am. Acad. Child Psychiatry* 20:167-83.
144. Sturzenberger, S., P. D., Cantwell, J. Burroughs, B. Salkin, and J. K. Green. 1977. A follow-up study of adolescent psychiatric inpatients with anorexia nervosa. *J. Am. Acad. Child Psychiatry* 16:703-15.
145. Schwartz, D. M., and M. G. Thompson. 1981. Do anorectics get well? Current research and future needs. *Am. J. Psychiatry* 138:319-23.
146. Steinhausen, H. C., and K. Glanville. 1983. Follow-up studies of anorexia nervosa: A review of research findings. *Psychol. Med.* 13:239-49.

2

Characteristics of Bulimia

James E. Mitchell, M.D., and Richard L. Pyle, M.D.

Bulimia is an eating disorder characterized by a pattern of episodic binge-eating. Patients with this disorder are aware that their eating pattern is abnormal, but they feel unable to stop eating voluntarily. Their binge-eating is a solitary behavior frequently followed by depression and remorse. They are chronically concerned about their weight, often inducing vomiting or abusing laxatives to prevent weight gain or to promote weight loss.[1,2]

The Diagnosis of Bulimia

Two diagnostic systems are widely used to diagnose patients who are not actively anorectic but who demonstrate bulimic characteristics. One clinical syndrome was originally delineated by Russell in 1979[3] and subsequently discussed by Fairburn.[4,5] Russell set forth three inclusion criteria for identifying patients with this problem, which he termed "bulimia nervosa": 1) The patient suffers from powerful and intractable urges to overeat. 2) The patient seeks to avoid the "fattening" effects of food by inducing vomiting or abusing purgatives or both. 3) The patient has a morbid fear of becoming obese.

Russell stressed the relationship between the problem of bulimia nervosa and anorexia nervosa and in his initial report considered the former a variant of the latter.

The American approach to the problem has been somewhat different, focusing on the binge-eating behavior itself. The most recent edition of the American Psychiatric Association's Diagnostic and Statistical Manual included bulimia as a separate eating disorder and stipulated the following diagnostic criteria:[1]

A. Recurrent episodes of binge eating (rapid consumption of a large amount of food in a discrete period of time, usually less than two hours).
B. At least three of the following:
    (1) consumption of a high-caloric, easily ingested food during a binge
    (2) inconspicuous eating during a binge
    (3) termination of such eating episodes by abdominal pain, sleep, social interruption, or self-induced vomiting.
    (4) repeated attempts to lose weight by severely restrictive diets, self-induced vomiting, or use of cathartics or diuretics
    (5) frequent weight fluctuations greater than ten pounds due to alternating binges and fasts
C. Awareness that the eating pattern is abnormal and fear of not being able to stop eating voluntarily.
D. Depressed mood and self-deprecating thoughts following eating binges.
E. The bulimic episodes are not due to anorexia nervosa or any known physical disorder.

Although these criteria were proposed before much research on nonanorectic bulimia had been published, they are quite useful in the light of later studies. There has been concern about their vagueness and lack of specificity, however, particularly because frequency parameters are not stipulated. Epidemiological investigations have shown that binge-eating is relatively common in young females in the general population and does not necessarily indicate significant impairment.[6-12]

In the Russell criteria,[3] the inclusion of vomiting or laxative abuse suggests the delineation of a smaller, more highly characterized group of patients because these associated behaviors are much less common than binge-eating in the general population.[9] The DSM-III criteria are built around the central problem of binge-eating, and they may identify quite a few people in the "normal" population depending upon who is interpreting the criteria.[7,9] The two criteria can also be compared on the basis of weight. Bulimic symptoms can be seen in patients with anorexia nervosa.[13] Although the DSM-III criteria exclude patients with anorexia nervosa, no consideration is given to the possible differentiation of normal weight bulimics, who tend to self-induce vomiting or abuse laxatives, from overweight patients, who may only binge-eat and may not self-induce vomiting or abuse laxatives. This latter group would not be identified as having bulimia nervosa using the Russell criteria.[3]

Other terms have been suggested to describe these patients. Marlene

Boskind-Lodahl has suggested the term "bulimarexia" to describe an apparently similar condition.[14] In a series of articles dealing with possible neurophysiological changes in patients with certain eating problems, Green and Rau have used the term "compulsive eating disorder" to describe patients who appear to have clinical symptoms resembling those seen in DSM-III bulimia.[15-17] Hilde Bruch has used the term "thin-fat" people to describe patients who have some similar characteristics.[18] The list of terms continues to grow.

Because this semantic confusion is common in the medical literature on bulimia, any discussion of bulimia must begin with a clarification of terms. In this chapter, the term *bulimia* will be used to imply the DSM-III diagnosis of the syndrome, any other usage will be so indicated.

Epidemiology of Bulimia

Efforts to determine the frequency of bulimia have been hindered by several problems. The diagnostic confusion has been paralleled by problems in defining bulimic behaviors when designing questionnaires. For example, no two researchers define an eating binge the same way or even use the same parameters. Some have suggested that the amount of food eaten is the important variable, whereas others have focused on the way the food is eaten, such as in a compulsive, rapid fashion. Because of this lack of agreement, different researchers have used different definitions, leading to a problem in comparing studies. With the exception of two reports,[10,12] surveys to date have involved only college students. Also, the inherent limitations of questionnaire studies—such as relying on subjective report—must be considered. All these problems limit our knowledge about the incidence of bulimia and bulimic behaviors in the general population; however, the available information suggests that it is a very common disorder.

An early report by Stangler and Printz[19] first suggested the magnitude of the problem. These authors found that 3.8% of a consecutive series of 500 students being seen for emotional problems at a student health service had received a diagnosis of bulimia; this represented 5.3% of the females seen. Subsequent investigations are summarized in table 3. The early study by Hawkins and Clement[6] involved a questionnaire survey of 247 psychology students. About half of the males and nearly four-fifths of the females admitted to binge-eating behavior; however, less than 10% admitted to vomiting, and only 8 females and 1 male admitted to vomiting after binge-eating episodes. A subsequent study[7] of 355 students at a northeastern university also found a high rate of binge-eating behavior in a college population (68.1% of the females and 60.2% of the males). Thirteen per-

Table 3. Epidemiology of Bulimia

	Total		Binge-Eat		Bulimia	
Study	Female	Male	Female	Male	Female	Male
Hawkins and Clement[6] (N = 247; response rate not stated)	73.7%	26.3%	79.0%	49.0%		
Halmi, Falk, and Schwartz[7] (N = 355; 66% response)	59.8%	33.4%	68.1%	60.2%	19.0(1.7)%[a]	6.1%
Sinoway[8] (N = 1,172; 65% response)	100.0%	0	47(25)%[b]		13.7%[c]	
Pyle et al.[20] (N = 1,355; 98.3% response)	42.4%	57.6%	57.4%	41.0%	7.8(1.1)%[d]	1.4%
Cooper and Fairburn[10] (N = 369; 96.1% response)	100.0%	0	26.4%[e]		1.9%[f]	
Clarke and Palmer[11] (N = 206; 76% response)	100.0%	0	46.2%[g]			
Johnson et al.[12] (N = 1,268; 100% response)	100.0%	0	57.0%			

[a] The 1.7% vomit at least once a week.
[b] The 25% are "true" binge-eaters, using clarification question.
[c] Bulimarexia.
[d] The 1.1% binge-eat at least once a week and also induce vomiting and use laxatives once a week.
[e] Current, 20.9%; 7.3% at least weekly.
[f] Bulimia nervosa.
[g] Current, 30.2%; 7.1% at least weekly.

cent of those surveyed (19% of the females and 6.1% of the males) met all the major symptoms of bulimia as defined by DSM-III, but only 6 of the 355 admitted to vomiting at least once week as part of their eating problem. Sinoway[8] reported a survey of 1,172 female college students. Forty-seven percent of this group admitted to binge-eating, but only 25% were believed to practice "true binge-eating" on the basis of subsequent clarification questions in the questionnaire. Of those surveyed, 13.7% met the major criteria for bulimarexia as defined by Marlene Boskind-Lodahl.[14] Two studies from Great Britain have also documented a fairly high rate of bulimic symptoms in college students and in women attending a family planning clinic.[10,11]

Johnson et al. surveyed 1,268 adolescent high school females and found that 57% admitted to binge-eating episodes and that 8% appeared to meet DSM-III criteria for bulimia.[12] Using the additional frequency criteria of episodes of binge-eating at least once a week, the prevalence dropped to 4.9%.

Our survey of 1,355 freshman students at a midwestern university[20] found that a high percentage of subjects admitted to binge-eating episodes (57.4% of the females and 41% of the males). The questionnaire that we used represented a modification of DSM-III criteria; overall, 7.8% of the females and 1.4% of the males probably would have met DSM-III criteria on clinical grounds based on their responses to the questions.

As part of our investigations, we also administered the instrument to a series of 37 female bulimic patients seen in our eating disorders clinic.[20] We then attempted to derive criteria to differentiate a group of the surveyed students who might most closely resemble our patients. Although 7.8% of the female college students appeared to meet DSM-III criteria for bulimia, only 4.5% met the criterion of weekly binge-eating, and only 1.1% met the more rigorous criteria of weekly binge-eating combined with weekly self-induced vomiting or laxative abuse. However, all of the 37 female bulimic patients surveyed in our clinic met the inclusion criterion of weekly binge-eating, and 91.9% ($n=34$) met the more rigorous criteria.

These findings suggest that the primary differentiating symptom in the DSM-III criteria for bulimia—binge-eating—is relatively common in young adult college students. But patients with bulimia demonstrate both a high incidence and frequency of other abnormal eating-related behaviors, such as self-induced vomiting and laxative abuse. When more rigid criteria are used to select a group of students who resemble a bulimic patient group, the apparent frequency of the bulimia syndrome decreases considerably. In our study, about 1% of the females and 0.3% of the males met such rigorous criteria.[20]

Taken together, the available epidemiological studies suggest the following three conclusions. First, binge-eating episodes, as loosely defined in most questionnaire studies, are relatively common in the young adult college population and may actually be present in over half of young women. The presence of these behaviors, however, does not necessarily indicate a clinically significant eating disorder. Second, studies to date indicate that between 8% and 14% of young women (and between 1% and

10% of young men) may meet DSM-III criteria for bulimia. This finding may reflect the vagueness of the DSM-III criteria as well as the high prevalence of presumed abnormal eating behaviors in the general population. If more rigid criteria are used, a much smaller prevalence is identified. Finally, the eating behaviors observed in bulimic patients may represent the extreme end of a spectrum of abnormal eating and eating-related behaviors. Obviously, some system needs to be developed that encompasses the notion of this spectrum, including normal variation and pathological extreme.

A last important point about epidemiology is the growing concern that bulimia nervosa or bulimia may be increasing in the general population. Fairburn[21] speculated that increased publicity may be encouraging more people to seek help. At this time, however, it is unclear whether the apparent increase in cases represents a change in incidence or simply the fact that people are now coming for help. Both explanations may be valid. Certainly, the cultural preoccupation with thinness and physical attractiveness may be having dramatic effects on the prevalence of this disorder.[14]

Clinical Characteristics of Bulimia

Much of the published work on bulimia nervosa has been devoted to clinical description.[3,21-29] The major series of patients with bulimia, bulimia nervosa, or related problems that have been reported in the medical literature are summarized in table 4.

Russell[3] originally described the diagnosis of bulimia nervosa in 1979 and reported a series of 30 patients. Fairburn added 11 patients with the same diagnosis.[5] Our group originally reported a series of 34 cases[9] and subsequently reported an additional 168;[28] these were all patients who had been seen for evaluation in an outpatient eating disorders clinic. Abraham and Beumont[25] reported on a series of 32 patients diagnosed as "binge-eaters." Most recently, Herzog[27] has also reported a series of patients seen in an outpatient eating disorders program and diagnosed as bulimic.

Two large community survey studies have also been reported. Fairburn and Cooper[5] solicited subjects through advertisements in a women's magazine. Of the 600 individuals responding to this solicitation, 499 were believed to fulfill the criteria for bulimia nervosa. Johnson et al.[26] mailed questionnaires to 454 patients who had written their eating disorders program requesting information regarding bulimia. Of the 68% who responded, 67% met DSM-III criteria for bulimia and were included in the series.

The mean age of these patients when they come for treatment or are

Table 4. Major Studies of Patients with Bulimia and Related Disorders

Study	Age[a] Mean	Age[a] Onset Eating Disorder	Age[a] Onset Bulimia	Anorexia History	Binge-Eat Once/Day or More	Binge-Eat Once or Several Times/Week	Vomit Once/Day or More	Vomit Once or Several Times/Week	Abuse Laxatives Once/Day or More	Abuse Laxatives Once or Several Times/Week	Abuse Diuretics Once/Day or More	Abuse Diuretics Once or Several Times/Week
Russell[b]		18.8	21.2	80%								
Fairburn[c]		16.1	17.1	55%								
Pyle, Mitchell, and Eckert[d]	24[e]	18[e]		47%[f]	56%	44.1%	47.1%	41.2%	2.9%	11.8%		
Abraham and Beumont[g]	24		17	28%	100%		53%					
Fairburn and Cooper[h]	23.8		18.4	43%	27.2%	32.6%	56.1%	17.5%		18.8%		
Johnson et al.[i]	23.7		18.1	5%	51.5%	41.8%	59.2%	28.6%	24.5%	30.2%		
Herzog[j]	24.6		18.4									
Mitchell et al.[k]	24		20		63.8%	26.7%	56.6%	23.2%	7.9%	17.8%	3.0%	4.2%

a Onset ages given as averages.
b Reference 3. N = 30 (28 females, 2 males); diagnosis of bulimia nervosa.
c Reference 4. N = 11 (all females); diagnosis of bulimia nervosa.
d Reference 9. N = 34 (all females); diagnosis of bulimia.
e Median.
f "Probable" or "possible" cases.
g Reference 25. N = 32 (30 females, 2 males); diagnosis of binge-eating.
h Reference 5. N = 499 (all females), obtained by advertisement; diagnosis of bulimia nervosa.
i Reference 26. N = 316 (all females), obtained from mail contact; diagnosis of bulimia.
j Reference 27. N = 30 (29 females, 1 male); diagnosis of bulimia.
k Reference 28. N = 168 (164 females, 4 males); diagnosis of bulimia.

identified through community surveys is about 24 (table 4). Eating problems seem to begin during adolescence, usually between ages 16 and 20. The development of the binge-eating pattern seems to antedate the development of vomiting behavior.[5]

According to most studies, identified patients with bulimia or bulimia nervosa binge-eat at least once a day and also induce vomiting at least once a day. About 20% to 40% of patients abuse laxatives at least once a week for weight control purposes, and a smaller percentage uses diuretics.

A history of anorexia nervosa is very common in these patients. The minimal figure reported to date was 5% in the Johnson et al. community survey.[26] In studies involving patients seen for therapy, 30%-80% of patients gave a history compatible with a diagnosis of previous anorexia nervosa.

The critical behavior required for the diagnosis of bulimia by the DSM-III criteria is that of the binge-eating episode itself. The term *binge-eating* has unfortunately been used in various ways, and its definition remains unclear. Most binge-eating episodes involve the ingestion of excessive quantities of food, and—as will be detailed later in this chapter—the amount of food ingested may indeed be very large;[30,31] however, not all patients ingest large amounts of food.[5,31] A characteristic underlying some of the current thinking about binge-eating in bulimics is the notion that patients experience a distressing sense of loss of control when they are engaging in this behavior.[22] Other defining variables include the secretive nature of the eating episodes, their precipitation by stressful events, the compulsive way in which the food is taken, and the fact that the patient can easily differentiate a binge-eating episode from other eating behavior.

How does the problem of bulimia start? Onset is frequently associated with dieting behavior; 34%-88% of patients with bulimia indicate the onset of symptoms after a period of dieting.[24-26] However, many patients with bulimia are chronically concerned about their weight and may have been dieting much of the time prior to the onset of the bulimia. We do not know whether the dieting episode preceding the onset of bulimia differs from the usual dieting pattern for these people. Our group reported a history indicating traumatic events preceding the onset of bulimia in many of the patients in our initial series.[9] In particular, these patients reported histories of loss or separation prior to onset. Common losses mentioned were moving away from home or the breakup of a romantic relationship.

Many patients who develop bulimia have had periods of being overweight. Halmi, Falk, and Schwartz[7] have shown that bulimic symptoms are more likely to appear in students who at some time have been overweight or tended to be at the heavy end of their normal weight range. Johnson et al.[26] found that about half of their group had been overweight.

Regardless of the initiating events, the bulimic behavior pattern appears over time to assume an independent existence and to become a regular pattern in the patient's life.

What precipitates individual binge-eating episodes? Sometimes the episodes are planned in advance and are not related to stress, but it is useful to examine the emotional state of patients immediately before the binge-eating takes place. Patients frequently report feeling anxious and tense,[25] experiencing a craving for certain foods or an uncontrollable appetite.[9] They also report a variety of other negative emotional states, including unhappiness.[9] Having eaten something "forbidden" or considered fattening also appears to be a strong precipitant for many patients to binge-eat.[25] For others, any food intake—such as a normal meal—may develop into a binge-eating. This finding of loss of control lends support to the restraint hypothesis outlined by Wardle and Beinart,[32] which suggests that the behavior can be precipitated by prior intake of high-caloric foods and by anxiety. These factors seem to predispose to a sense of loss of control that is closely associated with binge-eating behavior. For the person involved, the choice is between binge-eating and fasting.

During binge-eating episodes, patients with bulimia tend to consume high-carbohydrate or high-fat foods that are easy to eat and that do not require much preparation or chewing.[31] Commonly eaten foods include ice cream, bread or toast, candy, doughnuts, and soft drinks.[31] Patients with bulimia frequently binge-eat foods that they avoid at other times because they fear their high-caloric nature. Other patients, however, binge-eat on what they believe to be more healthy foods (like fresh fruits and vegetables), or they simply turn a regular meal into a binge by enlarging the quantity of food to be eaten.

The size of binge-eating episodes varies considerably. Russell originally reported that some of the patients he studied had consumed as many as 5,000-20,000 calories in a binging episode.[3] Johnson et al.[26] indicated that the average binge in their population was about 4,800 calories, with a range of 1,000 to 55,000. Our group[31] asked 25 patients to record what they ate during each binge-eating episode. The average caloric intake during a binge was 3,415 calories, with a range of 1,200 to 11,500. We later monitored the binge-eating behavior of 6 patients on a research ward and found a mean caloric intake per binge of 4,470 calories (unpublished study). We also found that the mean amount of vomitus produced during emesis after the binge was nearly 2.5 liters of fluid. This study also established that patients with bulimia tended to have larger binge-eating episodes than they had estimated was their typical pattern in advance, despite being monitored in the hospital.

Bulimic individuals can binge-eat at any time during the day, but they tend to do so late in the day when they return home from work or school. Most patients report that they eat very rapidly during an episode, without really tasting the food. Many watch television or read while binge-eating. Afterwards, patients frequently report a sense of relief but also may feel uncomfortable and experience feelings of guilt, worry, and being "too full." The duration of binge-eating episodes varies considerably: a typical episode appears to last less than 2 hours. Of the 40 patients studied by our group,[31] the mean duration was 1.18 hours, with a range of 15 minutes to 8 hours. Abraham and Beumont reported binge durations of anywhere from 15 minutes to as long as 2 weeks.[25] Eating behavior not associated with binge-eating has also been a source of some concern because patients with bulimia eat abnormally at other times as well. Patients with bulimia will commonly fast for prolonged periods when not binge-eating in an attempt to compensate for presumed caloric excess during a binge-eating episode. They may eat only very small amounts at other times; many never eat breakfast.

Most patients with bulimia induce vomiting, abuse laxatives, or abuse diuretics in an attempt to prevent weight gain from excess caloric intake or to promote weight loss. The vomiting behavior usually becomes coupled to the binge-eating. The use of laxatives and diuretics and the self-induced vomiting predispose these patients to a variety of medical complications, which will be reviewed in chapter 3.

A variable related to abnormal eating patterns is the frequent weight swings seen in patients with bulimia.[1,22,25] These patients tend to be very sensitive about their weight, and minor weight fluctuations are perceived by tightness of clothes. Like most anorexia nervosa patients, they frequently weigh themselves. Weight fluctuations can cause considerable concern and may exacerbate abnormal eating-related patterns. Patients with bulimia may also have a faulty perception of their body size relative to its weight,[5,22] a problem similar to the distortion seen in anorexia nervosa patients.

Associated Symptoms

A symptom very commonly seen in patients with bulimia is depression,[2,3,9] which frequently develops secondarily. As the bulimic behaviors assume increased importance, social and family relationships, work or job performance, and self-esteem all suffer. Herzog[27] reported that 75% of 30 patients with bulimia had significant depressive symptoms; Johnson and Larson[33] found that bulimic women reported feeling sadder, lonelier, and weaker than controls. Our group[34] reported that the mean depression score on the Minnesota Multiphasic Personality Inventory

(MMPI) in 30 patients with bulimia was 74.6, indicating significant elevation and a considerable depressive symptomatology. Hudson, Pope, and Jonas reported that fully 80% of a series of 70 patients with bulimia met DSM-III criteria for major affective disorder using the National Institutes of Mental Health Diagnostic Interview Schedule.[35] These and other reports have underscored this strong association between depression and bulimia.

What this means in clinical terms is still unclear. Several threads of evidence need to be considered in examining the association between bulimia and depression. First, depression is also commonly seen in patients with anorexia nervosa.[36] Longitudinal studies indicate a high rate of depression at follow-up in patients with anorexia nervosa.[37] Second, family histories suggest an increased incidence of affective disorders in relatives of patients with anorexia nervosa and bulimia,[37-39] pointing to a possible familial relationship between affective disorders and these eating disorders. Third, nonsuppression on the dexamethasone suppression test (DST) is commonly seen in many patients with either anorexia nervosa or bulimia.[40,41] Nonsuppression on the DST is commonly seen in patients with significant endogenous depression, but in other conditions as well.[42] Does DST nonsuppression indicate a possible underlying affective disorder in some of the patients? Fourth, there is the growing interest in the use of antidepressant drugs—both monoamine oxidase inhibitors and tricyclic/tetracyclic antidepressants—in the treatment of anorexia nervosa and bulimia. Several studies suggest the effectiveness of these agents in treating bulimic patients.[43-46] This material is reviewed in chapter 6.

How much of the depression seen in association with bulimia is secondary to the physical and psychosocial sequelae of the illness, and how much represents a primary endogenous depression? The available evidence suggests a link between bulimia and depression in some individuals, and we believe that this area must be vigorously investigated.

In addition to depression, impulsivity is another problem frequently described in patients with bulimia—most dramatically illustrated by the impulsive eating binge itself. Shoplifting is another example.[5,8-9,47] Patients with bulimia are frequently reported to have problems with stealing. Not surprisingly, the item most often stolen is food.[9] Patients will steal other items as well, however, such as clothes or cosmetics. Items may be stolen for personal use or to sell to buy food. In our experience, patients with laxative abuse problems frequently develop a pattern of stealing this particular commodity, perhaps out of embarrassment. Stealing has also been reported in bulimic anorexia nervosa subjects.[11] In the epidemiological survey of our group,[20] the "bulimic" student group identified by the questionnaire was more likely to report stealing behavior than the "nonbulimic" students (those who failed to meet DSM-III criteria using the same instrument).

Chemical abuse also appears to be associated with bulimia. Whether this reflects more generalized problems with impulse control is not clear. Eight of the original 34 patients in our series of patients with bulimia had previously completed chemical dependency treatment, and an additional patient was believed to be alcoholic.[9] Herzog[27] reported that 10 of the 30 bulimic patients in his series reported alcoholism in at least one first-degree family member, suggesting a familial relationship between bulimia and alcoholism. The abuse of food in bulimia and the abuse of alcohol or other drugs may have common features. Similarities between bulimia and alcohol abuse have been discussed in detail in a previous paper.[34] The similarities include loss of control over the use of the substance, preoccupation with the use, use of the substance to cope with stress or negative feelings, reenforcing nature of the behavior, secretiveness, social isolation, and legal and occupational consequences.

Our group reported a comparison of MMPI test results between a group of women with bulimia who had no history of problems with drug and alcohol abuse and women with alcohol or drug abuse problems who were in treatment.[34] Women with alcohol or drug abuse problems scored significantly higher on the MacAndrews Scale of the MMPI, a scale used to identify patients with alcohol abuse problems and considered by some investigators as a measure of characteristics associated with addiction in general. The mean MMPI profiles, however, and the distribution of MMPI code types were quite similar between the two groups.

Another problem mentioned in association with bulimia has been self-cutting or self-mutilation.[47-49] The frequency of this type of behavior in patients with bulimia and the general population has not been adequately studied.

Clinical Course

Little is known about the longitudinal course of bulimia. Many patients evidently experience an initial weight loss when they first become bulimic. Because many women engage in bulimic behaviors in hopes of losing weight, this initial weight loss probably reinforces the behavior. Fairburn[22] reported that the nadir of weight is reached at about 12 months. After that time, patients seem to begin gaining weight again. In our experience, this may be accounted for by changes in the binge-eating episodes. As patients progress in the course of the illness, the frequency of the binge-eating episodes and the amount of food consumed during a binge-eating episode seem to increase. However, a small percentage of patients with bulimia actually stop the binge-eating yet continue to induce vomiting after meals.[28] Most patients have been ill for several years before seeking help. We have treated patients who have been actively bulimic on a nearly daily basis for more than 20 years.

Personality and Adjustment

Unfortunately, very little is known about the background or families of origin of patients who eventually develop bulimia. We originally reported that 94% of our patients came from intact homes.[9] Herzog, however, reported that 50% of the 8 adolescent bulimic females in his study had a history of parental divorce, chronic illness, or death in their families, suggesting more severe familial pathology.[50]

Weiss and Ebert compared 15 normal-weight bulimic subjects and 15 controls matched for age, socioeconomic status, and IQ.[51] The bulimics demonstrated significantly more psychopathology and gave histories suggesting more stealing behavior, more impulsive behavior, and more menstrual disturbances. They also consistently rated themselves as sicker on all psychometric scales.

Adverse social consequences frequently develop as part of the pattern of bulimic behaviors.[2,26] Johnson and Berndt[52] have shown that individuals with bulimia using a structured self-rating scale report increased impairment in social adjustment when compared with a normal community sample. The bulimics demonstrate a pattern of responses similar to that of a group of alcoholic patients.

One of the parameters most commonly affected is social relationships. Patients with bulimia frequently report that they have experienced interpersonal difficulties with family, friends, or "significant others" in their life. They may develop problems with work or school; students frequently report that their academic performance suffers. Many report financial problems because of the costs involved. Some have to take second jobs. In a few cases, we have treated individuals who have had to declare bankruptcy because of the financial problems resulting from the habit.[2]

Bulimic patients report that the disorder interferes a great deal with other aspects of their life (97% of surveyed subjects), with social relationships (94%), and with family relationships (94%).[25] Johnson and Larson[33] also found that bulimic behavior leads to decreased social contact with others.

Marlene Boskind-Lodahl reported that these patients experience few satisfactory love relationships.[14] This observation has not yet been substantiated, but more information is needed about the effects of bulimia on marital relationships. There is evidence of sex role problems as well. Rost,

Neuhaus, and Florin recently reported that women with bulimia tend to follow a role concept of passivity, dependence, and unassertiveness. These conclusions were based on a comparison of responses by bulimic women and matched controls on instruments designed to measure sex role attitudes and behavior.[53]

The results of psychological testing have suggested some similar psychological characteristics in many of these patients. Our group[34] examined the MMPI results of 81 bulimics, a sample excluding patients with a history of drug abuse problems. The composite MMPI profile demonstrated elevations on scales 2,4,7, and 8, which suggests problems with depression, impulsivity, anger, anxiety, and social withdrawal. Norman and Herzog[54] reported that scale 4 (psychopathic deviant) was the most common peak scale in 14 normal-weight bulimic subjects, again suggesting problems with impulsivity, anger, and rebelliousness.

Identification of Patients with Bulimia

Bulimia is not a rare disorder, but patients with this problem frequently hide it from their doctors. Health professionals who work with young females should routinely inquire about abnormal eating patterns because these problems are common and serious enough to be major health concerns. Results of laboratory analysis of physical examination may also suggest the diagnosis. Elements suggestive of bulimia that are present on physical examination or laboratory testing are reviewed in chapter 3.

When asking about eating behaviors, health professionals can use certain general topics of questioning to identify the patients who have profound problems with eating. As when discussing other topics that are uncomfortable for some patients, a direct, nonjudgmental approach is usually best in order to elicit the necessary data. One can ask whether the patient has binge-eating episodes and what the usual pattern is. Inquiry about the use of laxatives and self-induced vomiting should be routine. A history concerning any significant weight change will also prove useful.

When the examining professional has evidence suggesting an underlying eating disorder, more detailed questioning is indicated. Areas to be covered should include the following:

A. History of eating pattern
   1. Was the patient ever underweight or overweight?
   2. What were the highest and lowest adult weights and when did they occur?
   3. What was the eating pattern like before the onset of the eating problems?

4. What circumstances surrounded the onset of the eating problems?
5. What has the eating pattern been like since the onset of the eating problems? Does the patient eat normal meals? How often? Does the patient binge-eat? What are the amounts and types of food ingested during an eating binge? Where does the patient binge-eat? What factors seem to precipitate binge-eating episodes? Does the patient engage in any diets or fasts?

B. History of associated characteristics
1. Vomiting—What is the frequency and how does the patient induce the vomiting?
2. Laxative usage (frequency, type, dosage)?
3. Use of diuretics (frequency, type, dosage)?
4. Use of amphetamines or over-the-counter stimulant drugs (frequency, type, dosage)?
5. Exercise pattern—Is there evidence of hyperactivity?
6. Body weight distortion—Does the patient feel fat when thin?
7. Menstrual history—are amenorrhea or irregular menses present?
8. Preoccupation with food?
9. Mood changes, Particularly as related to depression?
10. Sleep pattern—Any evidence of insomnia? Night binge-eating?
11. Stealing behavior?
12. Alcohol or drug abuse?

C. History of associated social complications
1. Problems at work, school?
2. Problems in relationships?

One may also ask about the presence of affective disorders, eating problems, and drug abuse in relatives because of the suggested familial relationships among these disorders.

Related Eating Problems

A major problem in diagnosing and working with patients with eating disorders is the lack of a reliable classification system. Unfortunately, there are several other eating problems that must be considered. In addition to bulimia nervosa,[3] anorexia nervosa,[13] bulimia,[2] bulimarexia,[13,55] and binge-eating,[25] several other symptoms or syndromes have been described in the literature that probably overlap with bulimia. These include self-induced vomiting,[56] the dietary chaos syndrome,[57] psychogenic vomiting[58,59] and the laxative abuse syndrome.[60] For example, patients with psychogenic vomiting frequently vomit in response to stress, but they are reported not to evidence serious psychological conditions. The authors reviewing this problem noted that it is much more common in women.[58,59] How similar is this syndrome to bulimia? The laxative abuse syndrome, another example of a related problem,[60] is described in association with depression, personality disorder, and anorexia nervosa. It presents a clinical picture that might be considered a variant of bulimia in some patients.[60] The present review indicates that there is considerable overlap between normal weight bulimia, bulimia nervosa, and these related clinical problems.

Summary and Conclusion

A classification system clearly needs to be developed that considers eating pattern, weight, and the presence or absence of certain other abnormal eating-related behaviors such as self-induced vomiting, laxative abuse, or diuretic abuse. Communication problems among investigators, clinicians, and patients will continue until such a system is developed.

Available epidemiological research strongly suggests that the major symptom of bulimia—binge-eating—is relatively common in the general population and that the syndrome of bulimia as defined by DSM-III[1] is also surprisingly common among young women. However, it is not necessarily the presence of binge-eating or even of other abnormal eating-related problems that identifies individuals in the general population who resemble the patients seen for bulimia. In patients, these behaviors have escalated out of control in terms of frequency and eventually come to replace or perhaps crowd out normal eating patterns.

Although we do not know much about the longitudinal course of this illness, it appears that it usually starts in late adolescence in individuals who may have had a problem with being overweight when younger. Stressful events may precipitate the onset. Individuals may originally lose weight when they become bulimic but most eventually start to gain weight. In many patients who come for treatment, bulimia has led to social, financial, and, in some cases, legal difficulties. The clinical picture in some ways resembles the clinical picture of patients addicted to drugs or alcohol.

There are some important suggestions in the literature that bulimia may be related on a familial basis to other substance abuse problems (such as alcoholism) and to mood disorders. Further research is needed to clarify these relationships.

Some of the most important questions remain to be answered. Why do bulimic-type behaviors that are fairly common in the general population escalate out of control in a subgroup of people and eventually come to dominate the individual's life? Do certain personality variables or life stresses predispose to this course? The number of patients seeking help for bulimia has increased dramatically in the last several years. Does this reflect an increasing incidence of this disorder? If so, what are the cultural determinants of this change and what could be done to reverse the trend? What happens to these patients, with or without treatment? Are they at higher risk for affective disorder episodes later in life?

Clinicians and researchers are faced with a special challenge when working with the problem of bulimia. If the incidence of the disorder is indeed increasing, and if the determinants of this increase can be understood, health professionals may be able to suggest preventative measures or to identify precursors of the behavior so that early identification and intervention can be achieved.

REFERENCES

1. American Psychiatric Association. 1980. *Diagnostic and statistical manual of mental disorders.* 3rd ed. Washington, D.C.
2. Mitchell, J. E., and R. L. Pyle. 1982. The bulimia syndrome in normal weight individuals: A review. *Int. J. Eating Disorders* 1:61-73.
3. Russell, G. 1979. Bulimia nervosa: An ominous variant of anorexia nervosa. *Psychol. Med.* 9:429-48.
4. Fairburn, C. G. 1980. Self-induced vomiting. *J. Psychosom. Res.* 24:193-97.
5. Fairburn, C. G., and P. J. Cooper. 1982. Self-induced vomiting and bulimia nervosa: An undetected problem. *Br. Med. J.* 284:1153-55.
6. Hawkins, I. I., and P. F. Clement. 1980. Development and construct validation of a self-report measure of binge eating tendencies. *Addict. Behav.* 5:219-26.
7. Halmi, K. A., J. R. Falk, and E. Schwartz. 1981. Binge-eating and vomiting: A survey of a college population. *Psychol. Med.* 11:697-706.
8. Sinoway, C. G. 1982. The incidence and characteristics of bulimarexia in Penn State students. Paper presented at the annual convention of the American Psychological Association, Washington, D.C.
9. Pyle, R. L., J. E. Mitchell, and E. D. Eckert. 1981. Bulimia: A report of 34 cases. *J. Clin. Psychiatry* 42:60-64.
10. Cooper, P. J., and C. G. Fairburn. 1983. Binge-eating and self-induced vomiting in the community—a preliminary study. *Br. J. Psychiatry* 142:139-44.
11. Clarke, M. G., and R. L. Palmer. 1983. Eating attitudes and neurotic symptoms in university students. *Br. J. Psychiatry* 142:399-404.
12. Johnson, C. L., C. Lewis, S. Love, M. Stuckey, and L. Lewis. 1983. A descriptive survey of dieting and bulimic behavior in a female high school population. Report of the Fourth Ross Conference in Medical Research, September 1983.
13. Casper, R. C., E. D. Eckert, K. A. Halmi, S. C. Goldberg, and J. M. Davis. 1980. Bulimia—its incidence and clinical importance in patients with anorexia nervosa. *Arch. Gen. Psychiatry* 37:1030-40.
14. Boskind-Lodahl, M. 1976. Cinderella's stepsisters: A feminist perspective on anorexia nervosa and bulimia. *J. Women Culture Soc.* 2:342-56.
15. Rau, J. H., and R. S. Green. 1975. Compulsive eating: A neuropsychologic approach to certain eating disorders. *Compr. Psychiatry* 16:223-31.
16. Rau, J. H., and R. S. Green. 1978. Soft neurologic correlates of compulsive eating. *J. Nerv. Ment. Dis.* 166:435-37.

17. Rau, J. H., F. A. Struve, and R. S. Green. 1979. Electroencephalographic correlates of compulsive eating. *Clin. Electroencephalogr.* 10:180-89,
18. Bruch, H. 1973. *Eating disorders.* New York: Basic Books.
19. Stangler, R. S., and A. M. Printz. 1980. DSM-III: Psychiatric diagnosis in a university population. *Am. J. Psychiatry* 137:937-40.
20. Pyle, R. L., J. E. Mitchell, E. D. Eckert, P. A. Halvorson, P. A. Neuman, and G. M. Goff. 1983. The incidence of bulimia in freshman college students. *Int. J. Eating Disorders* 2:75-85.
21. Fairburn, C. G., P. J. Cooper, and M. O'Connor. 1983. Publicity and bulimia nervosa. *Br. J. Psychiatry* 142:101-2.
22. Fairburn, C. G. 1982. Binge-eating and bulimia nervosa. *S. K. and F. Publications* 1:1-20.
23. Fairburn, C. G. 1982. Bulimia: Its importance and management. *Arch. Neurol.* 39:735-36.
24. Fairburn, C. G. 1982. Binge eating and its management. *Br. J. Psychiatry* 141:631-33.
25. Abraham, S. F., and P. J. V. Beumont. 1982. How patients describe bulimia or binge eating. *Psychol. Med.* 12:625-35.
26. Johnson, C. L., M. K. Stuckey, L. D. Lewis, and D. M. Schwartz. 1983. Bulimia: A descriptive survey of 316 cases. *Int. J. Eating Disorders* 2:3-16.
27. Herzog, D. B. 1982. Bulimia: The secretive syndrome. *Psychosomatics* 23:481-87.
28. Mitchell, J . E., R. L. Pyle, E. D. Eckert, D. Hatsukami, and R. Lentz. 1983. Electrolyte and other physiological abnormalities in patients with bulimia. *Psychol. Med.* 13:273-78.
29. Johnson, C. 1982. Anorexia nervosa and bulimia. In *Promoting adolescent health: A dialog on research and practice,* ed. T. J. Coates. New York: Academic Press.
30. Willard, S. G., R. H. Anding, and D. K. Winstead. 1983. Nutritional counseling as an adjunct to psychotherapy in bulimic treatment. *Psychosomatics* 24:545-51.
31. Mitchell, J. E., R. L. Pyle, and E. D. Eckert. 1981. Frequency and duration of binge-eating episodes in patients with bulimia. *Am. J. Psychiatry* 138:835-36.
32. Wardle, J. and H. Beinhart. 1981. Binge-eating: A theoretical review. *Br. J. Clin. Psychol.* 20:97-109.
33. Johnson, C., and R. Larson. 1982. Bulimia: An analysis of moods and behavior. *Psychosom. Med.* 44:341-51.
34. Hatsukami, D., P. Owen, R. Pyle, and J. Mitchell. 1982. Similarities and differences on the MMPI between women with bulimia and women with alcohol or drug abuse problems. *Addict. Behav.* 7:435-39.
35. Hudson, J. I., H. G. Pope, and J. M. Jonas. 1983. Bulimia: A form of affective disorder? Paper presented at the annual meeting of the American Psychiatric Association, 4 May, New York.
36. Eckert, E. D., S. C. Goldberg, K. A. Halmi, R. C. Casper, and J. M. Davis. 1982. Depression in anorexia nervosa. *Psychol. Med.* 12:115-22.
37. Cantwell, D. P., S. Sturzenberger, J. Burroughs, B. Salkin, and J. K. Green. 1977. Anorexia nervosa—an affective disorder? *Arch. Gen. Psychiatry* 34:1087-93.
38. Winokur, A., V. March, and J. Mendels. 1980. Primary affective disorder in relatives of patients with anorexia nervosa. *Am. J. Psychiatry* 137:695-98.
39. Hudson, J. I., H. G. Pope, J. M. Jonas, and D. Yurgelun-Todd. 1983. Family history study of anorexia nervosa and bulimia. *Br. J. Psychiatry* 142:133-38.
40. Gerner, R. H. and H. E. Gwirtsman. 1981. Abnormalities of dexamethasone suppression test and urinary MHPG in anorexia nervosa. *Am. J. Psychiatry* 138:650-53.
41. Hudson, J. I., H. G. Pope, J. M. Jonas, P. S. Laffer, M. S. Hudson, and J. C. Melby.

1983. Hypothalamic-pituitary-adrenal axis: Hyperactivity in bulimia. *Psychiatry Res.* 8:111-17.

42. Gwirtsman, H., R. H. Gerner, and H. Sternbach. 1982. The overnight dexamethasone suppression test: Clinical and theoretical review. *J. Clin. Psychiatry* 43:321-27.

43. Walsh, B. T., J. W. Stewart, L. Wright, W. Harrison, S. P. Roose, and A. H. Glassman. 1982. Treatment of bulimia with monoamine oxidase inhibitors. *Am. J. Psychiatry* 139:1629-30.

44. Pope, H. G., and J. I. Hudson. 1982. Treatment of bulimia with antidepressants. *Psychopharmacology* 78:176-79.

45. Pope, H. G., J. I. Hudson, and J. M. Jonas. 1983. Antidepressant treatment of bulimia: Preliminary experience and practical recommendations. *J. Clin. Psychopharmacology* 3:274-81.

46. Pope, H. G., J. I. Hudson, J. M. Jonas, and D. Yurgelun-Todd. 1983. Bulimia treated with imipramine: A placebo-controlled double-blind study. *Am. J. Psychiatry* 140:554-58.

47. Nogami, Y., and F. Yabana. 1977. On kibarashi-gui (binge eating). *Folia Psychiatr. Neurol. Jpn.* 31:159-66.

48. Simpson, M. A. 1973. Female genital self-mutilation. *Arch. Gen. Psychiatry* 29:808-10.

49. Pao, P. N. 1969. The syndrome of delicate self-cutting. *Br. J. Med. Psychol.* 42:195-206.

50. Herzog, D. B. 1982.. Bulimia in the adolescent. *Am. J. Dis. Child.* 136:985-89.

51. Weiss, S. R., and M. H. Elbert. 1983. Psychological and behavioral characteristics of normal weight bulimics and normal weight controls. *Psychosom. Med.* 45:293-303.

52. Johnson, C., D. J. Berndt. 1983. Preliminary investigation of bulimia and life adjustment. *Am. J. Psychiatry* 140:774-77.

53. Rost, W., M. Neuhaus, and I. Florin. 1982. Bulimia nervosa: Sex role attitude, sex role behavior, and sex role related locus of control in bulimarexic women. *J. Psychosom. Res.* 26:403-8.

54. Norman, D. K., and D. B. Herzog. 1983. Bulimia, anorexia nervosa, and anorexia nervosa with bulimia: A comparative analysis of MMPI profiles. *Int. J. Eating Disorders* 2:43-52.

55. Boskind-Lodahl, M., and W. C. White. 1978. The definition and treatment of bulimarexia in college women: A pilot study. *J. Am. Coll. Health Assoc.* 27:84-86.

56. Rich, C. L. 1978. Self-induced vomiting: Psychiatric considerations. *JAMA* 239:2688-89.

57. Palmer, R. L. 1979. The dietary chaos syndrome: A useful new term? *Br. J. Med. Psychol.* 52:187-90.

58. Hill, O. W. 1968. Psychogenic vomiting. *Gut* 9:348-52.

59. Rosenthal, R. H., W. L. Webb, and L. D. Wruble. 1980. Diagnosis and management of persistent psychogenic vomiting. *Psychosomatics* 21:722-30.

60. Oster, J. R., B. J. Materson, and A. I. Rogers. 1980. Laxative abuse syndrome. *Am. J. Gastroenterol.* 74:451-58.

3

Medical Complications of Anorexia Nervosa and Bulimia

James E. Mitchell, M.D.

The eating disorders of anorexia nervosa and bulimia are associated with potentially serious medical risks. Certain physical conditions can mimic either disorder, and a variety of medical complications can develop from the anorectic or bulimic behaviors.

This chapter reviews the medical complications and the physical conditions that may mimic these problems. Because anorexia nervosa has been studied as a distinct entity for many years, we have much more information about its complications than about those of nonanorectic bulimia.

Anorexia Nervosa

Most of the physical abnormalities demonstrated in anorectic patients resemble those described in starved or semistarved normals, and they are thus most likely secondary to the starvation process itself.[1] For example, the endocrine abnormalities demonstrated in anorexia nervosa patients are usually very similar to the abnormalities demonstrated in patients who are being starved. [1-6] Review of the starvation literature, however, is beyond the scope of this chapter.

The signs and symptoms commonly associated with anorexia nervosa are shown in table 5, as based on research involving several series of cases of patients reported in the medical literature.[7-11] Frequency of these signs and symptoms varies widely, partly because of the criteria used and the rigor with which they are sought. Amenorrhea is invariably present, and constipation is also common. Hypotension, hypothermia, dry skin, bradycardia, and lanugo have all been demonstrated in most patients in at least one of these studies. Some of these signs will be discussed in more detail under the specific organ systems involved.

Table 5. Signs and Symptoms of Anorexia Nervosa

Signs	
Bradycardia	25-90%
Hypotension	20-85
Hypothermia	15-85
Lanugo	20-80
Dry skin	25-60
Edema	20-25
Petechiae	10
Symptoms	
Amenorrhea	100
Constipation	40-100
Excess energy	35
Abdominal pain	20
Cold intolerance	20
Lethargy	20

Note: Shown as percentages of patients reporting these symptoms or manifesting these signs on physical examination. Rounded to nearest multiple of 5%.

Hematologic Abnormalities

Several hematologic abnormalities have been described in patients with anorexia nervosa; the most frequent is leukopenia, which is often accompanied by a relative lymphocytosis. Carryer, Berkman, and Mason described this pattern in 1959,[12] reporting that 15 of 26 patients with anorexia nervosa had a lymphocytosis greater than 4,000; 9 had a leukopenia of less than 5,000. Various other authors have noted similar patterns in subgroups of their patients with anorexia nervosa.[8,13-16]

Rieger, Brady, and Weisberg[17] compared hematologic indices between 34 patients with anorexia nervosa and 34 normal controls. Hematologic values were within normal limits, but hemoglobin, hematocrit, and levels of white blood cells were all relatively lower in patients with anorexia nervosa than in controls; a relative lymphocytosis was also present in the anorexia nervosa group.

Bowers and Eckert[18] compared hematologic indices between 68 patients with anorexia nervosa and a group of matched control patients who had a variety of other psychiatric diagnosis. The anorexia nervosa patients had significantly decreased leukocyte counts compared with controls. The absolute neutrophil, lymphocyte, and monocyte counts were also lower than in controls; this pattern was characterized as panleukopenia.

In the Bowers and Eckert study,[18] 3 of 25 subjects had platelet counts less than 150,000 mm.[3] Thrombocytopenia has also been reported in patients with anorexia nervosa by Lampert and Lau.[19]

Because the hematologic changes have been shown to improve with weight gain, they are presumed to result from the attendant malnutrition.[14,15] For example, Halmi and Falk[15] documented a significant increase in neutrophil counts with a significant decrease in percentage of lymphocytes accompanying treatment response in anorexia nervosa patients.

Bone marrow findings have been reported in several series of patients with anorexia nervosa. In 1972, Mant and Faragher[20] reported marked hypocellularity of the bone marrow and the presence of gelatinous acid mucopolysaccharide in the aspirants of 6 patients. This pattern was believed secondary to the starvation. Other series of bone marrow findings have been reported by Lambert and Lau;[19] Cornbleet, Moir, and Wolf;[21] similar to those of Mant and Faragher,[20] Kubanek et al.;[14] Amrein et al.;[22] and Myers et al.[16] These changes have been shown to be reversible with weight gain.[14]

The hemotologic changes seen in patients with anorexia nervosa have led to concern that they may be at increased risk for infection. Additional concern has been raised by the reports that peripheral granulocyte cells obtained from anorexia nervosa patients have a reduced killing rate for *Staphylococcus aureus* and *Escherichia coli* in vitro.[23,24] However, Bowers and Eckert[18] examined the clinical histories for infection in a group of 68 patients and compared them with a group of matched controls. Although the patients with anorexia nervosa had lower leukocyte counts, there was no significant difference between the two groups in rate of infections.

Immune system functioning has also been studied in patients with anorexia nervosa. Golla et al.,[25] reporting on lymphocyte functioning in 9 patients, found them to have an intact cell-mediated immune system, normal T-lymphocyte populations, and unimpaired proliferative lymphocyte responsiveness to mitogenic stimulation. Responsiveness was actually significantly increased in the anorectic patients, with a regression toward control values with weight gain. Pertshuk et al.,[26] studying cellular immunity in 22 patients with anorexia nervosa, found that they continue to manifest immunocompetency as evidenced by delayed hypersensitivity responses until they become severely emaciated. Although only 1 of 14 patients above 60% IBW (ideal body weight) was anergic, 5 of 8 patients below this level demonstrated anergy. Anorectics have also been shown to develop hemagglutination inhibition titers equal to or higher than controls in response to influenza vaccine.[27]

Clotting mechanisms in patients with anorexia nervosa have been studied by some authors. Investigations of the fibrinolytic enzyme system found a significantly higher mean level of plasminogen activator and a significantly lower mean level of fibrinogen concentration in the anorexia nervosa group compared with controls.[28] There were no significant differences for plasminogen and fibrin degradation products. Reduced serum levels of certain serum complement proteins have also been reported in anorexia nervosa.[29,30]

Renal Complications

Elevated serum blood urea nitrogen (BUN) levels have frequently been described in patients with anorexia nervosa. Warren and Van de Wiele[8] reported that 40.5% of 42 patients had BUN levels greater than 20. This BUN elevation has been ascribed to dehydration.[15] As would be expected, serum creatinine levels have usually been reported to be normal.

More sophisticated renal function tests have not been reported in any large series of patients. Aperia, Broberger, and Fohlin[31] studied 12 adolescent patients with anorexia nervosa (8 females and 4 males) and compared the results of the testing with results obtained from matched healthy controls. Glomerular filtration rate and renal blood flow were generally reduced in anorexia patients. Urinary concentrating capacity was also studied following water deprivation and vasopressin augmentation. Although the authors commented that the urinary concentrating capacity was moderately depressed both before and after vasopressin augmentation, there were no significant differences compared with control values.

Wigley[32] reviewed 17 case reports of patients with anorexia nervosa who had developed hypokalemic alkalosis and found a history of some kind of renal problem in 8 of these cases. Wigley added 3 additional cases that suggested an association between renal problems and anorexia nervosa. Autopsy findings in 1 of these cases showed marked vacuolization of the cells lining the proximal convoluted tubule. Wigley suggested that these changes might be secondary to the potassium depletion seen in this patient.

Mecklenburg et al.[33] reported that 4 of 5 subjects with anorexia nervosa demonstrated an increase in urine osmolality greater than 9% (suggesting partial diabetes insipidus) following water deprivation and subsequent vasopressin administration. Vigersky et al.[34] reported similar findings in 8 of 21 patients with anorexia nervosa. These data suggest that a subgroup of patients with anorexia nervosa may have a partial diabetes insipidus. Gold et al.[35] studied plasma and cerebrospinal fluid arginine vasopressin in patients with anorexia nervosa and found abnormal responses to intravenous hypertonic saline infusions; most, if not all, of the subjects also had increased urinary output.

Metabolic Complications

Elevated serum cholesterol has been reported frequently in patients with anorexia nervosa.[36,37] Klinefelter originally made this observation in a series of 98 patients with anorexia nervosa.[38] Mordasini, Klose, and Greten[39] subsequently reported additional studies demonstrating elevated cholesterol levels in anorexia nervosa compared with normal controls. Halmi and Fry[37] noted considerable scatter in cholesterol values and reported that frank hypercholesterolemia was relatively uncommon in anorectics. They also found no difference in serum cholesterol between bulimic and restrictor subgroups of anorectics.

The etiology of this relative cholesterol elevation remains unclear. Nestel[36] suggested that the hypercholesterolemia reflected diminished cholesterol and bile turnover and demonstrated that bile acid excretion was reduced in two anorectic patients with elevated cholesterol. Mordasini et al.[39] hypothesized that a diminished cholesterol turnover secondary to delayed low-density lipoprotein metabolism would explain the cholesterol elevations. This suggests a type II pattern of hypercholesterolemia. Serum triglyceride levels have been reported to be normal.[40]

Elevated serum carotene levels have also been reported in anorexia nervosa patients.[8,41,42] Robboy, Sato, and Schwabe[41] compared 8 patients with anorexia nervosa, 10 controls, and 76 patients who manifested cachexia secondary to organic causes. The anorexia nervosa patients displayed significantly increased levels of beta carotene, retinyl esthers, retinol, and retinoic acid. These authors interpreted these data to suggest that the hypercarotenemia seen in some anorexia nervosa patients was due to either increased carotene with vitamin A intake or some acquired defect in the utilization or metabolism of vitamin A. Other authors have also suggested that increased intake might explain some cases of hypercarotenemia.[42] Bhanji and Mattingly[43] reported that carotene levels were higher in anorexia nervosa patients who were restricters compared with those who induced vomiting or abused laxatives. Casper et al.[44] reported normal plasma vitamin A levels with retinol binding protein in patients with anorexia nervosa compared with controls.

Another metabolic abnormality demonstrated in patients with anorexia nervosa involved the trace metal zinc; zinc deficiency has been suggested as a possible contributing factor to the development and maintenance of anorexia nervosa.[45,46] This suggestion stems from a presumed relationship between taste impairment and zinc deficiency. Casper et al.[47,48] measured trace materials in female patients with anorexia nervosa and attempted to correlate these changes with abnormalities in taste function. In the anorexia nervosa patients, plasma zinc, urinary zinc, and urinary copper levels were depressed whereas the zinc and copper content of hair was normal compared with normal controls. The anorexia nervosa patients demonstrated hypogeusia (decreased taste) on taste testing. Plasma zinc levels, however, did not correlate with taste recognition scores. Nine patients were retested after discharge and taste function was improved at that time. It was concluded that the zinc and copper deficiencies and the hypogeusia reflected the self-imposed nutritional restrictions of anorexia; no relationship was demonstrated between hypozincemia and impaired taste. Esca et al.[49] described a case of acrodermatitis enteropathica secondary to zinc deficiency in a patient with anorexia nervosa.

Liver function abnormalities have been ascribed in a minority of patients with anorexia nervosa. Halmi and Falk[15] reported that some patients with anorexia nervosa have elevated liver function tests prior to treatment. However, they found that the mean levels of these enzymes increased significantly during treatment. This suggested fatty degeneration of the liver secondary to refeeding as the probable cause. Kanis et al.[50] also reported a rise in serum alkaline phosphatase during treatment. Cravario, Cravetto, and Autino[51] reported a study of liver functions in 27 patients with anorexia nervosa. They found normal liver functions (including serum transaminase, alkaline phosphatase, serum bilirubin, and Bromsulfalein determinations). Nordgren and von Scheele[52] suggested malnutrition as a cause of altered hepatic and pancreatic function in two patients with anorexia nervosa.

Wachslicht-Rodbard et al.[53] reported increased insulin binding to erythrocytes in patients with anorexia nervosa. Binding characteristics normalized following refeeding of these patients. Their interpretation of the scatchard analysis indicated that the changes in binding characteristics reflected an actual increase in the number of receptors rather than a change in receptor affinity, although this conclusion has been debated.[54] Kanis et al.[50] and Halmi and Falk[15] found serum albumin and total serum protein to be normal in patients with anorexia nervosa.

Gastrointestinal Problems

Because of the markedly abnormal eating behaviors seen in patients with anorexia, one area of particular concern has been the consequences of such behaviors on gastrointestinal physiology. Silverstone and Russell in 1967[55] reported one of the original studies in this area. Using a pressure transducer, these authors recorded gastric contractions and found no differences in gastric motility between 8 patients with anorexia nervosa and 10 controls. Five patients were retested after weight gain. They then demonstrated a slight decrease in gastric motility, but the differences were still not significant when compared with controls.

Dubois et al.[56] using a dye dilution technique measured gastric hydrogen output, fluid output, intergastric volume, and fractional emptying rates in 15 patients with anorexia nervosa and 11 controls. They demonstrated a decreased fractional emptying rate and a decreased hydrogen ion output in the anorexia nervosa patients compared with controls. The peak pentagastrin-stimulated hyrogen ion output was only 64% of control values. The peak gastric fluid output was significantly reduced. When retested after weight gain, patients demonstrated an improvement in fractional emptying time toward control values, but the difference between patients and controls was still significant; gastric hydrogen ion output and fluid output had not improved significantly. Decreased gastric secretion in anorexia nervosa has also been demonstrated by Kishi et al.[57]

Using a gamma camera technique, Saleh and Lebwohl[58] studied gastric retention of technetium-99 labeled meals in patients with anorexia nervosa. Seven subjects (5 females and 2 males) showed delayed gastric emptying compared with controls. These patients were reevaluated after receiving 10 mg of metoclopramide 30 minutes prior to testing; metoclopramide is a dopamine-blocking agent that has peristalsis-inducing actions. Five of the 7 patients demonstrated improvement in gastric emptying. The 7 patients were then treated with metoclopramide. On follow-up one month into treatment, all 7 patients indicated subjective improvement in gastric functioning. These authors concluded that the metoclopramide might be a useful adjunct in the treatment of anorexia nervosa, particularly as a pharmacological aid to improve upper gastrointestinal functioning.

Using a Scinti-scanning method, Holt et al.[59] measured test meal gastric emptying rate in 10 patients with anorexia nervosa and 12 control volunteers. These authors found impaired gastric emptying in patients with anorexia nervosa compared with controls.

Based on the studies reported to date, some patients with active anorexia nervosa appear to have demonstrable impaired gastric functioning while low in weight. These changes may include delayed gastric emptying, decreased hydrogen ion output, and decreased gastric fluid output. These parameters change in the direction of normalization with weight gain, but they have not yet been documented to be completely reversible.

A serious complication of both anorexia nervosa and bulimia is acute gastric dilatation.[60-70] This complication can result in gastric rupture and death. Saul, Dekker, and Watson reviewed the literature on gastric dilatation and noted that there had been 66 cases of spontaneous rupture of the stomach reported.[71] About half of these cases appeared to be related to ingestion of large amounts of food and/or acute gastric dilatation. Eleven of the cases had been diagnosed as having anorexia nervosa; most of these were patients who were undergoing refeeding.[61,64,66,67,72] The mechanism appeared to be a dilatation of the stomach with obstruction of gastroeso-phageal junction because a decompression tube could not be passed. Mar-kowski has documented the development of gastric dilatation in prisoners of war undergoing refeeding.[60]

Sialodenosis has been demonstrated in several patients with anorexia nervosa and with nonanorectic bulimia. More than 20 cases of salivary gland enlargement have been reported in the medical literature in these patients.[73-76] The clinical picture is one of painless swelling of the salivary glands, the parotid glands being most frequently affected but others impli-cated as well.[77] The mechanism of the parotid gland swelling is unclear; the problem has been variously attributed to high carbohydrate intake, alkalosis, and malnutrition.[78] Levin et al.[75] reported biopsy findings in one case, which revealed normal tissue. Walsh, Croft, and Katz[76] reported three parotid gland biopsies that demonstrated asymptomatic, noninflam-matory salivary gland enlargement with one case evidencing scattered inflammatory cells. The incidence of this problem and its correlation with abnormal eating behavior or weight pattern is unknown.

A case of pancreatitis appearing concurrently with anorexia nervosa has also appeared.[79] A recent report found reduced echogenicity of the pancreas in 3 of 10 patients with anorexia nervosa on ultrasound evalua-tion, suggesting possible pathological changes in this organ.[80] The abnor-mality corrected with weight gain.

Another medical concern in patients with anorexia nervosa is the problem of the superior mesenteric artery syndrome. This syndrome can be con-fused clinically with either anorexia nervosa or bulimia. The syndrome involves vascular compression of the third portion of the duodenum. Patients present with vomiting, abdominal pain, and, if the problem has become chronic, weight loss.[81] The compression, which results from me-chanical pressure caused by the structures contained in the root of the mesentery—particularly the superior mesenteric neurovascular bundle—upon the duodenum, can be intermittent and positional. This problem has also been described in patients following severe weight loss not associated with anorexia nervosa, such as in bedridden, injured patients.[82] The con-dition sometimes can be managed supportively but may require surgical intervention. The weight loss of anorexia nervosa may actually predispose to this condition, particularly in those patients confined to bed rest.[83,84] Therefore, the superior mesenteric artery syndrome may mimic the symp-toms of anorexia nervosa and should be considered in the differential diagnosis of that illness. Because the weight loss of anorexia nervosa may increase the likelihood of patients developing the syndrome, particularly if they are at bed rest, a change in clinical status with the onset of vomiting and abdominal pain in an anorexia nervosa patient should raise the suspi-cion of the possibility of compression of the duodenum.

In summary, abnormalities of gastric physiology (such as delayed gastric emptying and decreased hydrogen ion and fluid output) have been documented in anorectic patients when they are low in weight. The superior mesenteric artery syndrome can either predispose to anorexia nervosa or mimic it. Gastric dilatation, with a risk of gastric rupture and death, is a potential problem in patients with anorexia nervosa being refed or in patients who binge-eat. Some patients demonstrate sialodenosis.

Cardiopulmonary Complications

A growing number of studies indicate that the cardiovascular system can be affected by anorexia nervosa. Electrocardiographic (EKG) abnormalities have been described in about half of such patients.[85,86] The EKG changes most commonly described have been changes in T-wave morphology or ST segment depression.[85,86] Bradycardia is frequently mentioned,[87] although tachycardia has also been described.[86] The bradycardia is believed to reflect the decreased metabolism in these patients, functioning as an adaptation to the starvation; the tachycardia may reflect dehydration.

Several case reports suggest that patients with anorexia nervosa may be at increased risk for arrhythmias. Sinus arrest with ectopic atrial rhythm,[87] nodal escape beats with sinus bradycardia,[85] ventricular ectopy,[80] and probable junctional origin with retrograde atrial conduction[88] have all been reported. Although the most obvious explanation for these arrhythmias would be electrolyte abnormalities, such arrhythmias have been described in patients with demonstrated normal electrolytes.[88]

Circulatory dynamics have also been studied in patients with anorexia nervosa, using echocardiography. Gottdiener et al.[89] reported a decrease in cardiac chamber dimensions greater than expected after correction for body surface area in patients with anorexia nervosa. Kalager, Brubakk, and Basse[90] studied a series of 15 patients with anorexia nervosa and found that 87% had left ventricular functional impairment reflecting probable reduced cardiac contractility using systolic ejection time and cardiac output measures. Hypotension and peripheral edema have also been frequently reported in association with anorexia nervosa (table 5). Powers[91] recently reported three cases of heart failure in anorexia nervosa patients undergoing refeeding. Powers stressed the probable role of the increased metabolic demands in this situation (refeeding) as predisposing to this complication. A series of four cases of pericardial effusion in patients with anorexia nervosa has appeared.[92] The pathophysiology of this complication is unclear.

A few case reports of pneumomediastinum have been reported in anorexia nervosa patients or in patients with hyperemesis gravidarum.[93,94] This complication may be related to the vomiting but the pathophysiology remains unclear.

Dental Problems

Problems of dentition, which are quite common in anorexia nervosa patients, appear to be directly attributable to the abnormal behaviors involved in this syndrome. Hellstrom[95] described dental findings in a series of 39 patients with anorexia nervosa. Hurst, Crisp, and Lacey[96] described such findings in an additional 17 cases. In both reports, two major types of dental pathology were noted: the presence of a rapidly developing dental caries, presumably related to high carbohydrate intake; and the presence of perimyolysis, a dental condition that develops secondary to chronic regurgitation. Decalcification of the lingual, palatal, and posterior occlusal surfaces of the teeth were described. This pattern of decalcification differentiates the changes from those caused by acid ingestion because the distribution indicates that the acid is coming from the back of the mouth. The clinical appearance is one of erosion of the enamel and dentin. Contours appear rounded, and there is an absence of staining of the dental surfaces. Because the amalgams are relatively resistant to the acid, they end up looking like islands in the eroded enamel.[96] The pattern is fairly characteristic. This area has also recently been reviewed by Stege, Visco-Dangler, and Rye.[97]

Fluid and Electrolyte Disturbances

Several fluid and electrolyte disturbances have been described in anorexia nervosa patients. The metabolic abnormalities that develop in this condition are apparently the consquences of associated behaviors like laxative abuse, self-induced vomiting, and diuretic abuse, although prolonged fasting may contribute.

In the reported series of patients with anorexia nervosa, metabolic alkalosis is frequently the most common electrolyte abnormality described[8,98-102] Hypochloremia can also be seen in patients who induce vomiting secondary to a loss of gastric acid.[8] Potassium deficits have been demonstrated in a minority of these patients, apparently secondary to renal potassium losses. This renal potassium loss is promoted by the secondary hyperaldosteronism that results from the volume contraction seen in these patients. Hyponatremia is an uncommon finding.[8]

The alkalosis and potassium deficiency seen in anorexia nervosa may cause weakness and constipation, symptoms that mimic depression.[103] In severe cases, such abnormalities can predispose to cardiac arrhythmia or sudden death.[103] Therefore, electrolyte abnormalities are a source of concern with eating disorders. The issue of dehydration has been discussed in the section on renal complications.

Neurological Complications

The relationships between eating disorders and primary central nervous system (CNS) dysfunction has been particularly intriguing. The CNS dysfunction has been suggested as both the cause and consequence of eating disorders. Investigators have taken various paths to explore such relationships.

One approach has been to investigate electroencephalographic (EEG) patterns in patients with eating disorders. A systematic study in this area was published by Crisp, Fenton, and Scotton in 1968.[104] Crisp evaluated 32 patients with anorexia nervosa (31 females and 1 male) prior to treatment. Forty-nine percent manifested abnormal background activity; such changes were seen in only 22% of the controls. Thirty-one percent of the patients versus 9% of the controls had unstable EEG hyperventilation responses. The authors believed that there was a significant association betweeen the length of treatment, low serum electrolyte values, and these EEG abnormalities, and they stressed that such abnormalities could at least partially be accounted for by the metabolic disturbances seen in the patients. Most of the published research evaluating the relationship between abnormal eating patterns and EEG abnormalities involves patients with bulimia or compulsive eating disorders; it will be covered later in this chapter.

To explore possible relationships between CNS dysfunction and eating disorders, we need to examine clinical reports documenting neurological problems that present with abnormal eating behavior as a symptom. Many cases of patients with CNS space-occupying lesions, such as hypothalamic tumors, who have presented with a clinical picture suggestive of anorexia nervosa have appeared in the literature.[105,106] Because of such reports, the possibility of a primary CNS lesion must always be considered in patients presenting with the symptoms of anorexia nervosa or disordered eating.

Computerized axial tomography has also been used to evaluate possible CNS pathology in anorexia nervosa. Following reports of abnormal CAT scans in 4 patients,[107,108] Nussbaum et al.[109] reported scan results in a series of 14 patients, some of whom may not actually have met weight criteria for anorexia nervosa. Seven of these patients demonstrated abnormal scans evidencing cortical atrophy or ventricular dilatation. Controls were not used. Heinz, Martinez, and Haenggeli[108] and Sein, Searson, and

Nicol[110] have also reported EMI scan abnormalities suggesting cerebral atrophy in several cases of adolescent anorexia nervosa, with reversal to normal on repeat scanning following weight gain.

A case of Wernicke's encephalopathy in a patient with anorexia nervosa recently appeared.[111] The authors suggested that this may be an overlooked problem in these patients.

In summary, the question of EEG abnormalities in patients with anorexia nervosa requires further study. Certain neurological problems can mimic anorexia nervosa and must be considered in the differential diagnosis. Further work is indicated, using CAT scanning and perhaps PET scanning techniques, to evaluate CNS structure and function.

Endocrine Abnormalities

The endocrine system is the organ system that has been most intensively studied in anorexia nervosa. Numerous endocrine abnormalities have been documented in this group of patients. These will only be briefly reviewed; more detailed reviews are available.[112-114] Although several of the described abnormalities—like changes in thyroid function—contribute in a direct way to the clinical picture, the clinical significance of other abnormalities is unknown.[112,115]

Menstrual Functioning

Amenorrhea is a characteristic feature of anorexia nervosa. The most common pattern is one of secondary amenorrhea in patients who have experienced menarche, although primary amenorrhea can also be seen.[112] In a significant minority of cases, amenorrhea actually precedes weight loss by several months.[112] This finding has contributed to speculation that there is some primary hypothalamic dysfunction in anorexia nervosa. Patients with anorexia nervosa frequently resume menstruation after weight is restored.[112] However, improvement in anorectic attitudes and behaviors, in addition to weight gain, appears to be important in reestablishing regular menses.[116]

Gonadotropins and Gonadal Steriods

Studies of gonadotropins and gonadal steroids suggest hypofunctioning of the hypothalamo-pituitary-ovarian axis in this group of patients. Reduced levels of luteinizing hormone (LH) and follicle stimulating hormone (FSH) have been frequently reported,[117-125] although reports of normal or elevated values have also appeared.[126,127] Responsiveness of LH to luteinizing hormone releasing hormone (LHRH) has also been reported to be impaired in some patients with anorexia nervosa when they are low in weight, but results have been inconsistent.[127-132] Responsiveness to LHRH has been found to improve with weight gain[121,127,128,131,133] or with LHRH priming.[134] This has been interpreted as reflecting a possible underlying deficit in endogenous stimulation by LHRH; such a deficit would be suggestive of hypothalamic dysfunction. Urinary pituitary gonadotropins have been shown to be low in some patients with anorexia nervosa.[33,40]

Using serial monitoring techniques, researchers have found the LH secretory pattern to be "immature," i.e., to resemble the pattern seen in premenarcheal girls.[119,135,136] This LH secretory pattern "matures" with weight gain accompanied by symptomatic improvement;[133] weight gain alone may not be sufficient to correct the abnormality.[119]

Abnormalities in the hypothalamic responsiveness to the negative feedback effects of estrogen have also been reported.[137,138] Plasma and urine estrogen levels have been shown to be low[33,40,118,121-123,125] but to return toward normal with weight gain.[118] Abnormalities in the metabolism of estrogen have also been shown. Estrogen metabolism in these patients generates a relative decrease in estradiol and a relative increase in estrone. This pattern is opposite to that seen in obese women.[139]

Low testosterone levels have been demonstrated in several male patients with anorexia.[140-142]

Thyroid Functions

Thyroid function abnormalities have been commonly reported in patients with anorexia nervosa. The changes seen in these patients are generally believed to be adaptational to the starvation.

Low levels of serum T3 are seen fairly consistently in patients with anorexia nervosa when low in weight.[8,124,143-147] The T3 values probably represent a low T3 syndrome secondary to a decrease in the peripheral conversion of T4 to T3, a pattern adaptational to starvation.[143,148-150] The less active form, reverse T3, has been found to be elevated.[151] The T4 values are reported to be normal or low,[143,144,152] and the T3 to T4 ratio is reported to be low.[143]

Low thyrotropin (TSH) values have also been described in a few patients with anorexia nervosa.[40,143,144] A delay in the peak TSH response to thyrotropin-releasing hormone (TRH),[143,153] a delay in the fall of TSH,[146] and a blunted TSH response to the TRH[154] have all been demonstrated in some anorexia nervosa patients.

Growth Hormone

Fasting growth hormone levels have frequently been found to be elevated in anorexia nervosa patients,[40,117,120,154-158] a pattern that corrects with weight gain.[120] Several reports have documented a pathological growth hormone increase in response to TRH stimulation[154,157,159] or to glucose administration;[156,160] other investigators have failed to confirm these results.[117,161] An attenuated growth hormone response to insulin-induced hypoglycemia,[162] to apomorphine,[156] and to L-dopa[130] have also been reported. Mecklenburg et al.[33] found a normal increment in growth hormone following arginine or insulin infusion or during spontaneous hypoglycemia. The clinical implications of these growth hormone regulatory abnormalities are not clear.

Prolactin

Fasting prolactin levels have generally been found to be normal in patients with anorexia nervosa;[33,154,163-165] but elevated levels have been reported.[135] A paradoxical increase in prolactin has been reported in response to gonadotropin-releasing hormone in some patients.[166] Prolactin response to TSH and to sulpiride have been reported to be normal,[154,163,165] but an exaggerated response has been reported in at least two patients.[135]

Glucose

Fasting hypoglycemia has been documented by several authors in patients with anorexia nervosa.[33,40] Diabetic glucose tolerance curves have been observed in some patients[8] and have been shown to normalize with weight gain.[156] Flat glucose tolerance curves have also been reported.[8]

Adrenal Functions

Regulation of adrenal cortisol secretion has been demonstrated to be abnormal in many patients with anorexia nervosa. Several authors have reported elevated basal cortisol levels.[40,117,120,136,167] Some patients have been demonstrated to have inadequate cortisol suppression following dexamethasone[126,167,168] and to have disturbed secretory patterns of cortisol.[136,140,169] The elevated cortisol levels appear to reflect both an increase in secretion and a decrease in clearance of this substance.[76,170]

We do not know whether the lack of suppression on the dexamethasone suppression test seen in patients with anorexia nervosa correlates with depressive symptoms or some other abnormality, such as low weight or some other abnormal eating-related behavior.

Temperature Regulation

The regulation of temperature is another basic metabolic function under hypothalamic control. Body temperature regulation disturbances have been demonstrated in patients with anorexia nervosa. These studies have contributed to speculation that a hypothalamic problem might be involved.[171] Mecklenburg et al. in 1974[33] demonstrated that anorexia nervosa patients showed exaggerated fluctuations in core body temperature when exposed to extremes of temperature. The lowering of thresholds for thermoregulatory sweating and vasodilatation that has been demonstrated may contribute to the hypothermia seen in some of these patients.[172] Freyschuss, Fohlin, and Thoren[173] have also reported that patients with anorexia nervosa demonstrated reduced and irregular vasodilatation upon exposure to indirect heating.

Bulimia

Specific signs and symptoms associated with nonanorectic bulimia have not been adequately studied. Patients with this problem frequently complain of lethargy and impaired concentration. Abdominal pain is frequently reported following binge-eating and vomiting episodes. Insufficient data are available to adequately characterize the medical risk of bulimia; the available reports will be summarized by organ system.

Renal Complications

Our group[174] reported the results of laboratory analyses in a series of patients with either nonanorectic bulimia ($n = 158$) or atypical eating disorders ($n = 10$). Abnormal screening renal function tests were found in only 4 patients; one of these had a history of preexisting renal disease. The other 3 patients all had an elevated BUN with a normal serum creatinine. Our group also reported vasopressin augmentation to be less than 5% in 6 normal-weight bulimic subjects who were water deprived for a minimum of 16 hours prior to vasopressin administration.[175] These data indicate normal water concentrating ability in this small series of normal-weight bulimic subjects.

Gastrointestinal Problems

In their review of spontaneous rupture of the stomach, Saul, Dekker, and Watson[71] reported the case of a normal weight individual with a history of anorexia nervosa who overate excessively. This patient may have met criteria for bulimia. The patient developed infarction and perforation of the stomach followed by severe and irreversible shock. A case of gastric dilatation in a normal weight person with bulimia that was successfully managed medically has also been published.[176] These reports suggest that gastric dilatation and infarction are possible complications of bulimia as well as anorexia nervosa.

A case of a patient who was hospitalized on four occasions for episodes of acute pancreatitis following eating binges has been published.[177] The author excluded other common causes for the pancreatitis and was able temporally to correlate the bulimic behaviors to the episodes of pancreatitis.

Studies describing gastric physiology in patients with bulimia have not yet been reported.

Fluid and Electrolyte Disturbances

Fluid and electrolyte abnormalities are also commonly encountered in patients with bulimia.[174] Our group reported on laboratory studies in a series of patients with bulimia ($n = 158$) and atypical eating disorders ($n = 10$).[174] Of these patients, 84.5% were vomiting on a regular basis and 37.5% were abusing laxatives. Eighty-two of the 168 patients demonstrated some electrolyte abnormality on routine screening. Metabolic alkalosis (27.4%), hypochloremia (23.8%), and hypokalemia (13.7%) were the most common abnormalities. An attempt was made to correlate abnormal electrolytes to abnormal eating behaviors. Patients who reported that they induced vomiting at least daily were significantly more likely to manifest alkalosis than patients reporting less frequent self-induced vomiting behavior. Metabolic acidosis was described in a few patients; fasting-induced metabolic acidosis or acidosis secondary to acute diarrhea from laxatives were suggested causes.

Neurological Complications

Rau and Green have published extensively on the possible association between eating disorders and EEG abnormalities in a series of articles exploring the hypothesis that some demonstrable neurophysiological dysfunction underlies "compulsive eating" problems.[178-180] The overview article summarizes their experience with 79 patients.[181] Thirteen of this group were underweight and 19 were overweight; 64.4% of the sample had abnormal EEGs. The abnormalities most commonly seen were paroxysmal dysrhythmias. The most common EEG abnormality found was the 14 and 6 per second spike pattern. This pattern has been demonstrated to be present in some normal adolescents[182] and some normal adults.[183] It is currently a matter of debate as to whether or not this pattern is more common in psychiatric populations.[184] It is unclear whether this EEG abnormality is actually associated with behavioral abnormalities.[185-187]

Our group reported EEG investigations in a series of 25 patients who satisfied DSM-III criteria for bulimia.[188] The EEG tracings were read twice by electroencephalographers blind to diagnosis. Both readings concurred that 21 of the tracings were normal and that 4 were abnormal. The authors concluded that only a minority of patients who met DSM-III criteria for bulimia actually had demonstrable EEG abnormalities.

There have also been reports of bulimic symptoms in patients not of low weight who have been found to have primary neurological problems, including Huntington's chorea,[189] following amygdalectomy,[190] following lobotomy,[191] and as a postictal phenomenon.[192] Bulimic-type symptoms have also been described in association with CNS tumors.[193,194] Bulimic symptoms can also be seen in association with hypersomnia in the Klein-Levin syndrome and in patients with parkinsonism, where improvement in eating followed treatment for the primary illness.[195]

Hematologic Abnormalities

A single case of a patient with bulimia nervosa who manifested a hemorrhagia tendency and was found to have a deficiency of vitamin K-dependent coagulation factors has appeared.[196] The presumed mechanism was deficient intake of the necessary food.

Endocrine Abnormalities

Only a limited number of endocrine investigations have been reported to date in patients with bulimia. The available studies suggest certain abnormalities that will be discussed below. Testing to date, however, has suggested maintenance of normal endocrine functioning in many patients with bulimia.

Menstrual functions have been reported to be irregular in nonanorectic bulimia, but prolonged amenorrhea does not appear to be as widespread as it is in anorexia nervosa. The relationship between eating patterns and the menstrual cycle remains an interesting one deserving further study. Gonadotropins and gonadal steroid levels have not been reported.

Glucose and insulin levels have not been adequately characterized in patients with bulimia.

Our group reported thyroid functions in a series of 86 patients who met DSM-III criteria for bulimia or atypical eating disorder.[174] Sixteen patients (18.6%) had abnormal thyroid function tests on screening examination; all but one, however, were subsequently felt to have normal thyroid functions after physical examination and TSH determination. One case was diagnosed as true hypothyroidism. Gwirtsman et al.[197] reported blunted TSH response (change in TSH of less than 5) to TRH in 8 of 10 patients with bulimia. Our group[175] reported normal TSH responsiveness to TRH in 5 of 6 normal weight subjects with bulimia. Gwirtsman et al. also reported an increase in growth hormone in 2 of 3 subjects following TRH administration.

Table 6. Major Medical Complications of Anorexia Nervosa

Hematologic	Leukopenia, relative lymphocytosis
	Thrombocytopenia
	Hypocellularity of the bone marrow
	Decreased granulocyte killing rate
Renal	Elevated BUN (dehydration)
	Partial diabetes insipidus
Metabolic	Hypercholesterolemia
	High serum carotene
	Low plasma zinc, urinary zinc, and urinary copper
	Abnormal liver function tests
	Increased insulin erythrocyte binding
Gastro-intestinal	Altered gastric emptying
	Decreased gastric acid output
	Decreased gastric fluid output
	Swelling in salivary glands
	Elevated serum amylase
	Superior mesenteric artery syndrome
	Gastric dilatation, rupture
Cardiovascular	Abnormal EKG
	Arrhythmias, bradycardia, hypotension
	Altered circulatory dynamics
	Pericardial effusion
	Edema
Dental	Caries
	Perimyolysis
	Decalcification
Fluid and electrolyte	Dehydration
	Alkalosis
	Hypochloremia
	Hypokalemia
Central nervous system	Abnormal EEG
	Abnormal CAT scan

We also reported elevated fasting prolactin concentrations in 3 of 6 subjects of normal weight with bulimia; 5 of the 6 subjects demonstrated normal prolactin responsiveness to TRH stimulation.[175]

Dexamethasone suppression results have been reported in several series. A significant number of patients with nonanorectic bulimia appear to be nonsuppressors on the DST (56% of 9 subjects reported by Hudson, Laffer, and Pope in 1982;[198] 47% of 47 subjects reported by Hudson, Pope, and Jones in 1983;[199] 67% of 18 reported by Gwirtsman et al. in 1982;[197] and 50% of 28 subjects reported by Mitchell et al.[200]). Cortisol secretory patterns have not been reported.

Table 7. Endocrine Abnormalities Associated with Anorexia Nervosa

Gonadal steroids	Low LH, FSH
	Immature LH pattern
	Impaired response to LHRH
	Low urinary gonadotropins, estrogens
	Abnormal estrogen metabolism
Thyroid	Low T3, high reverse T3
	Impaired TRH responsiveness
Growth hormone	Elevated basal levels
	Pathological responsiveness to TRH, glucose
Prolactin	Pathological responsiveness to LHRH
Glucose	Fasting hypoglycemia
	Abnormal glucose tolerance test
Adrenal	Elevated cortisol
	Change in cortisol metabolism, secretion
	Positive dexamethasone suppression test

Discussion

The major medical complications of anorexia nervosa and bulimia are summarized in tables 6-8. We can see that these disorders are clearly not medically benign conditions. We have considerable information about anorexia nervosa, and we know it can prove fatal. The major reasons for death include inanition, fluid and electrolyte abnormalities, and suicide; the overall mortality varies from 0% to 19% in reported series.[201,202] Not

Table 8. Major Medical Complications of Bulimia

Renal	Elevated BUN (dehydration)
Gastro-intestinal	Swelling in salivary gland
	Elevated serum amylase
	Gastric dilatation, rupture
Dental	Caries
	Perimyolysis
	Decalcification
Fluid and electrolyte	Dehydration
	Alkalosis
	Hypochloremia
	Hypokalemia
Central nervous system	Abnormal EEG
Endocrine	Impaired TRH responsiveness
	Pathological growth hormone responsiveness to glucose
	Elevated basal prolactin
	Positive dexamethasone suppression test

enough is known to estimate the mortality from bulimia. Considering the reports of serious electrolyte abnormalities and gastric dilatation in these patients, one would sadly predict that fatalities have and will occur.

Certain general guidelines can be offered concerning the physical and laboratory assessment of patients with anorexia nervosa and bulimia (table 9). A careful medical history and physical examination are an important part of the evaluation process. Careful attention should be given to the state of hydration and inanition, oral hygiene, cardiac functioning, and vital signs. Is there significant hypotension or bradycardia? Careful neurological assessment is indicated to rule out the primary neurological lesion that might present with disordered eating as a symptom.

Table 9. Physical and Laboratory Assessment
of Anorexia Nervosa and Bulimia Patients

Physical examination

Vital signs
State of hydration
Degree of inanition
Oral hygiene
Cardiac functioning
Evidence of neurological dysfunction

Laboratory

Routine
  CBC
  Screening renal function tests
  Screening liver function tests
  Serum glucose
  Serum electrolytes
  Thyroid functions
Recommended as routine in some treatment centers
  Skull films with sella views
  Visual fields
  CAT scan
  Prolactin
  LH, FSH

Routine screening laboratory work appears indicated, as outlined in table 9. Skull films with sella views combined with visual fields or, as an alternative, CAT scans are done routinely at some centers to screen for CNS and pituitary abnormalities. Some clinicians also include basal prolactin levels as a measure of pituitary function.

Regardless of the routine screening tests used, a careful history and physical examination remain the most useful methods to evaluate these patients. Evidence of an atypical presentation should alert the evaluating physician of the necessity for a vigorous pursuit of other possible etiologies.

REFERENCES

1. Barbosa-Saldivar, J. L., and T. B. Van Itallie. 1979. Semistarvation: An overview of an old problem. *Bull. N.Y. Acad. Med.* 55:744-97.
2. Keys, A., A. Henshel, and H. L. Taylor. 1947. The size and function of the human heart at rest in semi-starvation and in subsequent rehabilitation. *Am. J. Physiol.* 50:153-69.
3. Pimstone, B. L., G. Barbezat, J. D. L. Hansen, and P. Murray. 1968. Studies on growth hormone secretion in protein-calorie malnutrition. *Am. J. Clin. Nutr.* 21:482-87.
4. Smith, S. R., P. J. Edgar, T. Pozefsky, M. H. Chhetri, and T. E. Prout. 1974. Growth hormone in adults with protein-calorie malnutrition. *J. Clin. Endocrinol. Metab* 39:53-62.
5. Smith, S. R., T. Bledsoe, and M. K. Chhetri. 1975. Cortisol metabolism and the pituitary-adrenal axis in adults with protein-calorie malnutrition. *J. Clin. Endocrinol. Metab.* 40:43-52.
6. Vigersky, R. A., A. E. Andersen, R. H. Thompson, and D. L. Loriaux. 1977. Hypothalamic dysfunction in secondary amenorrhea associated with simple weight loss. *N. Engl. J. Med.* 297:1141-45.
7. King, A. 1963. Primary and secondary anorexia nervosa syndromes. *Br. J. Psychiatry* 109:470-79.
8. Warren, M. P., and R. L. Van de Wiele. 1973. Clinical and metabolic features of anorexia nervosa. *Am. J. Obstet. Gynecol.* 117:435-99.
9. Halmi, K. A. 1974. Anorexia nervosa: Demographic and clinical features in 94 cases. *Psychosom. Med.* 36:18-26.
10. Silverman, J. A. 1983. Anorexia nervosa: Clinical and metabolic observations. *Int. J. Eating Disorders* 2:159-66.
11. Schwabe, A. D., B. M. Lipe, R. J. Chang, M. A. Pops, and J. Yager. 1981. Anorexia nervosa. *Ann. Intern. Med.* 94:371-81.
12. Carryer, H. M., J. M. Berkman, and H. L. Mason. 1959. Relative lymphocytosis in anorexia nervosa. *Staff Meet. Mayo Clin.* 34:426-32.
13. Pearson, H. A. 1967. Marrow hypoplasia in anorexia nervosa. *J. Pediatr.* 71:211-15.
14. Kabanek, B., H. Heimpel, G. Paar, and A. Schoengen. 1977. Hematologische Veranderungen bei anorexia nervosa. *Blut* 35:115-24.
15. Halmi, K. A., and J.R. Falk. 1981. Common physiological changes in anorexia nervosa. *Int. J. Eating Disorders* 1:16-27.
16. Myers, T. J., M. D. Perkerson, B. A. Witter, and N. B. Granville. 1981. Hematologic findings in anorexia nervosa. *Conn. Med.* 45:14-17.
17. Rieger, W., J. P. Brady, and E. Weisberg. 1978. Hematologic changes in anorexia nervosa. *Am. J. Psychiatry* 135:984-85.
18. Bowers, T. K., and E. Eckert. 1978. Leukopenia in anorexia nervosa. *Arch. Intern. Med.* 138:1520-23.
19. Lampert, F., and B. Lau. 1976. Bone marrow hypoplasia in anorexia nervosa. *Eur. J. Pediatr.* 124:65-71.
20. Mant, M. J., and B. S. Faragher. 1972. The haematology of anorexia nervosa. *Br. J. Haematol.* 23:737-49.
21. Cornbleet, P. J., R. C. Moir, and P. L. Wolf. 1977. A histochemical study of bone marrow hypoplasia in anorexia nervosa. *Virchows Arch.* 374:239-47.

22. Amrein, P. C., R. Friedman, K. Kosinski and L. Ellman. 1979. Hematologic changes in anorexia nervosa. *JAMA* 241:2190-91.
23. Gotch, F. M., C. J. F. Spry, A. G. Mowat, P. B. Beeson, and I. C. M. Maclennan. 1975. Reversible granulocyte killing defect in anorexia nervosa. *Clin. Exp. Immunol.* 21:244-49.
24. Palmblad, J., L. Fohlin, and M. Lundstrom. 1977. Anorexia nervosa and polymorphonuclear (PMN) granulocyte reactions. *Scand. J. Haematol.* 19:334-42.
25. Golla, J. A., L. A. Larson, C. F. Anderson, A. R. Lucas, W. R. Wilson, and T. B. Tomasi. 1981. An immunological assessment of patients with anorexia nervosa. *Am. J. Clin. Nutr.* 34:2756-62.
26. Pertschuk, M. J., L. O. Crosby, L. Barot, and J. L. Mullen. 1982. Immunocompetency in anorexia nervosa. *Am. J. Clin. Nutr.* 35:968-72.
27. Armstrong-Esther, C. A., A. H. Crisp, J. H. Lacey, and T. N. Bryant. 1978. An investigation of the immune response of patients suffering from anorexia nervosa. *Postgrad. Med. J.* 54:395-99.
28. Ogston, D., and W. B. Ogston. 1976. The fibrinolytic enzyme system in anorexia nervosa. *Acta Haematol.* 55:230-33.
29. Kim, Y., and A. F. Michael. 1975. Hypocomplementemia in anorexia nervosa. *J. Pediatr.* 87:582-85.
30. Wyatt, R. J., M. Farrell, P. L. Berry, J. Forristal, M. J. Maloney, and C. D. West. 1982. Reduced alternative complement pathway control protein levels in anorexia nervosa: Response to parenteral alimentation. *Am. J. Clin. Nutr.* 34:973-80.
31. Aperia, A., O. Broberger, L. Fohlin. 1978. Renal function in anorexia nervosa. *Acta Paediatr. Scand.* 67:219-24.
32. Wigley, R. D. 1960. Potassium deficiency in anorexia nervosa, with reference to renal tubular vacuolation. *Br. Med. J.* 2:110-13.
33. Mecklenburg, R. S., D. L. Loriaux, R. H. Thompson, A. E. Andersen, and M. B. Lipsett. 1974. Hypothalamic dysfunction in patients with anorexia nervosa. *Medicine* 53:147-59.
34. Vigersky, R. A., D. L. Loriaux, A. E. Andersen, and M. Lipsett. 1975. Anorexia nervosa: Behavioral and hypothalamic aspects. *Clin. Endocrinol.* 5:517-35.
35. Gold, P. W., W. Kaye, G. L. Robertson, and M. Ebert. 1983. Abnormalities in plasma and cerebrospinal-fluid arginine vasopressin in patients with anorexia nervosa. *N. Engl. J. Med.* 308:1117-23.
36. Nestel, P. J. 1973. Cholesterol metabolism in anorexia nervosa and hypercholesterolemia. *J. Clin. Endocrinol. Metab.* 38:325-28.
37. Halmi, K., and M. Fry. 1974. Serum lipids in anorexia nervosa. *Biol. Psychiatry* 8:159-67.
38. Klinefelter, H. F. 1965. Hypercholesterolemia in anorexia nervosa. *J. Clin. Endocrinol. Metab.* 25:1520-21.
39. Mordasini, R., G. Klose, and H. Greten. 1978. Secondary type II hyperlipoproteinemia in patients with anorexia nervosa. *Metabolism* 27:71-79.
40. Hurd, H. P., P. J. Palumbo, and H. Gharib. 1977. Hypothalamic-endocrine dysfunction in anorexia nervosa. *Mayo Clin. Proc.* 52:711-16.
41. Robboy, M. S., A. S. Sato, and A. D. Schwabe. 1974. The hypercarotenemia in anorexia nervosa: A comparison of vitamin A and carotene levels in various forms of menstrual dysfunction and cachexia. *Am. J. Clin. Nutr.* 27:362-67.
42. Laszlo, J. E. 1981. Vitamin A (carotene) and anorexia. *Med. J. Aust.* I:146.
43. Bhanji, S., and D. Mattingly. 1981. Anorexia nervosa: Some observations on "dieters" and "vomiters," cholesterol and carotene. *Br. J. Psychiatry* 139:238-41.

44. Casper, R. C., E. D. Eckert, K. A. Halmi, S. C. Goldberg, and J. M. Davis. 1980. Bulimia: Its incidence and clinical importance in patients with anorexia nervosa. *Arch. Gen. Psychiatry* 37:1030-40.
45. Bakan, R. 1979. The role of zinc in anorexia nervosa: Etiology and treatment. *Med Hypotheses* 5:731-36.
46. Horrobin, D. F., and S. C. Cunnane. 1980. Interactions between zinc, essential fatty acids and prostaglandins: Relevance to acrodermatitis enteropathica, total parenteral nutrition, the glucagonoma syndrome, diabetes, anorexia nervosa and sickle cell anemia. *Med. Hypotheses* 6:277-96.
47. Casper, R. C., B. Kirschner, and R. A. Jacob. 1978. Zinc and copper status in anorexia nervosa. *Psychopharmacol. Bull.* 14:53-55.
48. Casper, R. C., B. Kirschner, H. H. Sandstead, R. A. Jacob, and J. M. Davis. 1980. An evaluation of trace metals, vitamins, and taste function in anorexia nervosa. *Am. J. Clin. Nutr.* 33:1801-8.
49. Esca, S. A., W. Brenner, K. Mach, and F. Gschnait. 1979. Kwashiorkor-like zinc deficiency syndrome in anorexia nervosa. *Acta Derm. Venereol.* (Stockh.) 59:361-64.
50. Kanis, J. A., P. Brown, K. Fitzpatrick, D. J. Hibbert, D. B. Horn, I. M. Nairn, D. Shirling, J. A. Strong, and H. J. Walton. 1974. Anorexia nervosa: A clinical, psychiatric, and laboratory study. *Q. J. Med.* 43:321-38.
51. Cravario, A., C. A. Cravetto, and R. Autino. 1974. Studio della funzionalita epatica nell'anoressia nervosa. *Minerva Med.* 65:2990-95.
52. Nordgren, L., and C. von Scheele. 1977. Hepatic and pancreatic dysfunction in anorexia nervosa: A report of two cases. *Biol. Psychiatry* 12:681-87.
53. Wachslicht-Rodbard, H., H. A. Gross, D. Rodbard, M. H. Ebert, and J. Roth. 1979. Increased insulin binding to erythrocytes in anorexia nervosa. *N. Engl. J. Med.* 300:882-87.
54. Jameson, L. 1979. Insulin binding in anorexia nervosa. *N. Engl. J. Med.* 301:386-87.
55. Silverstone, J. T., and G. F. M. Russell. 1967. Gastric "hunger" contractions in anorexia nervosa. *Br. J. Psychiatry* 113:257-63.
56. Dubois, A., H. A. Gross, M. H. Ebert, and D. O. Castell. 1979. Altered gastric emptying and secretion in primary anorexia nervosa. *Gastroenterology* 77:319-23.
57. Kishi, S., Y. Kitamura, H. Seki, S. Ito, K. Eto, M. Arizumi, K. Takeuchi, M. Nokihara, and H. Mori. 1980. Gastric secretory capacity in anorexia nervosa. *Tokushima J. Exp. Med.* 27:29-35.
58. Saleh, J. W. and P. Lebwohl. 1980. Metoclopramide-induced gastric emptying in patients with anorexia nervosa. *Am. J. Gastroenterol.* 74:127-32.
59. Holt, S., M. J. Ford, S. Grant, and R. C. Heading. 1981. Abnormal gastric emptying in primary anorexia nervosa. *Br. J. Psychiatry* 139:550-52.
60. Markowski, B. 1947. Acute dilatation of the stomach. *Br. Med. J.* 2:128-30.
61. Russell, G. F. M. 1966. Acute dilatation of the stomach in a patient with anorexia nervosa. *Br. J. Psychiatry* 112:203-7.
62. Evans, D. S., 1968. Acute dilatation and spontaneous rupture of the stomach. *Br. J. Surg.* 55:940-42.
63. Conrad, C., and M. T. Andersen. 1976. Akut ventrikelatoni efter umodeholden fodeindtagelse. *Ugeskr. Laeger* 138:2007-8.
64. Jennings, K. P., and A. M. Klidjian. 1974. Acute gastric dilatation in anorexia nervosa. *Br. Med. J.* 1:477-78.
65. Costanzo, J., N. Cano, G. Faugere, A. D'Orso, R. Guidicelli, and A. Gauthier. 1975. Dilatation aigue gastrique et anorexie mentale. *Nouv. Presse Med.* 4:509.
66. Bossingham, D. 1977. Acute gastric dilatation in anorexia nervosa. *Br. Med. J.* 2:959.

67. Brook, G. K. 1977. Acute gastric dilatation in anorexia nervosa. (a) *Br. Med. J.* 2:499-500.
68. Brook, G. K. 1977. Acute gastric dilatation in anorexia nervosa. (b) *Br. Med. J.* 2:1153.
69. Lebriquir, M., E. Moirot, J. M. Droy, J. Ph. Rogez, and J. Leroy. 1978. Dilatation aigue gastrique et anorexie mentale. *Sem. Hop. Paris* 54:1175-76.
70. Matikainen, M. 1979. Spontaneous rupture of the stomach. *Am. J. Surg.* 138:451-52.
71. Saul, S. H., A. Dekker, and C. G. Watson. 1981. Acute gastric dilatation with infarction and perforation. *Gut* 22:978-83.
72. Scobie, B. A. 1973. Acute gastric dilatation and duodenal ileus in anorexia nervosa. *Med. J. Aust.* 2:932:34.
73. Dawson, J., and C. Jones. 1977. Vomiting-induced hypokalemic alkalosis and parotid swelling. *Practitioner* 218:267-68.
74. Simon, D., P. Laudenbach, M. Lebovici, and P. Mauvais-Jarvis. 1979. Parotidomegalie au cours des dysorexies mentales. *Nouv. Presse Med.* 9:2399-2402.
75. Levin, P. A., J. M. Falko, K. Dixon, E. M. Gallup, and W. Saunders. 1980. Benign parotid enlargement in bulimia. *Ann. Intern. Med.* 93:827-29.
76. Walsh, B. T., C. B. Croft, and J. A. Katz. 1981-82. Anorexia nervosa and salivary gland enlargement. *Int. J. Psychiatry Med.* 11:255-61.
77. Anders, D., D. Harms, O. Kriens, and H. Schmidt. 1975. Zur frage der sialadenose als sekundarer organmanifestation der anorexia nervosa—beobachtungen en einem 13jahrigen knaben. *Klin. Padiatr.* 187:156-62.
78. Bernard, J. D., and M. A. Shearn. 1974. Psychogenic pseudo-Sjogren's syndrome. *West J. Med.* 120:247-48.
79. Schoettle, U. C. 1979. Pancreatitis: A complication, a concomitant, or a cause of an anorexia nervosalike syndrome. *J. Am. Acad. Child Psychiatry* 18:384-90.
80. Cox, K. L., R. A. Cannon, M. E. Ament, H. E. Phillips, and C. B. Schaffer. 1983. Biochemical and ultrasound abnormalities of the pancreas in anorexia nervosa. *Digestive Dis. Sci.* 28:225-29.
81. Akin, J. T., Jr., S. W. Gray, and J. E. Skandelakis. 1976. Vascular compression of the duodenum: Presentation of ten cases and review of the literature. *Surgery* 79:515-22.
82. Wayne, E., R. E. Miller, and B. Eiseman. 1971. Duodenal obstruction by the superior mesenteric artery in bedridden combat casualties. *Ann. Surg.* 174:339-45.
83. Pentlow, B. D., and R. G. Dent. 1981. Acute vascular compression of the duodenum in anorexia nervosa. *Br. J. Surg.* 68:665-66.
84. Sours, J. A., and L. J. Vorhaus. 1981. Superior mesenteric syndrome in anorexia nervosa: A case report. *Am. J. Psychiartry* 138:519-20.
85. Thurston, J., and P. Marks. 1974. Electrocardiographic abnormalities in patients with anorexia nervosa. *Br. Heart J.* 36:719-23.
86. Palossy, B., and M. Oo. 1977. ECG alterations in anorexia nervosa. *Adv. Cardiol.* 19:280-82.
87. Fohlin, L. 1977. Body composition, cardiovascular and renal functions in adolescent patients with anorexia nervosa. *Acta Paediatr. Scand. Suppl.* 268:7-19.
88. Mitchell, J. E., and R. Gillum. 1980. Weight-dependent arrhythmia in a patient with anorexia nervosa. *Am. J. Psychiatry* 137:377-78.
89. Gottdiener, J. S., H. A. Gross, W. L. Henry, J. S. Borer, and M. H. Ebert. 1978. Effects of self-induced starvation on cardiac size and function in anorexia nervosa. *Circulation* 58:425-33.
90. Kalager, T., O. Brubakk, and H. H. Basse. 1978. Cardiac performance in patients with anorexia nervosa. *Cardiology* 63:1-4.
91. Powers, P. S. 1982. Heart failure during treatment of anorexia nervosa. *Am. J. Psychiatry* 139:1167-70.

92. Silverman, J. A., and E. Krongrad. 1983. Anorexia nervosa: A cause of pericardial effusion? *Pediatr. Cardiol.* 4:125-27.
93. Donley, A. J., and T. J. Kemple. 1978. Spontaneous pneumomediastinum complicating anorexia nervosa. *Br. Med. J.* 1:1604-5.
94. Chatfield, W. R., J. D. P. Bowditch, and C. A. Forrest. 1979. Spontaneous pneumomediastinum complicating anorexia nervosa. *Br. Med. J.* 1:200-201.
95. Hellstrom, I. 1977. Oral complications in anorexia nervosa. *Scand. J. Dent. Res.* 85:71-86.
96. Hurst, P. S., A. H. Crisp, and J. H. Lacey. 1977. Teeth, vomiting and diet: A study of the dental characteristics of seventeen anorexia nervosa patients. *Postgrad. Med. J.* 53:298-305.
97. Stege, P., L. Visco-Dangler, and L. Rye. 1982. Anorexia nervosa: Review including oral and dental manifestations. *J. Am. Dent. Assoc.* 104:648-52.
98. Sunderman, F. W., and E. Rose. 1948. Studies in serum electrolytes. XVI. Changes in the serum and body fluids in anorexia nervosa. *J. Clin. Endocrinol. Metab.* 8:209-20.
99. Elkinton, J. R., and E. J. Huth. 1958. Body fluid abnormalities in anorexia nervosa and undernutrition. *Metabolism* 5:376-403.
100. Wolff, H. P., P. Vecsei, F. Kruck, S. Roscher, J. J. Brown, G. O. Dusterdieck, A. F. Lever, and J. I. S. Robertson. 1968. Psychiatric disturbance leading to potassium depletion, sodium depletion, raised plasma-renin concentration, and secondary hyperaldosteronism. *Lancet* I:257-61.
101. Wallace, M., P. Richards, E. Chesser, and O. Wrong. 1968. Persistent alkalosis and hypokalaemia caused by surreptitious vomiting. *Q. J. Med.* 37:577-88.
102. Warren, S. E., S. M. Steinberg. 1979. Acid-base and electrolyte disturbances in anorexia nervosa. *Am. J. Psychiatry* 136:415-18.
103. Webb, W. L., and M. Gehi. 1981. Electrolyte and fluid imbalance: Neuropsychiatric manifestations. *Psychosomatics* 22:199-203.
104. Crisp, A. H., G. W. Fenton, and L. Scotton. 1968. A controlled study of the EEG in anorexia nervosa. *Br. J. Psychiatry* 114:1149-60.
105. Lewin, K., D. Mattingly and R. R. Millis. 1972. Anorexia nervosa associated with hypothalamic tumor. *Br. Med. J.* 2:629-30.
106. Weller, R. A., and E. B. Weller. 1982. Anorexia nervosa in a patient with an infiltrating tumor of the hypothalamus. *Am. J. Psychiatry* 139:824-26.
107. Enzmann, D. R., and B. Lane. 1977. Cranial computer tomography findings in anorexia nervosa. *J. Comput. Assist. Tomogr.* 1:410-14.
108. Heinz, E. R., J . Martinez, and A. Haenggeli. 1977. Reversibility of cerebral atrophy in anorexia nervosa and Cushing's syndrome. *J. Comput. Assist. Tomogr.* 1:415-18.
109. Nussbaum, M., I. R. Shenker, J. Marc., and M. Klein. 1980. Cerebral atrophy in anorexia nervosa. *J. Pediatr.* 96:867-69.
110. Sein, P., S. Searson, and A. R. Nicol. 1981. Anorexia nervosa and pseudo-atrophy of the brain. *Br. J. Psychiatry* 139:257-58.
111. Handler, C. E., and G. D. Perkin. 1982. Anorexia nervosa and Wernicke's encephalopathy: An underdiagnosed association. *Lancet* 2:771-2.
112. Garfinkel, P. E., G. M. Brown, and P. L. Darby. 1981. The psychoendocrinology of anorexia nervosa. *Int. J. Ment. Health* 9:162-93.
113. Walsh, B. T. 1980. The endocrinology of anorexia nervosa. *Psychiatr. Clin. North Am.* 3:299-312.
114. Beumont, P. J. V. 1979. The endocrinology of anorexia nervosa. *Med. J. Aust.* 1:611-13.
115. Neufeld, N. D. 1979. Endocrine abnormalities associated with deprivation dwarfism and anorexia nervosa. *Pediatr. Clin. North. Am.* 26:199-208.

116. Falk, J. R., and K. A. Halmi. 1982. Amenorrhea in anorexia nervosa: Examination of the critical body weight hypothesis. *Biol. Psychiatry* 17:799-806.
117. Brown, G. M., P. E. Garfinkel, N. Jeuniewic, H. Moldofsky, and H. C. Stancer. 1977. Endocrine profiles in anorexia nervosa. In *Anorexia nervosa,* ed. R. A. Vigersky. New York: Raven Press.
118. Beumont, P. J. V., P. J. Carr, and M. G. Gelder. 1973. Plasma levels of luteinizing hormone and of immunoreactive oestrogens (oestradiol) in anorexia nervosa: Response to clomiphene citrate. *Psychol. Med.* 3:495-501.
119. Boyar, R. M., J. Katz, J. W. Finkelstein, S. Kapen, H. Weiner, E. D. Weitzman, and L. Hellman. 1974. Anorexia nervosa—immaturity for the 24-hour luteinizing hormone secretory pattern. *N. Engl. J. Med.* 291:861-65.
120. Garfinkel, P. E., G. M. Brown, H. C. Stancer, and H. Moldofsky. 1975. Hypothalamic-pituitary function in anorexia nervosa. *Arch. Gen. Psychiatry* 32:739-44.
121. Halmi, K. A., and B. M. Sherman. 1975. Gonadotropin response to LH-RH in anorexia nervosa. *Arch. Gen. Psychiatry* 32:875-78.
122. Sherman, B. M., K. A. Halmi, and R. Zamudio. 1975. LH and FSH response to gondadotropin-releasing hormone in anorexia nervosa: Effect of nutritional rehabilitation. *J. Clin. Endocrinol. Metab.* 41:135-42.
123. Nillius, S. J., and L. Wide. 1977. The pituitary responsiveness to acute and chronic administration of gonadotropin-releasing hormone in acute and recovery stages of anorexia nervosa. In *Anorexia nervosa,* ed. R. A. Vigersky. New York: Raven Press.
124. Vigersky, R. A., D. L. Loriaux, A. E. Andersen, and M. Lipsett. 1975. Anorexia nervosa: Behavioral and hypothalamic aspects. *Clin. Endocrinol. Metab.* 5:517-35.
125. Baranowska, B., and S. Zgliczynski. 1979. Enhanced testosterone in female patients with anorexia nervosa: Its normalization after weight gain. *Acta Endocrinol. (Copenh.)* 90:328-35.
126. Danowski, T. S., E. Livstone, A. R. Gonzales, Y. Jung, and R. C. Khurana. 1972. Fractional and partial hypopituitarism in anorexia nervosa. *Hormones* 3:105-18.
127. Wiegelmann, W., and H. G. Solbach. 1972. Effects of LH-RH on plasma levels of LH and FSH in anorexia nervosa. *Horm. Metab. Res.* 4:404.
128. Warren, M. P., R. Jewelweicz, I. Dyrenfurth, R. Ans, S. Khalaf, and R. L. Van de Wiele. 1975. The significance of weight loss in the evaluation of pituitary response to LH-RH in women with secondary amenorrhea. *J. Clin. Endocrinol. Metab.* 40:601-11.
129. Nillius, S. J., and L. Wide. 1977. The pituitary responsiveness to acute and chronic administration of gonadotropin-releasing hormone in acute and recovery stages of anorexia nervosa. In *Anorexia nervosa,* ed. R. A. Vigersky. New York: Raven Press.
130. Sherman, B. M., and K. A. Halmi. 1977. Effect of nutritional rehabilitation on hypothalamic-pituitary function in anorexia nervosa. In *Anorexia nervosa,* ed. R. A. Vigersky. New York: Raven Press.
131. Warren, M. P. 1977. Weight loss and responsiveness to LH-RH. In *Anorexia nervosa,* ed. R. A. Vigersky. New York: Raven Press.
132. Morimoto, Y., T. Oishi, N. Hanasaki, A. Miyatake, B. Sato, K. Noma, H. Kato, S. Yano, and Y . Yamamura. 1980. Interrelations among amenorrhea, serum gonadotropins and body weight in anorexia nervosa. *Endocrinol. Jpn.* 27:191-200.
133. Isaacs, A. J., R. D. G. Leslie, J. Gomez, and R. Bayliss. 1980. The effect of weight gain on gonadotrophins and prolactin in anorexia nervosa. *Acta Endocrinol. (Copenh.)* 94:145-50.
134. Yoshimoto, Y., K. Moridera, and H. Imura. 1975. Restoration of normal pituitary gonadotropin reserve by administration of luteinizing-hormone-releasing hormone in patients with hypogonadotropic hypogonadism. *N. Engl. J. Med.* 292:242-45.

135. Travaglini, P., P. Beck-Peccoz, C. Ferrari, B. Ambrosi, A. Paracchi, A. Severgnini, A. Spada, and G. Faglia. 1976. Some aspects of hypothalamic-pituitary function in patients with anorexia nervosa. *Acta Endocrinol. (Copenh.)* 81:252-62.

136. Boyar, R. M., and J. Katz. 1977. Twenty-four hour gonadotropin secretory patterns in anorexia nervosa. In *Anorexia nervosa,* ed. R. A., Vigersky. New York: Raven Press.

137. Wakeling, A., V. A. DeSouza, and C. J. Beardwood. 1977. Assessment of the negative and positive feedback effects of administered oestrogen on gonadotrophin release in patients with anorexia nervosa. *Psychol. Med.* 7:397-405.

138. Wakeling, A., W. DeSouza, and C. J. Beardwood. 1977. Effects of administered estrogen on luteinizing hormone release in subjects with anorexia nervosa in acute and recovery stages. In *Anorexia nervosa,* ed. R. A. Vigersky. New York: Raven Press.

139. Fishman, J., R. M. Boyar, and L. Hellman. 1975. Influence of body weight on estradiol metabolism in young women. *J. Clin. Endocrinol. Metab.* 41:989-91.

140. Lemaire, A., K. Ardaens, J. Lepretre, A. Racedot, M. Burat-Herbaut, and J. Burat. 1983. Gonadal hormones in male anorexia nervosa. *Int. J. Eating Disorders* 2:135-44.

141. McNab, D., and K. Hawton. 1981. Disturbances of sex hormones in anorexia nervosa in the male. *Postgrad. Med. J.* 57:254-56.

142. Wesselius, C. L., and G. Anderson. 1982. A case study of a male with anorexia nervosa and low testosterone levels. *J. Clin. Psychiatry* 43:428-29.

143. Miyai, K., T. Yamamoto, M. Azukizawa, K. Ishibashi, and Y. Kumahara. 1975. Serum thyroid hormones and thyrotropin in anorexia nervosa. *J. Clin. Endocrinol. Metab.* 40:334-38.

144. Moshang, T., J. S. Parks, L. Baker, V. Vaidya, R. D. Utiger, A. M. Bongiovanni, and P. J. Snyder. Low serum triiodothyronine in patients with anorexia nervosa. *J. Clin. Endocrinol. Metab.* 40:470-73.

145. Burman, K. D., R. A. Vigersky, D. L. Loriaux, D. Strum, Y. Y. Djuh, F. D. Wright, and L. Wartofsky. 1977. Investigations concerning thyroxine deiodinative pathways in patients with anorexia nervosa. In *Anorexia nervosa,* ed. R. A. Vigersky. New York: Raven Press.

146. Croxson, M. S., and H. K. Ibbertson. 1977. Low serum triiodothyronine (T3) and hypothyroidism in anorexia nervosa. *J. Clin. Endocrinol. Metab.* 44:167-74.

147. Moshang, T., and R. D. Utiger. 1977. Low triiodothyronine euthyroidism in anorexia nervosa. In *Anorexia nervosa,* ed. R. A. Vigersky. New York: Raven Press.

148. Vagenakis, A. G. 1977. Thyroid hormone metabolism in prolonged experimental starvation in man. In *Anorexia nervosa,* ed. R. A. Vigersky. New York: Raven Press.

149. Suda, A. K., C. S. Pittman, T. Shimizu, and J. B. Chambers. 1978. The production and metabolism of 3,5,3'-triiodothyronine and 3,3,5'-triiodothyronine in normal and fasting subjects. *J. Clin. Endocriol. Metab.* 47:1311-19.

150. Gardner, D. F., M. M. Kaplan, C. A. Stanley, and R. D. Utiger. 1979. Effect of triiodothyronine replacement on the metabolic and pituitary responses to starvation. *N. Engl. J. Med.* 300:579-84.

151. Wermuth, B. M., K. L. Davis, L. E. Hollister, and A. J. Stunkard. 1977. Phenytoin treatment of the binge-eating syndrome. *Am. J. Psychiatry* 134:1249-53.

152. Moore, R., and I. H. Mills. 1979. Serum T3 and T4 levels in patients with anorexia nervosa showing transient hyperthyroidism during weight gain. *Clin. Endocriol.* 10:443-49.

153. Casper, R. C., and L. A. Frohman. 1982. Delayed TSH release in anorexia nervosa following injection of thyroptropin-releasing hormone (TRH). *Psychoneuroendocrinology* 7:59-68.

154. Macaron, C., J. F. Wilber, O. Green, and N. Freinkel. 1978. Studies of growth hormone

(GH), thyrotropin (TSH) and prolactin (PRL) secretion in anorexia nervosa. *Psychoneuroendocrinology* 3:181-85.

155. Landon, J., F. C. Greenwood, T. C. B. Stamp, and V. Wynn. 1966. The plasma sugar, free fatty acid, cortisol, and growth hormone response to insulin, and the comparison of this procedure with other tests of pituitary and adrenal dysfunction of anorexia nervosa. *J. Clin. Invest.* 45:437-49.
156. Casper, R. C., J. M. Davis, and G. N. Pandey. 1977. The effect of the nutritional status and weight changes on hypothalamic function tests in anorexia nervosa. In *Anorexia nervosa,* ed. R. A. Vigersky. New York: Raven Press.
157. Gold, M. S., A. L. C. Pottash, D. R. Sweeney, D. M. Martin, and R. K. Davies. 1980. Further evidence of hypothalamic-pituitary dysfunction in anorexia nervosa. *Am. J. Psychiatry* 137:101-2.
158. De la Fuente, J., and L. Wells. 1981. Human growth hormone in psychiatric disorders. *J. Clin. Psychiatry* 42:270-74.
159. Maeda, K. 1976. Effects of thyrotropin-releasing hormone on growth hormone release in normal subjects and in patients with depression, anorexia nervosa and acromegaly. *J. Med. Sci.* 22:263-72.
160. Alvarez, L. C., C. O. Dimas, A. Castro, L. G. Rossman, E. F. Vanderlaan, and W. P. Vanderlaan. 1972. Growth hormone in malnutrition. *J. Clin. Endocrinol. Metab.* 34:400-409.
161. Frankel, R. J., and J. S. Jenkins. 1975. Hypothalamic-pituitary function in anorexia nervosa. *Acta Endocrinol. (Copenh.)* 78:209-21.
162. Brauman, H ., and F. Gregoire. 1975. The growth hormone response to insulin induced hypoglycaemia in anorexia nervosa and control underweight or normal subjects. *Eur. J. Clin. Invest.* 5:289-95.
163. Beumont, P. J. V., G. C. W. George, B. L. Pimstone, and A. I. Vinik. 1976. Body weight and the pituitary response to hypothalamic releasing hormones in patients with anorexia nervosa. *J. Clin. Endocrinol. Metab.* 43:487-96.
164. Caufriez, A., R. Wolter, C. Robyn, and M. L'Hermite. 1980. Prolactin secretion in anorexia nervosa. *Acta Psychiatr. Belg.* 80:546-50.
165. Giusti, M., G. Mazzocchi, R. Mortara, D. Mignone, and G. Giordano. 1981. Prolactin secretion in anorexia nervosa. *Horm. Metab. Res.* 13:585-86.
166. Beumont, P. J. V., S. F. Abraham, and J. Turtle. 1980. Paradoxical prolactin response to gonadotropin-releasing hormone during weight gain in patients with anorexia nervosa. *J. Clin. Endocrinol. Metab.* 51:1283-85.
167. Walsh, B. T., J. L. Katz, J. Levin, J. Kream, D. K. Fukushima, L. D. Hellman, H. Weiner, and B. Zumoff. 1978. Adrenal activity in anorexia nervosa. *Psychosom. Med.* 40:499-506.
168. Gerner, R. H., and H. E. Gwirtsman. 1981. Abnormalities of dexamethasone suppression test and urinary MHPG in anorexia nervosa. *Am. J. Psychiatry* 138:650-53.
169. Auerbach, M. 1977. Anorexia nervosa: Circadian rhythm of plasma hormones. *N. Engl. J. Med.* 296:1069.
170. Boyar, R. M., L. D. Hellman, H. Roffwarg, J. Katz, B. Zumoff, J. O'Connor, H. L. Bradlow, and D. K. Fukushima. 1977. Cortisol secretion and metabolism in anorexia nervosa. *N. Engl. J. Med.* 296:190-93.
171. Wakeling, A., and G. F. M. Russell. 1970. Disturbances in the regulation of body temperature in anorexia nervosa. *Psychol. Med.* 1:30-39.
172. Luck, P., and A. Wakeling. 1980. Altered thresholds for thermoregulatory sweating and vasodilatation in anorexia nervosa. *Br. Med. J.* 281:906-8.
173. Freyschuss, U., L. Fohlin, and C. Thoren. 1978. Limb circulation in anorexia nervosa. *Acta Paediatr. Scand.* 67:225-28.

174. Mitchell, J. E., R. L. Pyle, E. D. Eckert, D. Hatsukami, and R. Lentz. 1983. Electrolyte and other physiological abnormalities in patients with bulimia. *Psychol. Med.* 13:273-78.

175. Mitchell, J. E., and J. P. Bantle. 1983. Metabolic and endocrine investigations in women of normal weight with the bulimia syndrome. *Biol. Psychiatry* 18:355-65.

176. Mitchell, J. E., R. L. Pyle, and R. A. Miner. 1982. Gastric dilatation as a complication of bulimia. *Psychosomatics* 23:96-97.

177. Rampling, D. 1982. Acute pancreatitis in anorexia nervosa. *Med. J. Aust.* 2:194-95.

178. Green, R. S., and J. H . Rau. 1974. Treatment of compulsive eating disturbances with anticonvulsant medication. *Am. J. Psychiatry* 131:428-32.

179. Rau, J. H., and R. S. Green. 1975. Compulsive eating: A neuropsychological approach to certain eating disorders. *Compr. Psychiatry* 16:223-31.

180. Rau, J. H., and R. S. Green. 1978. Soft neurological correlates of compulsive eaters. *J. Nerv. Ment. Dis.* 166:435-37.

181. Rau, J. H., F. A. Struve, and R. S. Green. 1979. Electroencephalographic correlates of compulsive eating. *Clin. Electroencephalogr.* 10:180-89.

182. Lombroso, C. T., I. H. Schwartz, D. M. Clark, H. Muench, and J. Barry. 1966. Ctenoids in healthy youths. *Neurology (Minneap.)* 16:1152-58.

183. Long, M. T., and L. C. Johnson. 1968. Fourteen- and six-per-second positive spikes in a nonclinical male population. *Neurology (Minneap.)* 18:714-16.

184. Wegner, J. T., and F. A. Struve. 1977. Incidence of the 14 and 6 per second positive spike pattern in an adult clinical population: An empirical note. *J. Nerv. Ment. Dis.* 164:340-45.

185. Gibbs, E. L., and F. A. Gibbs. 1951. Electroencephalographic evidence of thalamic and hypothalamic epilepsy. *Neurology (Minneap.)* 1:136-44.

186. Struve, F. A., and P. R. Ramsey. 1977. Concerning the 14 and 6 per second positive spike cases in post traumatic medical-legal EEGs reported by Gibbs and Gibbs : A statistical commentary. *Clin. Electroencephalogr.* 8:203-5.

187. Maulsby, R. L. 1979. EEG patterns in uncertain diagnostic significance. In *Current practice of clinical electroencephalography,* ed. D. W. Klass and D. D. Daly. New York: Raven Press.

188. Mitchell, J. E., W. Hosfield, and R. L. Pyle. 1983. EEG findings in patients with the bulimia syndrome. *Int. J. Eating Disorders* 2:17-23.

189. Whittier, J . R. 1976. Asphyxiation, bulimia, and insulin levels in Huntington disease (chorea). *JAMA* 235:1423-24.

190. Sawa, M., Y. Ueki, M. Arita, and T. Harada. 1954. Preliminary report on the amygdaloidectomy on the psychotic patients, with interpretation of oral-emotional manifestation in schizophrenics. *Folia Psychiatr. Neurol. Jpn.* 7:309-29.

191. Hofstatter, L., E. A. Smolik, and A. K. Busch. 1945. Prefrontal lobotomy in treatment of chronic psychoses with special reference to section of the orbital areas only. *Arch. Neurol. Psychiatry* 53:125-30.

192. Remick, R. A., M. W. Jones, and P. E. Campos. 1980. Postictal bulimia. *J. Clin. Psychiatry* 41:256.

193. Kirschbaum, W. R., 1951. Excessive hunger as a symptom of cerebral origin. *J. Nerv. Ment. Dis.* 113:95-114.

194. Reeves, A. G., and F. Plum. 1969. Hyperphagia, rage, and dementia accompanying a ventromedial hypothalamic neoplasm. *Arch. Neurol.* 20:616-24.

195. Rosenberg, P., Y. Herishanu, and B. Beilin. 1977. Increased appetite (bulimia) in Parkinson's disease. *Am. Geriatr. Soc.* 25:277-78.

196. Niija, K., T. Kitagawa, M. Fujishita, S. Yoshimoto, M. Kobayashi, I. Kubonishi, H.

Taguchi, and I. Miyoshi. 1983. Bulimia nervosa complicated by deficiency of vitamin K-dependent coagulation factors. *JAMA* 250:792-93.

197. Gwirtsman, H . E., P. Roy-Byrne, J. Yager, and R. H. Gerner. 1983. Neuroendocrine abnormalities in bulimia. *J. Am. J. Psychiatrty* 140:559-63.

198. Hudson, J. I., P. S. Laffer, and H. G. Pope. 1982. Bulimia related to affective disorder by family history and response to the dexamethasone suppression test. *Am. J. Psychiatry* 139:685-87.

199. Hudson, J., H. G. Pope, and J. M. Jones. 1983. Hypothalamic-pituitary-adrenal axis: Hyperactivity in bulimia. *Psychiatry Res.* 8:111-17.

200. Mitchell, J. E., D. Hatsukami, R. Pyle, and L. Boutacoff. In press. The dexamethasone suppression test in bulimia.

201. Hsu, L. K. G. 1980. Outcome of anorexia nervosa. A review of the literature (1954 to 1978). *Arch. Gen. Psychiatry* 37:1041-46.

202. Schwartz, D. M., and M. G. Thompson. 1981. Do anorectics get well? Current research and future needs. *Am. J. Psychiatry* 138:319-23.

4

Psychodynamics of Anorexia Nervosa and Bulimia

Allan M. Josephson, M.D.

I feel as if everyone is making decisions for me. I feel out of control and I feel fat and . . . I don't want to eat. I almost hope I lost weight this weekend to show them [hospital staff]. . . . I feel lazy and fat and out of shape. I want to exercise but I better not because I didn't eat very much.

> Debbie, a 17-year-old hospitalized
> patient with anorexia nervosa.

I couldn't feel anything inside after that experience (of being corrected by a basketball coach). I felt empty and angry . . . so I ate and ate. While I was eating I'd feel physical pain but soon I didn't feel anything. . . . It [binge-eating] took the place of the other hurt. Vomiting hurt too but it made me lose weight . . . then I felt better.

> Carrie, a 15-year-old bulimic describing
> a binge-eating episode.

For both of these girls, the simple daily activity of eating has become intertwined with the expression of their feelings. Debbie's refusal to eat and Carrie's binge-eating are hardly random actions; they have particular, significant meanings for each girl. To understand Carrie and Debbie, one must consider the meaning of their eating behaviors as well as the behaviors themselves, the message as well as the presentation.

This chapter, then, focuses on the psychodynamics of anorexia nervosa and bulimia, stressing the purpose of these symptoms and their inextricable involvement in each individual's development. The term *psychodynamics,* used here in a general sense to connote the psychological forces that motivate an individual, does not represent any one school of thought. It does, however, emphasize the reciprocal relationship between the individual and his or her environment. Each person incorporates new events into a set of experiences, constructing, at the same time, a system of thought that will link and explain these disparate events. Because no two individuals have precisely the same experiences and learning patterns, interpretations of identical events may differ greatly. Psychodynamics proposes a fluid interplay of experience, interpretation, and action rather than a static, systemized notion of cause and effect.

Engel advocates a similar elasticity on a larger scale in his explanation of the biopsychosocial model.[1] Decrying the reductionism of the traditional biomedical model, he delineates a hierarchical scheme consisting at one extreme of subatomic particles and atoms and at the other of the biosphere and the society or nation. The individual, at the center of the system, is both a self-contained unit and a part of a larger organization, affecting and affected by all the other components. Engel points out that "Nothing exists in isolation. Whether a cell or a person, every system is influenced by the configuration of the system of which it is a part, that is, by its environment."[1] Concentrating exclusively on the organ or tissue level of the hierarchy, a physician can gain only a partial understanding of an individual's illness.

Although Engel uses a hypothetical example of a man suffering from chest pain to illustrate the importance of considering all aspects of a person's life in planning patient care, his approach is no less important for the patient suffering from anorexia nervosa or bulimia. The anorectic patient, for instance, may have a significant metabolic disturbance that influences behavior; the individual's ingrained patterns of response may, in turn, exacerbate the physical condition. Poor family relationships contribute to the patient's increasing debility. Moreover, cultural factors that dictate thinness as a model of beauty must also be considered.

Over the years, researchers have attributed anorexia nervosa to parental overprotectiveness, society's insistence on thinness in women, and biological vulnerability. In the context of the biopsychosocial model, none of these factors is sufficient because each focuses on one particular area of an individual's life to the exclusion of all others. Overprotective parents do not necessarily produce anorectic children, nor does our society produce an exclusively anorectic female population despite its preoccupation with thinness. However similar aspects of their personalities or families may be, anorectic and bulimic patients remain individual and unique; the entire gamut of their experiences and perceptions must be entertained.

In focusing specifically on the psychodynamics of anorexia nervosa and bulimia, the following discussion considers psychological factors within the larger context of the patient's physical, familial, and social world, emphasizing the connections and interactions of these realms.

Anorexia Nervosa

The literature on individual psychodynamics can be distilled into two major related areas. The first emphasizes traditional psychoanalytic concepts and the second emphasizes ego deficits,[2] impaired object relationships,[3] and self pathology.[4] Classic psychoanalytic theory equated eating behavior with the sexual instinct.[5,6] Adolescents who could not meet the demands of adult genitality were believed to have regressed to a primitive level of oral gratification in which eating and sexual pleasure were identical. Refusal to eat thus represented a defense against oral impregnation fantasies. Other writers began to shift to an examination of the parent-child relationship and the general relationship issues that they believed contributed to the development of anorexia nervosa.[7] The most widely known theoreticians in this area have been Palazzoli[8] and Bruch.[9,10] Although these authors write about anorexia nervosa, their formulations parallel other developments in psychoanalysis. They, as well as others,[11,12,13] have emphasized the impaired sense of self as a core problem in anorectic patients and have related this impairment to early experience.

Bruch's contributions in particular have been very influential and deserve special mention.[9,10] Although she initially used traditional psychoanalytic concepts, she found that her clinical data did not support the fear of oral impregnation as a motivating factor in the genesis of the disorder. Bruch still believed that the basic disturbance in anorexia nervosa was a psychological one, however. Through persistent observation, she began to see the patients' superior goodness as a defense against a profound sense of inadequacy and ineffectiveness. She believed that their symptoms were based on problems with early relationships rather than the result of instinctual drives and the ensuing defenses against them. To Bruch, these young women seemed hopelessly unable to meet the demands of adolescence and young adulthood and retreated from them. Early attachment to parents, Bruch believed, was disrupted by the parents' failure to respond appropriately to their child's cues, basing their responses on their own needs rather than those of the child. The parents regarded the child's subsequent growth and development as their achievement, not the child's. Observation of the communication patterns of these families suggested that parental misunderstanding of their child's developmental needs continued beyond infancy. When a clear expression of self became necessary in adolescence or young adulthood, these individuals tried frantically to define themselves. These observations led Bruch to shift her individual psychotherapeutic strategy from interpretation of symbolic content to an active attempt to help the patient deal with her life experiences, both past and present.

Family Interaction

Both clinical experience and child development research have contributed to the dramatic growth of family systems theory in the last 40 years.[14] In the late 1940s and in the 1950s, therapists who were making little progress with difficult patients in individual psychotherapy began to see these patients with their families. They were frequently surprised to discover extremely important elements of their patients' lives that had remained outside the focus of individual therapy.[15,16] Child development research confirmed this clinical experience by demonstrating that the child actively participates in the relationship with its parents, rather than only passively accepting care from them as had been previously believed. Healthy emotional development therefore depends on a consonant match between the child's temperament and the parents' capacity to adapt. With these presumptions, family assessment has now become common in the evaluation of many psychiatric disorders that have an onset in childhood and adolescence.

Because of the reciprocal nature of family relationships, dysfunctional family interaction both provokes anorexia nervosa and profits by it. Two widely known clinical researchers from very different settings—Palazzolli in Milan[8] and Salvador Minuchin in Philadelphia[17-19]—have developed surprisingly similar views about these families. Palazolli observed that they maintain a collective sense of family that renders individual self-interest or expression reprehensible.[8] No one takes a leadership or ownership role, not even concerning their own feelings or thoughts. This observation is similar to Minuchin's concept of enmeshment, which he describes as a protectiveness that exceeds normal parental concern. This overprotectiveness smothers the developmental process of moving away from family. The child in turn frequently elicits the overprotective stance by seeming unable to manage her life without close surveillance. Minuchin also noted that these families lack verbal methods to resolve conflict and have a forced, inflexible way of viewing problems. A specific conflict-avoidance pattern stabilizes the family structure: the anorectic child's behavior produces anxiety within the family and becomes the primary focus of parental concern, enabling the parents to avoid open marital conflict and other problems of their family life.

The observations of Palazolli and Minuchin are familiar to most clinicians who have worked with anorectics and their families. They are also consistent with the formulations of some psychodynamic theorists concerning the importance of impaired object relations in these patients. Although the formulations of family theorists have been criticized on grounds of observer bias, retrospective distortion, the lack of comparison samples of families, and the inherent difficulty in distinguishing cause from effect in family interaction,[20-22] there is support in the research literature for their conclusions. Morgan and Russell[23] determined that a significant number of interactional and relationship problems existed in these families before the onset of anorexia nervosa. Crisp, Harding, and McGuinness[24] documented that the functioning of other family members frequently deteriorates as anorectics gain weight. Finally, Hsu, Crisp, and Harding[25] found that poor outcome was associated with disturbed relationships between parents and between parents and patients prior to the onset of the illness.

Two important points emerge from an examination of this literature. First, abnormal family interactions do appear to shape the psyche and delay development in young adults. Clinical experiences with families of anorectic patients suggest that these family problems are more than a simple response to illness. The families may be markedly defensive and display gross misunderstanding of adolescent developmental norms and willful resistance to change. Second, it seems likely that family interactional factors are not necessarily specific, but rather permissive, for the development of anorexia nervosa. The deviant individuation process may follow many routes; refusing to eat is but one. Similar family interactional patterns may engender difficulties other than anorexia nervosa in a child. Any claim for specificity of these patterns in anorexia nervosa must be carefully examined.

The study of family interactions seems promising. Many clinicians agree that involvement of the family is an important aspect in the treatment of anorexia nervosa.[19] Integration of psychodynamic theories and observation of family interactions promises the most complete understanding of the anorectic patient.

Meaning of the Symptoms to the Individual

The individual symptoms of anorexia nervosa are difficult to understand when considered in isolation. As Bruch pointed out, we need a framework that can serve as "an indispensible guide through the maze of seemingly contradictory psychological responses."[10] Using the developmental model as such a guide, we can assess the purposes of specific symptoms and attempt a cohesive understanding of the patient's life and problems.

Briefly, development involves progress through successive stages. Developmental tasks confront the individual at each stage, with subsequent stages involving more complex tasks. Each stage is based on the preceding one and prepares for the succeeding one. Thus, if anything interferes with the completion of a developmental task, successful completion of subsequent tasks becomes more difficult. The mastery of developmental tasks by anorectic patients is compromised by the cumulative effect of early experience, ongoing experience in their families, or both.

Anorexia nervosa seems to begin as a solution to a developmental conflict centered on the mastery of four universal adolescent tasks: identity formation, separation from family and coming to terms with one's feelings about family, development of mature love relationships, and learning control of one's body.[26] So closely are these tasks linked that a person who has difficulty in one area will almost certainly have problems in the others. For instance, a young girl who makes only a few, hesitant efforts to separate from her family will be unlikely to develop an identity that is truly her own. She will be more likely to unquestionably adopt her family's attitudes, values, and habits. Anorectic patients experience conflicting emotions in attempting to separate from their families. Their dependency on parents is associated with anger, an emotion heightened by their awareness that peers are able to move away from parents. This anger is often replaced by panic when they attempt to be more independent, only to become painfully aware of their ineffectiveness. Many clinicians have emphasized the anorectic's inability to contend with the problems and opportunities of adolescence.[8-10,16] These patients are frequently described as immature and resistant to change, tenaciously clinging to the prerogatives of childhood. Wishing to return to their relatively uncomplicated earlier years, they do not engage in activities appropriate to their age level.

Although few of her patients with anorexia nervosa had overt behavior problems before the onset of their illness, Hilde Bruch maintained that problems did in fact exist. Described by their parents as ideal children, many of these young girls had been acquiescent and agreeable but had not learned to express themselves or develop interests of their own. Bruch noted that "the need for self-reliant independence, which confronts every adolescent, seemed to cause an insoluble conflict, after a childhood of robot-like obedience. They lack awareness of their own resources and do not rely on their feelings, thoughts and bodily sensations."[9] The overt problems, then, seem to begin when the young girl ceases to believe that her tractability and the approval of her parents will give her a secure sense of identity. Bruch points out that this gradual change underlies the often sudden onset of dieting. This onset is frequently triggered by a chance remark about weight or some trivial event that is experienced as a blow to self-esteem.

Inadequately prepared to grow emotionally as her peers are doing, the anorectic withdraws to a narrow world that she can control and understand. She concentrates on her weight with single-minded intensity, avoiding by her preoccupation the adolescent developmental tasks of dating, separation from family, and some degree of independence. Ironically, the weight loss that she believes will make her more attractive to people may further distance her from them. The weight loss can never in itself magically endow the anorectic with assurance and social acceptance, but it can isolate her by declaring her different and inaccessible.

Losing weight, however, is an achievement that does not depend on other people. Denying herself sustenance, she attains a sense of control and identity. She alone determines what she will weigh; the protests of her parents and friends only enhance her feeling of power. Because of the importance of her sense of control, gaining weight or acknowledging hunger threaten the anorectic's sole source of self-esteem. As these individuals gain weight, many believe their lives to be empty and without direction.

Other symptoms may serve a primarily defensive function. For example, perfectionism, obsessionality, and compliance may be defenses against emptiness and helplessness. These patients attempt to repair low self-esteem by "being good." The superiority that many anorectics manifest may be a defense against a sense of underlying vulnerability. They may, on the other hand, eschew "goodness" for negativism, their defiance another attempt to assert their identity.

Hyperactivity may help the patient deal with the panic and anxiety that accompany autonomous functioning. Anorectics are frequently ill at ease with unstructured time and become overly active to fill the time, as with the following patient seen at the University of Minnesota Hospitals:

> Debbie, a 17-year-old, felt trapped. She was about to enter her senior year in high school and was unsure of her career direction. She had always done what others had told her to do and her compliance had led to academic success. However, she was very uncertain about her choice of college, a choice she was expected to make without direct instruction from an authority figure. She began to lose weight, exercise excessively, and dramatically increase her physical activity. She felt free when running or exercising. "I feel like nothing else exists. . . . There's nothing on my mind."

This patient described her excessive activity as allowing her to avoid thinking about the decisions of young adulthood. The physical activity was not a temporary escape from the pressures of her life but rather a part of the pattern of excessive, maladaptive withdrawal.

Can refusing food be a solution to conflicts in development? One way to approach this question is to consider the meaning of food ingestion to the individual. Characteristics of food ingestion suggest that food refusal is likely to have psychodynamic meaning. Food, for example, represents nurturance. For the child, it is associated with parental caretaking; for the adult, it is associated with friendship. Eating is an autonomous activity;

its initiation and termination can be controlled only by the person eating. Thus, any individual with conflicts around issues of nurturance and autonomy is potentially at risk to misuse food. If an individual wishes to say something through his or her behavior, an activity that occurs frequently and has effects that can be readily observed by others would serve that purpose. Eating has those characteristics.

Meaning of the Symptoms to the Family

Like the anorectic herself, the parents endow their daughter's refusal to eat with meaning. While starvation brings a sense of achievement to the individual, it also engages family members, reinforcing the processes that may have initially led to a poor sense of self—specifically, overcontrol by parents. Even extremely "close-knit" families, who may not in fact be overcontrolling, can also induce guilt in the adolescent by unintentionally making her feel that it would be unfair to leave after the family has done so much for her. By refusing food, the anorectic forces her family to become more involved than is developmentally appropriate, subverting the development of her identity. Parents may interpret refusal of food, negativism, and anger to mean, "You don't love me anymore" or, "You are rejecting me." At times, it may appear that the anorectic's siblings and parents are more concerned about her weight loss than she is. Such a caretaking role for siblings further blurs generational role boundaries, as in the following clinical case:

> Cheri, a 16-year-old girl of passive temperament, seemed helpless to her family. Her mother, lonely due to her husband's emotional distance, became more and more invested in her daughter's life. Cheri's father was thus further excluded and had even more reason to remain distant. Cheri's 14-year-old brother received less attention and greatly enjoyed the freedom engendered by his mother's overinvolvement with his sister. Her assertive 17-year-old sister was able to resist her mother's overinvolvement but became excessively concerned with Cheri's welfare. Normal development tended to push the 16-year-old daughter away from her mother. However, the development of anorexia nervosa led the 16-year-old to remain closely involved with mother yet still have something that she alone controlled. When Cheri gained weight and began to distance herself psychologically from her mother, the family system floundered. Eventually, the mother and father began to confront the problems with their relationship, and the 14-year-old son was forced to give up some of his premature autonomy and tolerate increased surveillance by his parents. The older sister was expected to develop her own life and decrease her role as an ancillary caregiver.

The outcome of these interactions is predictable. The symptoms of the disorder inevitably lead to responses from the family that, unless resisted, become dysfunctionl for the adolescent. These symptoms may be quite resilient, however, because they exert a stabilizing effect on the family. In a sense, Cheri's illness benefited the members of her family by allowing them to avoid inadequacies of their own. As she began to improve, her family faced the difficult task of acknowledging their problems and attempting to resolve them. Each family is, of course, unique, their interactions complex and often subtle. No formula can entirely capture the interactions in the family of an anorectic. It is essential, however, that the family's influence be considered. As long as her illness buttresses the family's needs, the anorectic daughter will have great difficulty regaining health.

Treatment Implications

In addition to enhancing our understanding of eating disorders, the biopsychosocial approach can serve as a useful model when discussing treatment. The first consideration in the treatment of anorexia nervosa must be weight gain and metabolic stability. Behavior modification, pharmacotherapy, and nutritional support may all be necessary to correct profound biologic deficits,[27,28] which need to be improved before meaningful psychodynamic work can begin. This integration of biological, behavioral, and psychodynamic approaches reflects an appreciation of the independent functioning the eating symptomatology assumes during the evolution of the disorder. Like a drug addiction, anorexia nervosa often takes on a life of its own after the beginning stages of dieting. As a result, psychodynamic reasons that were involved in the initiation of anorexia nervosa may be less important in perpetuating it. Therefore, the initial intervention often must be behavioral. For some, behavioral interruption of this pattern and achievement of weight gain may suffice. For others—perhaps those who have experienced more deviant development—behavioral intervention is only the first step, and psychodynamic issues must later be addressed. Behavioral approaches can also be overemphasized; by relying only on behavioral techniques and emphasizing weight gain, the therapist may underestimate the anxiety the patient experiences with weight gain.[10,21] On the other hand, clinicians who solely emphasize psychodynamics may be ignoring the cognitive dysfunction that may make meaningful psychotherapy impossible in severely ill anorectics.

The key to setting goals for any psychodynamic intervention—individual, family, or milieu—is to consider what behavior is developmentally appropriate for the adolescent or young adult. Once this is decided, each intervention strategy can be focused toward correcting the deviant development, using the template of normal development as a guide. For example, as the anorectic increases her ability to express herself, the less she needs to cling to weight loss as the sole route to autonomy and selfhood. Interventions should provide support and encouragement for developmentally appropriate behaviors that move the patient toward competence and that are made independently. Family, individual, and milieu interventions can all follow such a strategy.

Psychodynamic Intervention: Family

For those individuals who are either living with or are actively involved with their family of origin, the usual first step in psychodynamic intervention is an attempt to interrupt the family influences that may be sustaining the weight loss. This does not imply that family intervention is more important than individual psychotherapy; each is equally important within the sequence. It is difficult, however, to keep an anorectic patient's weight stable without first addressing family influences. In addition, firsthand knowledge of the family is invaluable to the therapist in individual work with the patient.

The chief purpose of family therapy is active restructuring of family transactions,[18] shifting the emphasis from eating to interactional problems. The anorectic patient must be encouraged to take initiative in her life, one aspect of which is eating responsibly. Parents are directed to focus on concerns other than their anorectic daughter, to give the anorectic the message that her life and her eating patterns will be her responsibility. This task may be aided by the parents' wish to be free of the excessive dependency of their child and the anorectic's normal adolescent drive toward automony. Weight stabilization often occurs as the parents strengthen their own relationship and the anorectic increases her ability to express herself.

While attempting these interventions, clinicians inevitably confront resistance to change. This resistance logically takes two forms: resistance to individual change and resistance to changes that take place within other family members. Although both the anorectic and her parents desire change, they are often reluctant to give up the patterns established by the anorectic's illness. The adolescent wants freedom yet frequently does not want to relinquish the specialness that her illness has conferred on her. Parents often wish to distance themselves from their child; however, they frequently have trouble accepting ther fact that this means they must construct a new relationship pattern for themselves. The patient's improvement is frequently resisted by the family, and vise versa. When parents begin to allow their daughter autonomy, the anorectic often becomes increasingly helpless. Similarly, when the anorectic begins to demonstrate increased competence, the family may subtly devalue these efforts. Thus, both patient and family members actively participate in the maintenance of psychopathology. The therapist must help all family members to recognize their resistance to individual change and their resistance to change in others.

An adolescent's movement toward competence can be hard to discern because it is often expressed with ambivalence or hostility. Families frequently need to be reminded that some uncomfortable changes, such as increased argumentativeness, may really represent progress. Movement toward competence, for example, may be manifested by the patient arguing for discharge from hospital after she has gained weight. Arguing for extra privileges while continuing to lose weight, on the other hand, reflects ineffective decision making rather than assertiveness.

It is not particularly difficult to generalize from transactions around food to transactions around other family problems, although the conflict about food is the first theme to be addressed. Minuchin[17] has described his reenactment of family conflicts around eating via a family lunch session. We, as well as others,[29] believe that conflict emerges naturally in the treatment setting and does not need to be staged. The anorectic's refusal to take control of her life and the family's acceptance of her passivity may have several manifestations—the patient may lose weight, refuse to come back to the hospital after a pass, become suicidal, or demand that the family take care of her personal tasks.

Once the family knows that all members must be involved in treatment, they should be allowed to direct its course. The role of siblings and fathers is particularly important. A sibling's expression of age-appropriate autonomy strivings provides an effective role model for the anorectic and helps her parents understand the developmental needs of the anorectic. If the father has not been emotionally involved with the family, emphasizing the need for his presence and support can strengthen the parents' relationship, simultaneously reducing the mother's need to be overly involved in her daughter's life.

Specific helpful techniques described in the literature have been reviewed by Yager[20] and Lagos.[30] These include forcing each person to speak for himself or herself; qualifying any communication that appears to be spoken for someone else; interrupting overprotective behavior (such as someone helping an anorectic off with her coat); and dealing with nonverbal communications such as looks, grimaces, and smiles, with the question, "Have you something to say?" In this last situation, the therapist may also state that such indirect communication is too difficult to understand and will be ignored until a clearer model is chosen.

Problems inevitably arise in family sessions. For example, it is common for the anorectic adolescent to refuse to talk. When initial efforts to get the anorectic patient to talk are unsuccessful, no further attempts should be made. A therapist can give the anorectic inappropriate control of the session by repeatedly attempting to engage her, only to be defeated by her silence. This silence should be ignored and interaction with other family members pursued. When the patient demonstrates competence through verbalization of her concerns, she can again become part of the session.

Defensiveness within these families takes a variety of forms, but early confrontation of parents or children in therapy can alienate them. Many families are invested in thinking themselves without problems. On the other hand, families with a chronic anorectic member often have given up. They have learned to work around the disorder, to accept it, and finally to assume that things will always be as they are. Introducing hope in these demoralized families is difficult. A reinterpretation of the meaning of the anorectic's symptoms and an alteration of therapeutic strategy may be necessary.

Therapists must remember that the process of family change is arduous for parents as well as patients, and should anticipate the development of symptoms in the parents as an adolescent gains weight and begins to individuate. This phenomenon has been reported by Crisp, Harding and McGuinness.[24] We have found depression and chemical abuse to be common among parents in this situation. The intensity of these problems should not be underestimated. In cases of intense symbiosis between parent and child, a potential for self-destructive behavior in the parent should be considered.

How does the therapist know that he or she is on the right track? The first clear sign of progress is often some relaxation of the obsessionality of the adolescent concerning not only weight but other areas in life that were previously overcontrolled (e.g., school work). Spontaneity gradually replaces rigidity. This progress may appear to be laxity to the parents and may need to be interpreted as a sign of normalcy. In families with more significant psychopathology, another child may become a symptom bearer.

Psychodynamic Intervention: Individual

The verbal inactivity and passivity of these patients presents a major problem in individual therapy. Interpretations can be difficult to time properly; all too frequently, interpretations result in the anorectic believing the therapist to be controlling and all-knowing. This perception recapitulates the early experiences of these patients and confirms their belief that someone will always tell them what to do. The role of wise authority figure only fosters the anorectics dependency and must be resisted by the therapist. The nature of the patient's underlying personality structure and level of development should be carefully assessed prior to interpretation. Those with more primitive self pathology will need greater structure in therapy sessions.

Bruch has suggested that the therapist needs to be active in the therapy and to promote the patient's activity rather than simply offering interpretations.[10] Effort should be directed toward getting the patient to discuss experiences earlier in her development. This in itself may contribute to an alliance if the patient feels she is listened to in an empathic way. This alliance can then be used to correct cognitive distortions that the patient may have about her own competence, her ability to control her life, and her feelings of worth. Weight stability, increased self-expression, and reports of involvement in developmentally appropriate activities all suggest progress. They are usually correlated with a decreased preoccupation with weight.

Therapists can start with an individual intervention with adolescents and young adults who are not living at home, but one should not be too quick to exclude the family. Even in situations where a young adult is living outside the home, the family may represent an important avenue to psychological improvement.

Psychodynamics and Inpatient Management

A main goal of psychodynamic management of patients in the hospital is to look beyond the immediate concerns about weight and allow the ward milieu to deal with the development issues. In an ideal situation, one would see a gradual weight gain and metabolic stability that frees staff to deal with psychologic issues.

Autonomy must be promoted. Any reasonable action that the patient initiates or supports should be accepted, even if its rationale is not particularly coherent. For example, we generally let the patients set their own goal weight to be gained prior to discharge. Invariably, this is lower than ideal body weight but more than their admission weight. If the patient chooses a low discharge weight, the staff may believe that this is evidence that the anorectic should not be allowed a choice. To take this choice away, however, could undermine the anorectic's sense of self and may affirm their belief that they have nothing to offer and can have no control over their life.

The focus on assertiveness may include more than one choice of their own goal weight. The patient should be encouraged to make her own decisions and be able to justify them. This is best illustrated and most easily achieved around issues of emotional importance, like arguing for discharge. Even minor issues, though, such as requesting an hour pass when parents show up unexpectedly, should be considered evidence of independent decision making.

Staff can easily focus on the manipulative element in the anorectic's behavior and enter into power struggles over food intake.[22] In using the term "manipulator," the staff underestimates the patient's anxiety and panic, failing to recognize how the patient's sense of self disintegrates as she gains weight. Correspondingly, staff frequently do not detect moves toward psychological competence as they are often indirect and minimal. It is extremely easy for ward staff to become punitive over small amounts of weight loss rather than to appreciate a general trend toward weight gain. Weight loss just prior to the planned day of discharge presents a particular challenge. Staff often interpret such weight loss as the patient's attempt to test them, and they conclude that the patient should remain in the hospital. Rather than automatically assuming that the patient has regressed, the therapist should assess the problem. In our experience, an adolescent can usually go home even if a minor weight loss occurs. Staff should resist displaying the same overprotectiveness that has long characterized the patient's family.

On inpatient wards that have patients with diagnoses other than anorexia nervosa, nonanorectic patients can be used as role models. Anorectics usually see themselves as special and superior to patients with conduct disorders. Using such patients' expressivity and emotional availability as models, anorectics can learn new interpersonal techniques. This is often a first step in reducing the anorectic's defense of superior goodness.

Invasive treatments like nasogastric tubing are rarely needed. Although the ideal of autonomy must take second place to concerns about the patient's health, the issue of nasogastric tubing all too often occurs during a therapeutic impasse rather than a medical crisis, and such techniques can usually be avoided.

Finally, the inhospital psychodynamic management of these patients should be characterized by a gradual decrease in structure as the patient's independence increases. If the same level of structure that was needed at the time of admission is present at the time of discharge, it is unlikely that meaningful psychodynamic work has occurred.

Bulimia

There are very few studies of patients of normal weight with bulimic symptoms. Most of the literature has instead concentrated on the differences between anorectic patients who restrict their diets to avoid gaining weight (restrictors) and anorectics who binge-eat and vomit or abuse laxatives (bulimics).[31-33] Several investigators have noted that bulimic patients are more likely to become depressed than restrictors[31,32] and to show a greater incidence of problems with impulse control, such as kleptomania and alcoholism.[31-33]

Perhaps the most dramatic difference between the two groups, however, lies in their estimation of their own self-control. Maintaining a rigid limit to their intake of food, restrictors deny hunger. Their abstinence provides them with a sense of worth and achievement; they have succeeded in exercising control over part of their lives. The bulimics, on the other hand, maintain a low weight but episodically lose control over their eating. Rather than denying hunger, they give it inordinate importance. Although vomiting and laxative use impose some control after a binging episode, the bulimic's sense of power over her own weight seems to be more fragile than that of the restrictors. In their paper delineating the features of bulimia in anorexia nervosa, Casper et al. noted that in psychotherapy "fasting patients often disclosed that they cherished their hunger feelings and derived a sense of mastery from them, whereas bulimic patients tended to feel more irritable and restless when they were hungry."[32]

The personalities and experiences of individuals in the two groups also seem to diverge. The restricting anorectics tend to minimize their social interactions and remain sexually inactive; the bulimics appear to be more outgoing and more likely to have engaged in sexual relationships. Both groups prize achievement, however, and set high, if not impossible, standards for themselves.

Minimized by some investigators,[34,35] the distinctions between these two groups of patients obviously remain tentative. If the categories do have clinical relevance, they cannot be considered static; girls who as adolescents maintain a low body weight by restricting their diets may later indulge in binge-eating and vomiting. Distinguishing between the two groups, however, emphasizes the binge/purge cycle itself and permits some preliminary speculations about its importance both to the bulimic-anorectic and to the normal-weight bulimic.

In one of the few articles in the literature specifically concerned with psychodynamic issues in bulimia, Sugarman and Kurash describe the slow process of an infant's separation from her mother, maintaining that the bulimic patient as a child was unable to proceed beyond the initial phase of separation.[36] The authors believe that infants use their own body as the first transitional object because the body combines both a representation of self and the tactile and sensory features of an object. After this, toddlers ordinarily find transitional objects that are truly separate from themselves, becoming more autonomous in the process. The child thus uses a blanket or some other object to represent their mother, a more sophisticated cognitive process than the simple identification of mother with their own body. According to Sugarman and Kurash, the child who later becomes bulimic fails, because of parental overinvolvement or underinvolvement, to progress from the first stage of transitional objects to the second; therefore, she has difficulty establishing an identity independent of her mother.

During adolescence, the problems of identity and autonomy reemerge under the pressures of biological change. Because she has not adequately separated from her mother, the bulimic patient reverts to her early synthesis of mother with her own body. Sugarman and Kurash state: "It is likely that the acts of eating (in childhood) and later gorging (adolescence) become the need-gratifying activities which allow the bulimic to develop a sensorimotor representation of the mother. *Food is not the issue; rather it is the bodily action of eating which is essential in regaining a fleeting experience of mother*" (italics in original).[36] Because the image of mother evoked by binge-eating then threatens to submerge her tentative sense of self, the bulimic vomits to free herself of her mother's presence. Seligman[37] and Sights[38] have delineated similar theories.

Rather than concentrating on problems within a single developmental phase, Bruch describes cumulative difficulties in the infant's interaction with her parents.[39] The child learns to distinguish one feeling from another by gauging her parents' reactions to her cries or demands. If her parents consistently misinterpret her needs, the child herself will not be able to judge them accurately. Parents who frequently offer their child food as solace for an emotional injury, for instance, may convince the child that feelings of hunger concur with feelings of pain. According to Bruch, if "a mother's reaction is continuously inappropriate, be it neglectful, oversolicitous, inhibiting, or indiscriminately permissive, the outcome for the child will be a perplexing confusion. When he is older he will not be able to distinguish between being hungry or sated, or between nutritional need and some other discomfort or tension."[9] Without being able to reliably understand her own needs, the individual feels helpless to control or monitor them. Instead, she must adapt to the exigencies of her environment, prey to each successive change.

Casper et al. also emphasize the role of emotions in bulimic anorexia, but in a slightly different way.[32] They contend that although binge-eating begins as a response to the profound hunger of self-starvation, it soon acquires a psychological dimension. Discovering the calming effect of the process of eating, the bulimic binge-eats to assuage feelings of depression, guilt, or anxiety. The authors maintain that "bulimia followed by self-induced vomiting can be understood as a complex defense maneuver in which food is abnormally employed to relieve mildly disturbing impulses, feelings, and thoughts."[32] Their investigation of the progression in the bulimic's use of food complements Bruch's description of early developmental problems. Although they emphasize different aspects of the bulimic's illness, both Bruch and Casper et al. believe that bulimic anorectics binge-eat to avoid or solve problems. Russell, in addition, described minor dissociative reactions in these individuals, many patients being unaware of outside stimuli during a binge.[21]

Family Interaction

Although the literature regarding families of patients with bulimia is scant, two recent studies make some interesting observations and suggest areas for future research. To examine the validity of the distinction between restrictor and bulimic anorectics, Strober et al. assessed family characteristics through the use of the MMPI and structured interviews of parents of adolescent children with anorexia nervosa.[40] Parents of bulimics reported more difficulty with impulse control and expression of hostile impulses and more disturbances in affect compared with parents of restrictors. Most fathers of restrictors exhibited greater passivity and reserve than fathers of bulimics. Similarly, mothers of bulimics exhibited more pronounced depression, hostility, and lability compared with the mothers of restrictors, who were more introverted, submissive, and "neurotic." Although families with a bulimic child may share some of the core features of the families of restrictors, they express their feelings more openly, often with considerable lability.

In their study of normal-weight bulimics, Weiss and Ebert found that these individuals feel close to fewer relatives than normal-weight controls.[41] They also had significantly higher scores on negative attitudes toward their parents on the Anorectic Attitude Questionnaire. It is difficult to say whether these results might apply to bulimic anorectics as well as normal-weight bulimics. The Strober et al. data regarding family conflict in families of bulimic anorectics suggest that they might,[40] but further studies would be necessary to judge whether these characteristics correlate with the symptom of bulimia.

Meaning of the Symptoms for the Individual and the Family

At the most obvious level, episodes of binge-eating and purging signify loss of control. Compared with restrictor anorectics who are able to deny any vestiges of hunger, bulimics must, with each binging episode, face their inability to suppress their hunger. For individuals whose self-esteem revolves around their ability to maintain a particular weight, these episodes represent personal failure; they have been unable to live up to their own exacting standards. The bulimic anorectic's tendency to polarize values also intensifies her guilt. If she has abstained from food, she is admirable; if she eats, she is worthless. There seem to be no shades of gray, no forgiveness.

Although it is expressed in terms of food, loss of control for the bulimic patient seems to be fundamentally a loss of emotional control. Whether investigators believe that the symptoms of bulimia result from insufficient separation or from problems with learning to recognize hunger effectively, most regard binge-eating and purging as an attempt by the individual to handle her feelings. Sugarman and Kurash suggest that the bulimic maintains a tenuous equilibrium by alternatively incorporating and repudiating the image of her mother.[36] Only in eating can the bulimic lessen the distress of her separation from mother. According to Bruch's theories, eating relieves both psychic and bodily discomfort since hunger for the bulimic is virtually synonymous with emotions.[39] Based on our observations of patients in psychological treatment, the intensity of the individual's concentration on eating replaces the intensity of her feelings. Ordinary eating does not usually block or transform feelings; binge-eating, with its rapid, uncontrollable intake of food, renders the precipitating emotions secondary.

The following case vignette of a 15-year-old girl illustrates both the importance of the patient's perception of her self-control and her use of food to mollify her emotions.

Leslie started dieting when she was 15 after her older sister lost 10 pounds before a dance. She exercised strenuously and fasted for long periods of time, ending her fasts by binge-eating and vomiting. Gradually the binge-eating episodes became more frequent and the vomiting habitual. When her parents noticed her behavior they confronted her, making her promise to stop. Instead, her binge-eating and vomiting escalated until she was discovered vomiting at school and her parents were informed. Angry and frustrated, they obtained locks for their cupboards and refrigerator to force Leslie to abstain from binge-eating. When she was apprehended stealing food from a grocery store, her parents decided to seek treatment for her.

During therapy, Leslie claimed that she had to diet rigidly to maintain her weight at an acceptable level and that even a weight gain of a pound made her feel worthless. She would fast or eat minimal amounts of food for several days, but them would feel an uncontrollable anxiety which could only be appeased by eating rapidly and voluminously. "When I am eating I don't think about anything, don't feel anything. I only begin to feel guilty later when I think about what I've done."

The pursuit or avoidance of food directs Leslie's life; all her attention revolves around her ability to control her appetite. Unlike the restrictor anorectic, Leslie admits that she cannot regulate her eating, however important it is to her to retain a low body weight. Frightened by their daughter's actions, Leslie's parents succumbed to her preoccupation with control by locking their refrigerator and cupboards. The locks themselves have a symbolic as well as a punitive significance—as long as the doors are safely fastened, nothing can escape. Leslie seals off her emotional needs in much the same way; if they can be ignored or displaced by episodic binge-eating, she can maintain a welcome, albeit precarious, equilibrium. As devastating as unleashed eating may be to her self-esteem, it may well protect her from more difficult emotional assaults.

The following case of a 16-year-old, normal-weight bulimic girl suggests somewhat different psychodynamics. In this case, binge-eating and purging mitigated intense feelings.

Carrie was one of two children, adopted at infancy from biologic parents who had no history of mental disorder. Her mother was an unassertive, pleasant woman who had difficulty setting limits with the temperamentally assertive Carrie. Carrie's older sister, Sharon, of more compliant temperament, easily conformed to her mother's discipline. Father, a reserved farmer, was not involved in disciplining his daughters, leaving this task to mother.

As Carrie developed, the forcefulness of her emerging personality overwhelmed her mother's attempts to limit her. Carrie always seemed to get much of what she wanted. Her first mental health contact came at the age of 12 when she took 11 aspirin immediately after her parents informed her that she could not date a 17-year-old male. Intense rage seemed to accompany any significant limit-setting thereafter. A public reprimand from her basketball coach at age 14 led to intense feelings of rejection. She coolly accepted this but, in private, engaged in a major binge-eating episode. Binge-eating subsequently became associated with almost any event which threatened her sense of entitlement and specialness. Depression became intermingled with the rage and humiliation of not being accepted as particularly important by her peers.

Her family acquiesced to her demand that all sweets and high-caloric foods be removed from the house to decrease her temptation to binge-eat. On one occasion, mother's attempt to resist these demands resulted in Carrie breaking a window. Fearful of this incident, the family confronted Carrie less, becoming hostages to her tyrannical behavior.

Carrie described a "pain inside when I would binge, but that takes the place of the other hurt and makes me forget it." Her painful affects were blunted by the experience of binge-eating. She stated: "It feels so good to give in and eat. I just love to eat. Nothing else matters when I'm eating." While Carrie did not rigidly restrict her diet, thinness was her ideal. Purging was inevitable, particularly in view of her expressed attitude: "I want to be able to binge and be as thin as I want."

In contrast to Leslie, Carrie did not pursue weight loss as a primary route to identity. Carrie's narcissistic stance was reflected in her wish to enjoy the tension reduction of binge-eating without experiencing the consequence of weight gain. Carrie's family also became involved in sustaining her symptoms.

Because bulimics are almost invariably women, the binge-eating and purging cycles undoubtedly have a social as well as a psychodynamic component for the individual. Women who have difficulty establishing an identity for themselves are more likely to be influenced by a society that traditionally has expected women to abdicate their needs and desires in favor of their family's requirements. Presenting a feminist approach to bulimarexia, Boskind-Lodahl asserted that individuals with this problem lose weight to achieve a sense of power that is usually denied women.[42] Because the bulimarectic can demonstrate power only over her own body, she engages in a "struggle against a part of the self rather than toward a self." So closely are gender and identity aligned that a woman's sense of her own identity must suffer if her gender is consistently denigrated.

Treatment Implications

Because psychodynamic approaches emphasize the ways in which individuals are unique, any treatment must first consider each patient's specific qualities; no one type of treatment will suffice for all patients with bulimia. The following discussion offers general guidelines and suggests approaches, but it is not intended to be universally applicable.

Generally, the first step in the treatment of bulimia is interrupting the binge-purge cycle, which may have become habitual and far removed from its original purpose. Appropriate behavior modification techniques and medical management, at times involving hospitalization, are indicated. After medical stabilization, a psychodynamic assessment should be made to determine whether the bulimic symptoms have provided a solution to developmental conflicts. If they have, psychodynamic interventions may be necessary to begin to resolve the patient's problems.

Because bulimics are generally older than nonbulimic anorectics, family interventions have less utility. In patients still living with their family of origin, however, intervention should be considered with the family to restructure and reframe unhealthy transactions. Emphasis in family therapy must be given to decreasing the control that the bulimic has over her parents and siblings. Fearing that they will trigger a binge-eating episode, families many times do not confront demanding, egocentric behavior involving either food-related or general issues. The therapist should insist that the bulimic be responsible for her behavior. The bulimic may initially become angry and demonstrate increased binge-eating and other self-destructive behaviors when the therapist or family states this expectation. Hospitalization or temporary out-of-home placement may occasonally be necessary in these cases.

After family conflicts have been addressed, individual psychotherapy may begin. For adults living outside of their parents' home, this is the first step after medical stabilization. A developmental assessment, including evaluation of the patient's level of ego functioning, should be completed before proceeding with psychotherapy. In therapy the patient and therapist should actively explore early problems and current difficulties leading to the patient's loss of control over her eating. This in some cases may lead to a broadening of treatment.

Psychodynamic management of hospitalized bulimic patients presents special challenges. The extroverted, emotionally labile bulimic can be difficult to manage on a hospital unit. Peer pressure can be helpful, but it is sometimes neutralized by bulimics who can coerce more passive patients to ignore clandestine binge-eating. Patients and inexperienced staff need support to resist psychological intimidation by such patients. When ward structure makes the previous binge-purge cycle impossible, bulimics should be encouraged to verbalize their increased tension and anger, which may be dramatic.

Conclusion

Important questions about anorexia nervosa and bulimia remain to be answered. What is the prevalence of dysfunctional patterns of family interaction in the general population? Is the prevalence of these patterns higher in certain psychiatric conditions such as eating disorders? When does parental involvement become overprotection? Studies that use standardized measurements of family interaction to assess important variables, both before and after treatment, are needed. A more thorough study of the psychodynamics involved in bulimia would be welcome, as well as an investigation of the character and structure of families of bulimic women. In addition, a realistic consideration of these patients' perceptions of their own femininity would add a much needed social dimension to the current literature.

The breadth of the questions above suggests the latitude of the areas affected by these illnesses. However hard one may try, anorexia nervosa and bulimia refuse to conform to a simple, coherent system with straightforward implications for treatment. They may, in fact, best be treated by several different approaches, each geared to a specific aspect of the disease. Behavioral techniques may be required to interrupt a binge-purge cycle, for instance, but be insufficient for treating the underlying difficulties that plague these patients. The essence of psychodynamic formulation lies in its capacity to integrate the diverse elements of a patient's existence and specific symptomatology into a coherent whole. It is through such integration that psychodynamic formulation can most plainly illuminate what our patients—in masked, defended, and conflicted ways—are really saying to us when they misuse food.

REFERENCES

1. Engel, G. L. 1980. The clinical application of the biopsychosocial model. *Am. J. Psychiatry* 137:535-44.
2. Hartmann, H. 1964. Comments on the psychoanalytic theory of the ego. In *Essays on ego psychology.* New York: International Universities Press.
3. Kernberg, O. 1976. *Object relations theory and clinical psychoanalysis.* New York: Jason Aronson.
4. Kohut, H. 1977. *The restoration of the self.* New York: International Universities Press.
5. Freud, A. 1958. Adolescence. *Psychoanal. Study Child* 13:255-78.
6. Waller, J., M. R. Kaufman, and F. Deutsch. 1940. Anorexia nervosa: A psychosomatic entity. *Psychosom. Med.* 2:3-16.
7. Meyer, J. E., and L. A. Weinroth. 1957. Observations on psychological aspects of anorexia nervosa. *Psychosom. Med.* 19:389-98.
8. Palazzoli, M. S. 1978. *Self-starvation.* New York: Jason Aronson.
9. Bruch, H. 1973. *Eating disorders: Obesity, anorexia nervosa and the person within.* New York: Basic Books.
10. Bruch, H. 1982. Anorexia nervosa: Therapy and theory. *Am. J. Psychiatry* 139:1531-38.
11. Rizzuto, A. M., R. K. Peterson, and M. Greed. 1981. The pathological sense of self in anorexia nervosa. *Psychiatr. Clin. North Am.* 4:471-87.
12. Sours, J. A. 1981. Depression and the anorexia nervosa syndrome. *Psychiatr. Clin. North Am.* 4:145-58.
13. Wilson, C. P., C. C. Hogan, and I. L. Mintz. 1983. *Fear of being fat.* New York; Jason Aronson.
14. Broderick, C. B., and S. S. Schrader. 1980. A history of professonal marriage and family therapy. In *Handbook of family therapy,* ed. A. S. Gurman and D. P. Kniskern. New York: Brunner Mazel.
15. Bowlby, J. 1949. The study and reduction of group tension in the family. *Human Relations* 2:123-28.
16. Lewis, J. M., W. R. Beavers, J. T. Gossett, and V. A. Phillips. 1976. *No single thread: Psychological health in family systems.* New York: Brunner Mazel.

17. Minuchin, S., B. L. Rosman, and L. Baker. 1978. *Psychosomatic families.* Cambridge, Mass.: Harvard University Press.
18. Minuchin, S., L. Baker, B. Rosman, R. Liebman, L. Milman, and T. Todd. 1975. A conceptual model of psychosomatic illness in children: Family organization and family therapy. *Arch. Gen. Psychiatry* 32:1031-38.
19. Minuchin, S., and H. C. Fishman. 1981. *Family therapy techniques.* Cambridge, Mass.: Harvard University Press.
20. Yager, J. 1981. Anorexia nervosa and the family. In *Family therapy and major psychopathology,* ed. M. R. Lansky. New York: Grune and Stratton.
21. Russell, G. 1979. Bulimia nervosa: An ominous variant of anorexia nervosa. *Psychol. Med.* 9:429-48.
22. Rampling, D. 1978. Anorexia nervosa: Reflections on theory and practice. *Psychiatry* 41:296-301.
23. Morgan, H. G., and G. F. M. Russell. 1975. Value of family background and clinical features as predictors of long-term outcome in anorexia nervosa: Four year follow-up study of 41 patients. *Psychol. Med.* 5:355-71.
24. Crisp, A. H., B. Harding, and B. McGuiness. 1974. Anorexia nervosa: Psychoneurotic characteristics of parents: Relationship to prognosis. *J. Psychosom. Res.* 18:167-73.
25. Hsu, L. H. G., A. H. Crisp, and B. Harding. 1979. Outcome of anorexia nervosa. *Lancet* 1:61-65.
26. Lewis, M. 1982. Adolescence. In *Clinical aspects of child development: An introductory synthesis of psychological concepts and clinical problems.* Philadelphia: Lea and Febiger.
27. Segraves, R. T., and R. C. Smith. 1976. Concurrent psychotherapy and behavior therapy. *Arch. Gen. Psychiatry* 33:756.
28. Karasu, T. B. 1982. Psychotherapy and pharmacotherapy: Toward an integrative model. *Am. J. Psychiatry* 139:1102-13.
29. Stern, S., C. A. Whitaker, M. J. Hagemann, R. B. Anderson, and G. J. Bargman. 1981. Anorexia nervosa: The hospital's role in family treatment. *Family Process* 20:395-408.
30. Lagos, J. M. 1981. Family therapy in the treatment of anorexia nervosa: Theory and technique. *Int. J. Psychiatry Med.* 11:291-302.
31. Strober, M. 1983. The significance of bulimia in juvenile anorexia nervosa: An exploration of possible etiologic factors. *Int. J. Eating Disorders* 1:28-43.
32. Casper, R. C., E. D. Eckert, K. A. Halmi, S. C. Goldberg, and J. M. Davis. 1980. Bulimia: Its incidence and clinical importance in patients with anorexia nervosa. *Arch. Gen. Psychiatry* 37:1030-35.
33. Garfinkel, P. E., H. Moldofsky, and D. M. Garner. 1980. The heterogeneity of anorexia nervosa: Bulimia as a distinct subgroup. *Arch. Gen. Psychiatry* 37:1036-40.
34. Ben-Tovim, D. I., V. Marilov, and A. Crisp. 1979. Personality and mental state within anorexia nervosa. *J. Psychosom. Res.* 124:353-59.
35. Strober, M. 1980. Personality and symptomatological features in young, non-chronic anorexia nervosa patients. *J. Psychosom. Res.* 124:353-59.
36. Sugarman, A., and C. Kurash. 1981. The body as a transitional object in bulimia. *Int. J. Eating Disorders* 1:57-67.
37. Seligman, E. 1976. A psychological study of anorexia nervosa: An account of the relationship between psychic factors and bodily functioning. *J. Anal. Psychol.* 21:193-207.
38. Sights, J. R. 1982. Parental antecedents of bulimia. Ph.D. thesis, University of Virginia.
39. Bruch, H. 1981. Developmental considerations of anorexia nervosa and obesity. *Can. J. Psychiatry* 26:212-17.
40. Strober, M., B. Salkin, J. Burroughs, and W. Morrell. 1982. Validity of the bulimia-restrictor distinctions in anorexia nervosa. *J. Nerv. Ment. Dis.* 170:345-51.

41. Weiss, S. R., and M. H. Ebert. 1983. Psychological and behavioral characteristics of normal-weight controls. *Psychosom. Med.* 45:293-303.
42. Boskind-Lodahl, M. 1976. Cinderella's step-sisters: A feminist perspective on anorexia nervosa and bulimia. *J. Women Culture Soc.* 2:342-56.

Part 2

Treatment

5

Behavioral Treatment of Anorexia Nervosa and Bulimia

Dorothy Hatsukami, Ph.D

Behavior therapy assumes that most behaviors are acquired and can be changed through learning procedures.[1] The focus in treatment is on maladaptive behaviors that have to be decreased and adaptive behaviors that have to be increased or learned. Thus, attempts are made to change or acquire *behavior* rather than to alter the aspects in a person that underlie it.

This chapter describes the application of behavioral principles in the treatment of anorexia nervosa and bulimia by addressing basic concepts, detailing techniques like cognitive therapy and adaptive skills training, and reviewing treatment outcome studies.

General Principles of Behavioral Therapy

Behavioral therapy distinguishes two types of learning: respondent and operant conditioning. Respondent conditioning deals with stimuli—called *unconditional* stimuli—that automatically evoke responses—called *unconditioned* responses. For example, a loud noise (unconditioned stimuli) would automatically evoke a startle response (unconditioned response). The connection between an unconditioned stimulus and an unconditional response is automatic, not learned. Respondent conditioning involves a process whereby new stimuli gain the power to elicit respondent behaviors. In this process, a neutral stimulus (*conditioned stimulus*) is paired with the unconditioned stimulus. Pairing a conditioned stimulus with an unconditioned stimulus eventually results in the conditioned stimulus alone leading to what is now termed a *conditioned response*. The classic experiment[2] was one in which a little boy named Albert was presented a furry white rabbit (neutral stimulus) paired with noise (unconditioned stimulus), which automatically elicited a startle response (unconditioned response). Eventually the white rabbit (now termed a conditioned stimulus) evoked the startle response (now termed a conditioned response). Once the conditioning is well established, another stimulus can be conditioned to the already present conditioned stimulus. For example, Albert may also become anxious when he hears the word "rabbit" because that label has been paired with the real rabbit. This process is called *higher-order conditioning.*

In operant conditioning, behavior is increased or decreased by its consequences. If the consequence increases the behavior, then this process is termed *reinforcement.* Reinforcement can be a presentation of a favorable event (positive reinforcement) or removal of an aversive event (negative reinforcement). For example, alcohol may be a reinforcer because of the initial pleasant pharmacological effects (positive reinforcement) or because it temporarily relieves tension or depression—that is, removes an aversive state (negative reinforcement). If the consequence decreases the behavior, this is termed *punishment.* As with reinforcement, punishment may be produced either by the presentation or removal of an event. For example, both criticism (presentation of an aversive event) or social isolation (a removal of social reinforcement) are examples of punishment. Figure 1 illustrates the principles of reinforcement and punishment.

	"Pleasurable" event	"Aversive" event
Presentation	Positive reinforcement (increases behavior)	Punishment (decreases behavior)
Removal	Punishment (decreases behavior)	Negative reinforcement (increases behavior)

Figure 1. Consequences in operant conditioning paradigm

Antecedent events can also control behavior. *Stimulus control* develops when antecedent stimuli are associated with both the behavior and the subsequent reinforcing consequences with such frequency that the stimulus begins to elicit the behavior. For example, going past a bakery (antecedent stimulus) may facilitate an urge to binge-eat. Stimuli or antecedents can be external (social and situational) or internal (emotional, physiological, and cognitive).

Some behavioral therapists believe that merely changing the occurrence of a maladaptive behavior is not enough. They think that it is also essential to teach skills that foster more adaptive ways of functioning, such as rational thinking, assertiveness, social skills, or problem-solving skills.

Behavioral Treatment of Anorexia Nervosa

Both respondent and operant techniques have been used to treat anorexia nervosa, principally to facilitate weight gain and improve eating habits. Particular respondent techniques include systematic desensitization and response prevention. The operant techniques that are widely used involve positive or negative reinforcement of behaviors (weight gain) or punishment of maladaptive behaviors (weight loss). Cognitive therapy involves examining and challenging irrational thoughts and beliefs that facilitate anorectic behaviors; other behavioral techniques focus on the teaching of adaptive skills (e.g., assertion, social skills, family communications).

Respondent Model

Theorists who espouse the respondent model view anorexia nervosa as a conditioned fear or anxiety about gaining weight and becoming fat.[3,4] In other words, a process of higher-order conditioning has caused feelings of fear or anxiety to become conditioned to food intake that can lead to weight gain. Avoiding food intake and subsequent weight gain, therefore, reduces anxiety. Other theorists and researchers have questioned whether anorexia nervosa represents such a phobic disorder.[5,6] Salkind, Fincham, and Silverstone found that, unlike individuals with a phobic disorder, anorectic patients exhibited minimal physiological response as measured by skin conductance to phobia-related stimuli (food).[5]

Therapists following the respondent model of anorexia nervosa have used systematic desensitization and response prevention to treat these patients.[7] Systematic desensitization is the counterconditioning or inhibiting of the anxiety associated with a particular stimulus by substituting a relaxation response for it. One study used visual imagery to investigate the direct effects of counterconditioning anxiety towards food.[8] The patient was first taught to relax, then presented with a hierarchy of situations ranging from ones provoking little anxiety to others provoking the most anxiety. In carefully monitored steps, each associated with increasing levels of anxiety, she was instructed to visualize herself being called to the table, being at the table, eating, eating fattening foods, enjoying these foods, having eaten, and then going to stand before a mirror in her mother's bedroom perceiving that she was gaining weight. This procedure was undertaken in a systematic fashion with relaxation being used to minimize the anxiety experienced during each step; the next step in the hierarchy was not undertaken until the previous one was no longer associated with anxiety. All of the imagery was centered on the home situation to allow maximum generalizability. Over a 50-day-period, this patient's weight rose from 57 to 78 pounds.

In response prevention, the patient is exposed to the anxiety-provoking situation and not allowed to escape. Over time, the anxiety evoked by the situation is expected to dissipate. In a study conducted by Mavissakalian,[6] two subjects were prevented from compulsive exercising (an anxiety-reducing behavior) following a full meal. Exposure to the anxiety-provoking stimuli (food and weight) was maintained for 90 minutes. Over the course of time and numerous sessions (135 and 90 sessions, respectively), the patients were able to adapt to the condition after the initial experiences of intense distress. Both patients increased their weight during treatment.

Operant Model

According to the operant model, anorexia nervosa develops or is maintained because of the reinforcing consequences of the behavior. Positive reinforcers for anorexia nervosa include cultural values that place importance on thinness, praise from peers or family for losing weight early in the course of the illness, and the patient's own personal gratification and sense of accomplishment for the self-control exhibited by loss of weight.[9] Loss of weight can be a powerful reinforcer because it demonstrates a tangible success.[10] Finally, rejection of food may eventually be reinforced by the attention it produces from family, peers, or others.[11] Negative reinforcement for anorectic behaviors includes the avoidance of responsibility and demands accompanying biological and social maturity.[3] The patient may also be helping the family to avoid conflict by maintaining the symptoms, allowing parents to deny and avoid problems between them or with other siblings.[12,13]

A behavioral program based on the operant model attempts to change the contingencies of reinforcement by providing positive reinforcement for adaptive eating behaviors or weight gain; avoidance of a negative situation or negative reinforcement for adaptive eating behaviors or weight gain; or punishment for nonadaptive eating behaviors or weight loss. Past research on the treatment of anorexia nervosa has primarily used both positive and negative reinforcement approaches and punishment to increase adaptive eating habits and weight gain. Most of the techniques were originally designed for inpatient treatment, although some are adaptable to outpatient use.

Behavioral Contracts

Adaptive eating habits and weight gain are the typical treatment goals in an operant behavioral program for anorexia nervosa. The goals are met by establishing a behavioral contract or "written agreement specifying operationally defined behaviors and contingencies designed to promote behavior change."[14] Behavioral contracts provide an explicit commitment on the part of the patient for behavioral change. Furthermore, they specify clear goals that determine when the contract is fulfilled. Finally, the contract details contingencies of reinforcement between the patient and therapist that are designed to motivate and execute behavior change.[1,13,15] The contract typically includes a detailed description of the target behavior; reinforcement contingencies upon attainment of the target behavior; punishment upon failure to achieve the target behavior; frequency of reinforcement; and methods to observe, measure, and record the target behavior.

Target Behavior. When patients are placed on a reinforcement regimen, it is important to specify the behavior to be reinforced. Typically, reinforcement is contingent on weight gain. Some researchers have tried to reinforce eating behavior, such as mouthfuls of food, amount of food eaten, and number of consecutive meals in a restricted period of time.[16-19] In some instances, however, reinforcing *only* these behaviors has led to the maintenance of the targeted eating behaviors but with vomiting and subsequent loss of weight, to disposing of food surreptitiously, or to taking smaller mouthfuls of food.[16,17,18] Azerrad and Stafford[19] used a point system based on the amount of food eaten or types of food eaten, and they found this system more effective than making rewards contingent on amount of weight gain. Points redeemable for privileges, material items, or extended home visits were given immediately after the eating behavior rather than at the end of the day for weight gain. In general, reinforcement is probably best when it is based both on weight gain and specific components of eating behavior.

The contract should also establish the specific amount of weight gain necessary before reinforcement will be given. A typical rate of gain for hospitalized patients would be half a pound daily.[4,12,20-23] Other researchers and clinicians, with equal success, have reinforced approximately .1 kg/day[19,24,25], any weight gain[14,15], have increased the weight contingencies over time[25,26,27], or have increased reinforcements with greater amounts of weight gain (for example, an extra privilege for gaining one pound rather than the half-pound goal).[19,21,13] A reasonable *goal* weight is 90% of the average height-for-weight figure derived from actuarial tables.[9]

Types and Methods of Positive Reinforcements. The contract must establish the types of rewards to be used in reinforcing the anorectic patient. A typical reinforcement allows patients to obtain various privileges contingent upon a specified increase in weight.[4,12,16-28] The system of rewards can either be tailored to the patient or standardized for groups of patients. Tailored rewards allow patients to determine the type of reinforcement they would like to earn upon gaining the specified amount of weight.[18,23,24] Potent reinforcers for the patient may also be determined by observation during baseline of behaviors that occur at a high frequency.[4,16,21]

For example, physical activity has been found to be a strong reinforcer for some anorectic patients. Blinder, Freeman, and Stunkard[21] found that the anorectics among their patient population walked an average of 6.8 miles per day, whereas normal patients walked 4.9 miles per day. Given this data, the researchers allotted the anorectic patient 6 hours of unrestricted activity outside the hospital on any day when her weight gain was greater or equal to half a pound. The average weight gain of the three patients in this study was 3.9 pounds per week.

Standardized reinforcements are already determined by the staff.[12,20,22,25-28] The rewards may include physical activity, socializing off the ward, overnight or weekend passes, visits from peers or relatives, watching television, and receiving mail or phone calls.

The privileges can be given either directly after the weight gain or through a token economy system. Direct reinforcement of weight gain was studied by Brady and Rieger.[4] Patients were reinforced on a daily basis if their morning weights were at least half a pound more than their weights the previous morning. If the patients attained the required half-pound gain, they would have a 6-hour, off-ward pass for the day; if they failed to gain the weight, they were restricted to the ward for the day. A token economy system was developed by Parker, Blazer, and Wyrick.[23] The patient was reinforced for weight gain on a daily basis. If the patient maintained her weight, she was given one chip; if she increased her weight by half a pound, she was given 10 chips; if the patient increased her weight by 1 pound, she was given 10 chips plus a surprise in a box. The chips were then exchanged for certain privileges (table 10). Azerrad and Stafford used a similar token system, except that points instead of chips were dispensed.[19] The points were redeemable for frequently used items (hair curlers, writing paper, stamps), for special events (movies), and for purchasing items from stores or catalogs.

A token economy system has certain advantages. The use of tokens or points shortens the delay between target behavior and reinforcement, making the reinforcement more immediate and therefore more effective. Other advantages include the use of a single reinforcer that can be traded for other reinforcers selected by the patient and the minimal disruption of the performance of the target behavior when dispensing points or tokens. The primary disadvantage is the problem with generalization once the patient returns to the natural environment.[1]

Studies indicate that positive reinforcement is an effective means for weight gain. For example, Agras et al. examined the effects of positive

Table 10. Privileges Obtained in Exchange for Tokens

Privilege	No. Tokens	Time
Card playing. Patient's responsibility to find partners.	1	Per hr
Walk on campus. Must be accompanied by attendant. Patient makes arrangements with nurse for attendant to go along.	2	1 hr per day
Crocheting lesson	1	½ hr session per day
Dance lesson	1	½ hr session per day
Visit with parents up to 6 hr	1	Per hr
Work on needlepoint	1	Per hr

Source: Adapted from "Anorexia nervosa: A combined therapeutic approach," by J.B. Parker, D. Blazer, and L. Wyrich, *Southern Medical Journal* 70 (1977): 448-56.

reinforcement and noncontingent privileges on caloric intake and weight gain.[25] There were four sequential phases in this particular experiment: a baseline condition, reinforcement of weight gain, noncontingent reinforcement (privileges given whether or not weight was gained), and return to reinforcement. The effects of negative reinforcement (discharge from the hospital after reaching a particular goal) were removed by contracting for a 12-week stay whether or not the patient gained weight. The results are shown in figure 2. During the baseline phase, caloric intake and weight (0.03 kg/day) increased slightly. Introduction of the reinforcement phase lead to a faster increase in caloric intake and weight (0.25 kg/day). The noncontingent reinforcement phase led to a sharp decrease in caloric intake (0.1 kg/day), and reintroduction of contingent reinforcement led to further increased gains (0.25 kg/day). This study demonstrates the effectiveness of positive reinforcement and the importance of reinforcement in weight gain.

Negative Reinforcement and Punishment. Negative reinforcement and punishment have also been helpful in increasing the weight of anorectic patients. Negative reinforcement can take the form of removing an aversive situation by reaching the specified goal weight. For example, patients are placed in an isolated, stripped room where they must remain except for participation in occupational therapy projects or individual or group therapies.[16,18,22,25,27,28] To escape confinement to a barren room, patients are

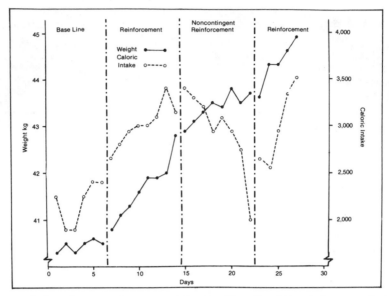

Figure 2. Data from experiment examining the effect of positive reinforcement in the absence of negative reinforcement. *Source:* "Behavior modification of anorexia nervosa," by W. S. Agras, D. H. Barlow, H. N. Chapin, G. G. Abel, and H. Leitenberg, *Archives of General Psychiatry* 30 (1974): 279-86. Copyright 1974, American Medical Association.

required to reach a specified goal weight. Other aversive situations include being confined to bed rest[12] and being tube fed.[28]

Another interesting but questionable form of negative reinforcement is the reduction in dose of chlorpromazine, a major tranquilizer, with weight gain. Blinder, Freeman, and Stunkard[21] treated an anorectic patient by reducing the drug dosage by 75% if the patient gained a quarter of a pound, 50% if the patient gained half a pound, and 25% if the patient gained three-quarters of a pound; the patient was given no drug if she gained 1 pound during the course of a day. This patient gained about 6 pounds per week. However, this method of reenforcement seems no longer acceptable according to contemporary standards concerning the use of psychotropic drugs.

Punishment presents an aversive stimulus to the anorectic patient whenever weight loss occurs. Thus, punishment is used to decrease the likelihood of weight loss. The aversive situations used as punishment are similar to those mentioned above: social isolation, tube feeding, confinement to bed rest.

Frequency of Reinforcement. The next important specification in a behavioral contract is frequency of reinforcement. Some therapists have reinforced patients on a daily basis[4,12,16,18,21-26] or at 5-day intervals;[27,28] others have combined both daily and weekly reinforcements.[24] Although the benefits of one schedule over another have not been comprehensively studied, daily reinforcement schedules seem to be more effective than, say, those based on 5 days.[22] General principle dictates that the more immediate the reinforcement, the greater its effectiveness.

Observation, Measurement, and Record. Finally, a contract must specify how the behavior is to be observed, measured, and recorded. Typically, a graph is used to record weight gain; it can include a line indicating the goal weight to be obtained during each weighing. The method by which the weight is measured and observed should be standardized. Researchers have favored weighing the patient at a specified hour each morning, after voiding but before breakfast.[4,12,19,24,25,28]

Informational feedback to the patient has been found to help weight gain. It would include such things as the number of mouthfuls the patient ingested, the number of calories, and weight. Agras et al. found that reinforcement plus feedback provide a greater increase in weight compared with reinforcement alone (fig. 3).[25] The experiment included five

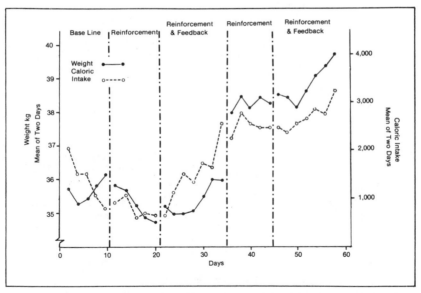

Figure 3. Data from experiment examining the effect of feedback on the eating behavior of a patient with anorexia nervosa. *Source:* "Behavior modification of anorexia nervosa," by W. S. Agras, D. H. Barlow, H. N. Chapin, G. G. Abel, and H. Leitenberg, *Archives of General Psychiatry* 30 (1974): 279-86. Copyright 1974, American Medical Association.

sequential phases: baseline, reinforcement, reinforcement and feedback, reinforcement, and reinforcement and feedback. There was minimal improvement in weight during the baseline and initial reinforcement phases; reinforcement plus feedback led to immediate increases in eating; removal of feedback led to no further gains in caloric intake and stabilization in weight; and, finally, a reinstitution of feedback led to further increases in weight and caloric intake.

Thus far, we have discussed the important components of a behavioral contract—establishing a goal weight, determining what behaviors to reinforce to attain the goal weight, the specific amount to reinforce, the types of reinforcements for the attainment of the specified goal, the frequency of reinforcement, and observation and measurement of the specified goals. Figure 4 provides an example of a contract that incorporates all the components discussed.

Goal

Attain goal weight

Desired Behavior

Gain weight at ½ lb per day until goal weight is reached

Approach	*Reinforcement*
1. Draw red ½ lb per day line on graph from base weight	
2. When weight is on or above contingency line, patient earns responsibility level according to guidelines below:	
A. Confined until 25% of goal weight	
B. At 25% (____lb) of goal weight.....................................	Four-hour pass, escorted with staff
C. At 50% (____lb) of goal weight.....................................	Four-hour pass, escorted with family
D. At 75% (____lb) of goal weight for 2 consecutive days...	Maintenance plan goes into effect
3. If patient is below contingency line:	Confined to unit No phone calls No visitors
4. Weigh at 6:30 a.m. every day in blue gown after voiding in the presence of two observers	
5. When weights obtained randomly during the day are below contingency, follow guidelines as in item 3	

Figure 4. Sample contract

Outpatient Treatment

Most of these behavioral techniques have been used on an inpatient basis. A few researchers and therapists have tried to apply behavioral techniques on an outpatient basis, and essentially the same principles are applied. One of the most important factors in the attempts to maintain or increase weight on an outpatient basis is a written contract indicating the goal weight, the expected number of pounds to be gained per week, a reinforcement and punishment system resulting from weight gain or weight loss respectively, and rehospitalization if the patient goes below a certain weight.

Halmi, Powers, and Cunningham[28] tried to increase weight with a behavioral approach after patients were discharged from the hospital. This individualized reinforcement program included such rewards as new clothes and special activities given by families for a gain of 1.1 pounds per week until the patient reached the normal weight range. Liebman, Minuchin, and Baker[12] required discharged patients to gain a minimum of 2 pounds per week in order to maintain normal activities. If the patient gained less, she was not allowed out of the house during the weekend and could not invite friends over to the house. Patients who gained more than 2.5 pounds could be active on Friday, Saturday, and Sunday nights. In addition to developing a contract and a reinforcement system, other successful components to ensure weight gain that we have found include a structured meal plan and establishing an eating situation that minimizes anxiety as much as possible—perhaps eating among peers or with other people. Because anorectics tend to distrust their own perceptions, a structured meal plan and recording of meals actually eaten seems to alleviate some of their fears about food intake.

Treatment Outcome

The effectiveness of behavioral treatment in comparison with other therapies is summarized from the data presented in an article by Agras and Werne[29] (tables 11 and 12). When we consider immediate outcome (table 11)—length of hospital days, average weight gain, and average weight gain per day—of the behavioral and traditional approaches, we see that the behavioral approach lends itself to shorter hospital stays (50 vs. 83.1 days), but that average weight gain and weight gain per day are similar. When we consider long-term outcome (table 12), we see a similar proportion of recovered or markedly improved patients (maintenance of normal or near normal weights, normal eating patterns, a return to menstruation, and substantially normal life adjustment) in both the behavioral and nonbehavioral approaches (45% vs. 47%) and a slightly higher proportion

Table 11. Immediate Outcomes of Traditional versus Behavioral Treatments

	Hospital Stay (Days)	Avg. Weight Gain (kg)	Weight Gain per Day (kg)
Traditional	83.1 (36-210)	8.3 (4.5-13.9)	.10 (.02-.29)
Behavioral	50.0 (32-77)	7.1 (5.1-12.4)	.15 (.13-.20)

Source: Data summarized from Agras and Werne.[29]

Table 12. Long-Term Outcomes of Nonbehavioral versus Behavioral Treatments

	Recovered or Markedly Improved	Improved	Not Improved	Deaths
Nonbehavioral	47%	21%	19%	9%
Behavioral	45	34	16	0

Source: Data summarized from Agras and Werne.[29]

of improved patients (residual problems especially in life adjustment) in the behavioral approach (33.8% vs. 21%). The results of the behavioral approach may be generally biased because of a shorter length of follow-up; however, a study undertaken by Garfinkel, Moldofsky, and Garner[30] comparing the two therapeutic modalities found no significant differences after a follow-up of some 58 weeks. Agras and Werne[29] point out that the similar outcome data may be attributed to the overlapping techniques employed in both approaches.

Cognitive Techniques

We have primarily addressed the use of behavioral techniques in weight gain. Among patients with anorexia nervosa, several areas in addition to weight gain may require extensive therapeutic work; weight gain cannot be the sole focus. Behavioral therapy has been criticized because it only deals with a rapid weight gain[31] and does not address cognitive misperceptions, interpersonal difficulties, and family problems.

Recently, some behavior therapists have recognized the importance of cognitive factors in the conceptualization and modification of behavior. The basic premise of cognitive therapy is that the thoughts, beliefs, and assumptions of individuals affect their feelings and behaviors.[32] Anorectics are believed to have cognitive distortions that maintain their maladaptive behaviors; excellent articles have been writteen about this area by Garner, Garfinkel, and Bemis[10] and Garner and Bemis.[9] Briefly, there are many erroneous thoughts and beliefs among anorectic patients that contribute to their behaviors. These need to be recognized, defined, and challenged so that they can be changed or abandoned. Several types of reasoning errors or styles of thinking are common among anorectic patients. One is dichotomous or all-or-nothing thinking: that is, thinking in absolute terms. This style of thinking may lead anorectic patients to entertain idealized notions of success and happiness and to feel like a complete failure if these notions are not realized. In addition, anorectics frequently see themselves and others as totally good or totally bad, or in total control or lacking any control. For example, one anorectic patient considered herself a failure and in total lack of control because she ate a bite of a cookie that was considered a forbidden food. To combat this all-or-nothing reasoning, patients are helped to develop realistic expectations.

Another type of erroneous thinking includes personalization and self-reference. The anorectic patient may believe that her behavior is the focus of other people's attention. This personalization often leads to the belief that it is necessary to maintain very high standards in order not to be disapproved of by others. A technique used to alter this faulty thinking involves "decentering,"[10] or applying the same stringent standards to other people as one does to one's own behavior.

A third type of common erroneous reasoning includes superstitious thinking. Unreasonable and irrational cause-and-effect relationships are developed. For example, the anorectic patient may think that if she eats any sweets she will gain 10 pounds the next day. The therapist's role is to provide feedback to help the patient recognize these distorted thoughts.

In addition to erroneous thoughts, anorectics frequently have faulty underlying assumptions, including the perception that weight, shape, or thinness is the sole determinant of self-worth. An anorectic patient remarked that she was surprised to discover that men can like women who are overweight. Other assumptions include the desirability for complete self-control and discipline, the assumption that perfect performance is necessary for self-fulfillment, and the belief that total approval from others must be obtained. Treatment of these underlying assumptions involves assisting the patient to recognize, then to support or challenge them. More adaptive underlying assumptions are then subsequently substituted.

Other Issues and Techniques

Anorectic patients have been found to experience interpersonal difficulties for several reasons. In fact, studies show that about 50% of the patients with anorexia have problems with social adjustment after treatment.[33,34] These patients need to develop interpersonal skills through assertiveness training and social and communication skills training that involve behavioral rehearsal of appropriate interactions. Videotaping may be a good medium for facilitating change. As a result of low self-esteem and social isolation consequent to the anorectic behavior, the patient may have difficulty generalizing adaptive social interactions to situations outside of therapy. Therefore, behavioral assignments describing self-initiated social activities may be important for these patients.[10] In addition, because the patient has typically experienced difficulty trusting his or her own judgment, the development of problem-solving skills may be essential. These patients also have a history of only limited amounts of outside activities. The therapist may take time to explore and increase the number of pleasurable activities as well as the number of areas—other than weight—in which the patient can gain mastery.

Finally, family therapy is often important to treatment. Family members need to be aware of their own misperceptions about the illness and to be educated about the problem. Furthermore, family behaviors that maintain or reinforce the eating disorder need to be explored and changed. Adaptive family behaviors include the avoidance of reinforcement of maladaptive eating behavior by making eating or weight an issue, discussion of only pleasant topics at meal times, maintenance of scheduled meals, avoidance of preparing special diets for the patient, and reinforcement of weight maintenance without overreaction.[14]

A strong source of positive reinforcement for improvement comes from the therapist and, if the patient is involved in a group, from other group members. Goals should be reasonable, with reinforcement of minimal steps. The reinforcement should be consistent, and agreements made on contracts must be followed through. The therapist should also be sure that the appropriate behaviors are being reinforced and should provide feedback to allow patients to test their own perceptions and alter their anorectic behaviors to more appropriate ones.

Behavioral Treatment of Bulimia

Much less has been published about the behavioral treatment of bulimia than of anorexia. During the past few years, bulimic patients have been treated with various types of approaches; in addition to behavioral therapy, these include insight therapy, support therapy, and an intensive treatment program combining both support and behavioral therapies. Behavioral therapeutic techniques that are widely used among individuals with addictive or excessive behaviors like alcohol abuse, smoking, and gross overeating have been applied to bulimic patients.[35-40] Our focus here is on the behavioral treatment of normal-weight individuals with bulimia who binge-eat and then vomit or abuse laxatives.

Behavioral Analysis of Bulimic Behavior

The operant model is useful in describing the maintenance of bulimic behavior and its treatment. A behavior is maintained by reinforcing consequences, and the consequences of bulimic behavior include both positive and negative reinforcements. Some of the reported reinforcing consequences of binge-eating include the ingestion of food as a pleasant event with associated pleasant sensations[41,42] and the ingestion of fattening foods without the fear of gaining weight.[42] Bulimic women also mention that binge-eating is reinforcing because it relieves tension or stress.[41,43] Several women have reported that binge-eating provides a distraction from aversive tasks or a means to avoid confronting a personal problem. They also mention that binge-eating and vomiting provides a structure in their lives, filling empty or transitional periods or helping them to escape from boredom. Others report that binge-eating and vomiting help to stop their mental preoccupation with food.[44]

Rather than the reinforcing consequences from binge-eating maintaining the bulimic behavior, however, it may be that the reinforcing consequences from vomiting maintain the binge-eating. In a study conducted by Johnson and Larson,[45] subjects with bulimia ($n = 15$) recorded moods before, during, and after binge-eating and vomiting. During a binge-eating episode, the subject's negative affects worsened; however, during vomiting, there was a reported increase in alertness and restoration of control and adequacy. Furthermore, the vomiting behavior provided discharge of anger as evidenced by a reduction of angry feelings. These researchers speculated that bulimic women continue to binge-eat so that they can vomit, rather than vomiting so that they can binge-eat. Vomiting has also been said to reduce the anxiety associated with weight gain after a binge-eating episode.[42] Once the individual learns that vomiting reduces anxiety after a binge, she is free from the fears that would inhibit overeating.[44]

Punishments are also associated with bulimic behavior. Binge-eating and self-induced vomiting have been reported to interfere with social relationships.[42,46] There are also potential occupational problems (missed work, inefficiency, problems with school),[46,47] physical problems (weakness, fatigue, dizziness, poor concentration, dental problems, electrolyte abnormalities, and other medical complications),[42,46-50] financial problems (because of the cost of food), and legal problems (as a result of shoplifting). There is a great deal of time lost in the mental preoccupation with food and the eating disorder, in addition to the time actually spent engaging in binging and vomiting behavior. There are also feelings of depression, guilt, anxiety, anger, and self-disgust resulting from the inability to control these episodes.[41,42,46-48] In spite of all these punishments, maladaptive behaviors continue because the strength of any reinforcer or punishment diminishes the farther it is removed from the actual behavior. Thus, immediate reinforcing consequences outweigh later maladaptive consequences.

Antecedent stimuli can also control behavior by facilitating its occurrence. Antecedents to binge-eating can be external cues (situational and social) or internal cues (emotional, cognitive, and physiological). An example of a situational cue would be time of day—such as midafternoon (2-4 p.m.) and early evening (6-8 p.m.), which are common binge-eating times.[45] Being alone in a house,[41,45,48] the accessibility of binge foods,[41] or eating small quantities of "forbidden" foods[41,42] may also provide cues for binge-eating. Other situational cues include a store that is typically associated with the purchase of binge foods and places associated with a high frequency of binge-eating, such as the kitchen, an automobile, or restaurants.[42] Social factors include interpersonal conflicts or stress[51] and occasions that call for socializing around food, such as holidays or parties. Emotional cues include extremely positive emotional arousal—days when the individual is feeling on top of the world—or negative emotional arousal—periods of anxiety, anger, frustration, boredom, depression, or disappointment.[41,46,48] Cognitive cues include preoccupation with food or eating, thoughts of deprivation as a result of high dieting standards, retaliatory thoughts, guilt-related thoughts, thoughts of lack of control over eating, thoughts of feeling fat, and negative self-reference thoughts.[41,42,52] Physiological cues include fatigue and hunger induced by fasting or excessively strict dieting.[41,47,48]

Behavioral Treatment

The behavioral treatment of bulimia has typically been undertaken on an outpatient basis, with both group and individual therapies. Components in our own program includes intervention directed at the behavior itself and its antecedents and consequences. Binge-eating is often the target behavior for intervention rather than the vomiting under the premise that cessation of binge-eating will stop the vomiting. For those patients who vomit nearly everything they eat, this approach may not be helpful. In these instances, vomiting is the primary focus of intervention. The techniques focusing on the modification of vomiting will be discussed later.

The goals of treatment can either be a gradual reduction of binge-eating and vomiting (or laxative use) or the abrupt cessation of binge-eating and associated behaviors at the onset of treatment or at a later date that is agreed upon. Presently, no data support one approach over the other in terms of treatment success, but our clinical impression is that abrupt cessation is more effective. Another goal was used in a study conducted by Mizes and Lohr[53] where "eating deviations"—defined as episodes of eating in addition to the four prescribed meal and snack times—were reduced. They found, however, that changing irregular eating habits may not be sufficient to change the frequency of binge-eating.

In the initial phases of intervention, patients are instructed in the principles of the functional analysis of behavior and given information about the nature and negative consequences that have been found among individuals with eating disorders.[54-56] They are told about the importance of making a commitment to change and that change is primarily a function of the initiative of the patient and utilization of methods of self-control. During this initial phase, baseline data are gathered as the individuals monitor their eating behavior: frequency of normal meals and snacks; binge-eating and vomiting, laxative use, or other means of ridding oneself of food or controlling weight; and the time and amount of food ingested. The individuals also record the antecedents associated with their normal and binge-eating episodes. (See fig. 5)[53-57] Individuals may monitor eating behaviors and antecedents throughout the course of the treatment or for the initial and last weeks. This assessment helps in determining the individual's pattern of eating behavior and the specific antecedent events that may be associated with binge-eating episodes.

After baseline data are collected, the next step is an analysis of the antecedent factors and the behavior itself, including a discussion of its consequences.[56] This analysis of antecedents and reinforcing consequences serves to direct the treatment intervention. For example, if the individual frequently binge-eats for relief of stress, the stress management may be an important component of the individual's treatment program. If the individual binge-eats when frustrated from interpersonal conflict and the binge-eating helps in avoidance of this problem, then assertiveness training and the teaching of communication skills would be indicated for this individual's treatment program. Exploring and discussing the *negative* consequences of the eating disorder are also important: by sharing these negative experiences, the shame and guilt that are often associated with the disorder may be alleviated, and the patient may be motivated to change the eating disorder when she is more cognizant of its adverse consequences.

Once the various components associated with the behaviors are analyzed, an intervention program is designed that seeks to change the eating behavior, to manipulate the antecedents and consequences, and to teach adaptive skills. Techniques from weight control treatment programs are often used in changing the eating behavior.[37-39] Patients are taught the importance of eating three meals a day and are encouraged to plan meals in advance, to develop routine schedules of eating, to focus on eating when eating, and to eat slowly.[42,53-56]

Time	Amount and Type of Food	Method of Ridding Food	Place	People	Feelings

Figure 5. Self-monitor record

Manipulating the antecedents involves breaking the relationship between the antecedent events and the bulimic behavior.[55-57] Individuals are taught to minimize cues related to binge-eating by removing food from all places in the house that are not appropriate storage areas; reducing the visual cues for eating; making junk or binge foods unavailable at home and in the immediate work area; staying out of the kitchen area as much as possible; eating in a designated eating place to break the association between various areas at home or work when eating; and preparing a shopping list before going to the grocery.[38]

They are taught to avoid situations most frequently associated with binge-eating: not to go into stores where binge foods are usually purchased, not to go past the candy machine, not to take a route that typically leads to restaurants or stores that are associated with binge-eating episodes. They are also taught to give themselves graduated increases in time before impulsively binging[57] or vomiting.[44,54]

Individuals are taught to use competing behaviors by scheduling activities at times that are associated with a high frequency of binge-eating. If binge-eating is common at a particular time of day, patients are encouraged to schedule another activity, such as jogging or going to the health spa. Arrangements can be made with a friend to help the patient follow through with completing the activity. Individuals are also encouraged to engage in activities that are associated with a low frequency of binging behavior—for example, studying in the library rather than in other settings where binge-eating is more common.

Exposure and response prevention is a method aimed toward preventing the undesired behavior from occurring. An example of this approach is illustrated in a study conducted by Smith.[57] An obese individual who engaged in binge-eating was encouraged to eat a certain amount of desirable foods during a therapy session. She was then instructed to refrain from eating any more of the food while being exposed to it for 30 minutes. She was further instructed to take the food home with her and continue her exposure to it for another 30 minutes and then to dispose of the remaining food without eating it. She was also encouraged to practice this procedure on a daily basis at home. Over the course of 8 months, the patient's binge-eating episodes decreased from daily to monthly.

The occurrence of behavior is obviously not simply a sequence of antecedent, behavior, and consequent events; behaviors are more complex. That is, a sequence of responses occurs in a fixed order with the last response in the chain being reinforced. This process is called chaining, in which the event that immediately precedes the reinforcement provides a signal for reinforcement and also becomes a reinforcer itself as a result of the frequent pairing of the signal with the reinforcer. In treatment, it is important to work backwards from the last responses and recognize the antecedent events that started the chain of events that led to binge-eating.

In figure 6 we see an example of chaining. The individual begins the morning without breakfast, leading to cognitions such as "I feel good not eating in the morning so that I can lose or maintain my weight." These cognitions lead to further resolve not to eat in the afternoon: "If I don't eat anything for lunch, I will feel better about myself." The individual then skips this meal, which leads to preoccupation with food, thoughts of inefficiency, and feelings of stress. Thoughts evolve into the perceived need to binge-eat, e.g., "I've had a stressful day, I deserve to binge." These thoughts lead to stopping at the grocery store or bakery after work, buying the binge-foods, going home, and binge-eating in the kitchen. Then vomiting leads to self-disgust and the resolve to attempt to control the eating the next day. Treatment involves the recognition of this chain and intervention by the patient in the early phases of the chain.[38] Typically, individuals are encouraged to plan alternate activities in the beginning phases of the chain. Alternate activities would be ineffective by the time the individual enters the grocery store. Thus, instead of skipping breakfast, the individual can start the day with a nutritious meal and plan to eat lunch.

Another facet in designing a treatment program involves the manipulation of consequences.[42,53,54,56] One way to increase adaptive behavior (that is, avoiding binge-eating and vomiting) is to reward it. Goals are broken down into small steps, such as not binging and vomiting for 1 day. The rewards should be contingent on the occurrence of the set behavior and be proximate to the completion of the adaptive behavior. Rewards can be either material or mental in nature. Figure 7 gives an example of a homework assignment given to patients to develop personal rewards. The individuals are taught to set up material rewards for themselves. These might include saving money (e.g., $5.00 per day) that was previously spent on binge-eating and using it to buy magazines, movies, or record albums. They are taught to make positive self-statements for the goals they have successfully completed. Furthermore, a social reinforcement system can be used because groups of bulimic individuals appear to provide strong reinforcement for adaptive behavior.

Covert sensitization is a punishment technique that has been used wherein patients visualize a negative imagery pertaining to the binge-eating and vomiting behavior.[58] They are asked to conjure up an image replete with aversive sensory details relating to their binge-eating or vomiting behavior. Often these individuals disengage themselves from the unpleasant aspects of their eating disorder. In the imagery, they are asked to visualize the actual act of binge-eating and vomiting. This image is

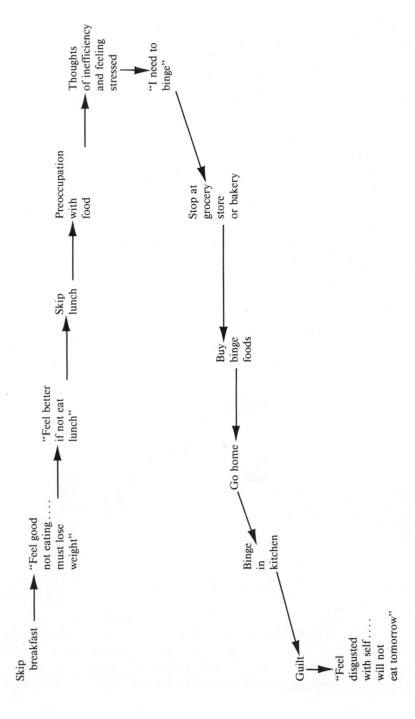

Figure 6. Behavioral chain leading to binge-eating and vomiting

---

Personal Rewards

Take a few minutes now to think of some good rewards for yourself. Start with material rewards. What things could you afford (in terms of money or time) that would be pleasant? What would you work for?

Remember that better rewards are those that are easily available. What are some material rewards tailor-made for you?

Think of at least five, and write them down here:

1. *Objects:* Magazines, record albums, books, cosmetics, clothing, games, gadgets, furniture.

2. *Stepping out:* Movie, restaurant, dance, play, museum, park, exhibit, fair, shopping, a tour.

3. *Miscellaneous:* Long-distance calls, money for special cause, gift for friend, money for special savings account.

4. *Social time:* Time with people to talk, play games, go somewhere, walk.

5. *Sit back and appreciate time:* Time for concentrating on something that is interesting to me: listening, reading a book, watching TV or people, reading letters.

6. *Do-my-own-thing time:* Time for those things that I never have time to do, like painting, drawing, sculpting, potting, writing, building something.

Now think of some possible mental rewards for yourself. Write at least five positive things that you could say when you have done something well:

1. "I really did well today."

2. "I handled the situation well."

3. "It took some doing to refuse that cake, but I did it!"

4. "That was pretty hard, but I managed not to binge!"

Figure 7. Homework for personal rewards

usually aversive and is considered to be a punishment and thereby to reduce the targeted behavior. They are asked to conjure up this image whenever they have a craving to binge-eat.

Other Techniques

Another component in treatment involves teaching adaptive skills.[53-56] Some individuals binge-eat because they lack the skills to cope with problematic areas in their life. A problem-solving approach (table 13) is taken in dealing with the individual's eating-related problems as well as problems in general.[15,59] The patient identifies feelings of distress and behaviors associated with these distressing emotions and is then instructed to define the situation that leads to these feelings and why the situation is upsetting. Once the problematic situation is identified, the individual is then asked

Table 13. Steps in Problem Solving

Identify feelings and behavior.
Define the problem:
  What has happened?
  What is upsetting about the situation?
Identify thoughts about the situation.
Determine whether thoughts are rational. Challenge thoughts:
  Are my thoughts realistic?
  Where is the evidence?
Substitute more adaptive or rational thoughts. Establish goals:
  What do I want?
  What would I prefer to happen?
Generate possible solutions.
Evaluate each alternative; choose the "best" alternative:
  How useful will this outcome be in solving my problem?
  How difficult will it be to do it?
  Do the benefits of this solution outweigh the possible costs?
Implement.
Verify after trying out a solution:
  What were the consequences of my action?
  Am I satisfied with the results?

to recognize thoughts that are associated with it. These thoughts are then challenged to determine whether or not they are rational. If the thoughts are irrational, the individual is taught to substitute more adaptive thoughts and establish goals to achieve a more desirable outcome to the problematic situation. Once the goals are determined, the individual generates as many solutions as possible, then chooses the best. The patient implements this solution and verifies whether the solution accomplished the original goal. If not, the individual attempts another solution.

Special attention is given to learning how to identify, evaluate, and challenge maladaptive thoughts that may predispose an individual to binge-eat. These thoughts may be food-related or not. Table 14 illustrates the types of food-related thoughts that may occur. As with anorectics, women with bulimia are taught to recognize not only thoughts but certain irrational beliefs or assumptions that may underlie them—for example, a need to be perfect or to obtain the approval of everybody.[60] Furthermore, they are also taught to recognize such styles of thinking as all-or-nothing, overgeneralizing, and jumping to conclusions with minimal evidence.[32,61] The patients are also taught the skills of relaxation, assertiveness, and communication.[56] Individuals with bulimia, like anorectics, have been found to be socially isolated. This isolation increases the probability of binge-eating. Furthermore, boredom has been noted as one of the precipitating factors in binge-eating.[45,56] Patients are thus encouraged to increase their level of socialization as well as of pleasurable activity.

Table 14. Food-Related Thoughts as Cues for Binge-Eating

Nostalgia: "I remember how great that piece of cake tasted. Life seemed more fun when I could eat what I wanted."

Testing yourself: "I haven't binged for three days—now I can control it and go by the bakery section to see what's there."

Crisis: "I've had a hard day. I deserve to binge under these circumstances."

Unwanted changes: "I've gained three pounds. I have no alternative but to binge and vomit."

Self-doubt: "I've tried to stop a million times and always failed—I'll fail again. I can't help myself."

Body and weight preoccupation: "I need to be on a strict diet to lose weight and look thin, but I can't control my eating. I might as well binge."

Deprivation: "Why can't I eat like a normal person?"

Treatment Outcome

Research literature concerning the behavioral treatment of binge-eating among bulimic and obese individuals is sparse. Most of the studies have incorporated techniques similar to those described above. The treatment outcome data are generally encouraging (table 15). Collective results show that by the end of treatment 13 of 15 patients experienced fewer than two binge-eating and vomiting episodes per month (at the onset of behavioral treatment the mean frequency was 19.1 ± 34.1 per week); 10 of 11 of these patients (follow-up data were missing for 2) maintained reduction at follow-up.

More recently, Johnson, Conners, and Stuckey[56] reported preliminary findings on 10 women with bulimia who underwent short-term group treatment based on a cognitive-behavioral model. All patients decreased the number of binge-purge episodes per week (10.33 pregroup vs. 2.4 postgroup) and increased the number of binge-free days per week (1.9 pregroup vs. 5.4 postgroup). The follow-up data showed that 4 patients continued to improve, 2 remained the same, and 4 declined since treatment. However, 9 of the patients continued to be improved in relation to their condition before treatment began.

Treatment of Vomiting

Some therapists focus primarily on the vomiting rather than binge-eating as the target of intervention. Most of this research has been conducted with individuals who vomit but who do not necessarily binge-eat. The behavioral methods that are used to decrease vomiting include: graduated response delay in the forced-vomiting response chain;[54,62] cognitive restructuring that involves disputing irrational beliefs related to vomiting

Table 15. Outcome of Behavioral Treatments for Bulimia and Vomiting

Study and Patient No.	Duration of Treatment (Months)	Frequency of Episodes		Follow-Up			No. Months to Follow-up
		At Onset of Treatment (per Week)	At End of Treatment (per Month)	Reduction Maintained			
				Yes	No	?	
Fairburn[55]							
1	6	28	0	✓			12
2	3	7	0	✓			12
3	12	>140	>150		✓		12
4	7	21	2	✓			12
5	5	10	0	✓			7
6	5	7	0	✓			12
7	5	7	0	✓			8
8	8	12	0	✓			12
9	8	14	0			✓	—
10	6	7	0	✓			4
11	6	5	0			✓	—
Long and Cordle[54]							
12	10	8	0	✓			9
13	3	11	1	✓			12
Mizes and Lohr[53]							
14	4	2	1		✓		1
Smith[57]							
15[a]	5	≥7	>8-12	✓			8

[a]Obese subject.

(particularly thoughts regarding body weight and size, and food intake) and replacing them with more adaptive beliefs;[52,62] preventing the vomiting response from occurring after the exposure to an ingestion of binge-type foods;[44] and aversive shock paired with mental images of the steps leading to vomiting.[63] All these case studies involved one patient, with individual sessions lasting between 1 month and 7 months on a daily,[63] every other day,[44] or weekly basis.[52,62] All these approaches demonstrated a reduction in vomiting (table 16). In three of four studies, vomiting was reduced to less than once per month; the other study demonstrated a clinically significant reduction. Furthermore, the patient in the study conducted by Rosen and Leitenberg,[44] also had binging episodes that reduced in frequency from seven episodes a week to two-three times a week. The follow-up data indicated that all the subjects maintained the reduction of vomiting.

In summary, behavioral techniques involved in the treatment of bulimia include an in-depth analysis of the binge-eating and vomiting behaviors, manipulation of antecedents and consequences to decrease the incidence of the episodes, and teaching of adaptive skills to help individu-

Table 16. Outcome of Behavioral Treatments for Vomiting

Study and Patient No.	Duration of Treatment (Months)	Frequency of Episodes		Follow-Up			
		At Onset of Treatment (per Week)	At End of Treatment (per Week)	Reduction Maintained			No. Months after
				Yes	No	?	Termination
Welch[62]							
1	5	28	0	✓			11
Grinc[52]							
2	7	12	0	✓			5
Rosen and Leitenberg[44]							
3	?	21	9.45	✓			10 (?)
Kenney and Solyom[63]							
4	1[a]	21	0	✓			3

[a]Twenty-two sessions.

als cope with problems that are often antecedents to the binge-eating episodes or that increase the reinforcing nature of the consequences. The skills are also important for helping to attain adaptive reinforcers. Thus far, the data indicate that binge-eating and vomiting behavior are significantly reduced in most individuals who receive behavioral treatment. But we do not know how a behavioral treatment approach compares with other approaches in treating bulimics, nor whether group treatment is more favorable than individual treatment. Furthermore, only a few research studies have sought to identify the techniques that are most effective. One study indicated that stimulus control did not reduce vomiting significantly unless it was paired with cognitive restructuring.[52] Another study found that stimulus control did not reduce binge-eating unless it was paired with relaxation.[53]

Future studies should include a larger sample size and a control or comparison treatment group. Several areas of study would be helpful: the best frequency and length of treatment, particular techniques that are most effective, and the relative success of treatment using an individual or group approach.

REFERENCES

1. Kazdin, A. E. 1980. *Behavioral modification in applied settings.* Homewood, Ill.: Dorsey Press.
2. Watson, J. B., and R. Rayner. 1920. Conditioned emotional reactions. *J. Exp. Psychol.* 3:1-14.
3. Crisp, A. H. 1970. Premorbid factors in adult disorders or weight with particular reference to primary anorexia nervosa (weight phobia). A literature review. *J. Psychsom.* 14:1-22.

4. Brady, J. P., and W. Rieger. 1972. Behavioral treatment of anorexia nervosa. In *Proceedings of the International Symposium on Behavior Modification.* New York: Appleton-Century-Crofts.

5. Salkind, M. R., J. Fincham, and T. Silverstone. 1980. Is anorexia nervosa a phobic disorder? A psychophysiological inquiry. *Biol. Psychiatry* 15:803-8.

6. Mavissakalian, M. 1982. Anorexia nervosa treated with response prevention and prolonged exposure. *Behav. Res. Ther.* 20:27-31.

7. Wolpe, J. 1958. *Psychotherapy by reciprocal inhibition.* Palo Alto, Calif.: Stanford University Press.

8. Hallsten, E. A. 1965. Adolescent anorexia nervosa treated by desensitization. *Behav. Res. Ther.* 3:87-91.

9. Garner, D. M., and K. M. Bemis. 1982. A cognitive-behavioral approach to anorexia nervosa. *Cognitive Ther. Res.* 6:123-50.

10. Garner, D. M., P. E. Garfinkel, and K. M. Bemis. 1982. A multidimensional psychotherapy for anorexia nervosa. *Int. J. Eating Disorders* 1:3-46.

11. Allyon, T., E. Haughton, and H. O. Osmond. 1964. Chronic anorexia: A behavioral problem. *Can. Psychiatry Assoc. J.* 9:147-54.

12. Liebman, R., S. Minuchin, and L. Baker. 1974. An integrated treatment program for anorexia nervosa. *Am. J. Psychiatry* 131:432-36.

13. Rosman, B., S. Minuchin, and R. Liebman. 1975. Family lunch session: An introduction to family therapy in anorexia nervosa. *Am. J. Orthopsychiatry* 45:846-53.

14. Epstein, L. H., and R. R. Wing. 1979. Behavioral contracting: Health behaviors. *Clin. Behav. Ther. Rev.* 1:1-22.

15. Goldfried, M. R., and G. C. Davison. 1976. *Clinical behavior therapy.* New York: Holt, Rinehart and Winston.

16. Bachrach, A. J., W. J. Erwin, and J. P. Mohr. 1965. The control of eating behavior in an anorexic by operant conditioning techniques. In *Case studies in behavior modification,* ed. L. P. Ullman and L. Krasner. New York: Holt, Rinehart and Winston.

17. Lobb, L. G., and H. H. Schaeffer. 1972. Successful treatment of anorexia nervosa through isolation. *Psychol. Rep.* 30:245-46.

18. Bhanji, S., and J. Thompson. 1974. Operant conditioning in the treatment of anorexia nervosa: A review and retrospective study of 11 cases. *Br. J. Psychiatry* 124:166-72.

19. Azerrad, J., and R. L. Stafford. 1969. Restoration of eating behavior in anorexia nervosa through operant conditioning and environmental manipulation. *Behav. Res. Ther.* 7:165-71.

20. Bianco, F. J. 1972. Rapid treatment of two cases of anorexia nervosa. *J. Behav. Ther. Exp. Psychiatry* 124:166-72.

21. Blinder, B. J., D. M. A. Freeman, and A. J. Stunkard. 1970. Behavior therapy of anorexia nervosa: Effectiveness of activity as a reinforcer of weight gain. *Am. J. Psychiatry* 126:1093-98.

22. Eckert, E. 1981. Behavioral modification in anorexia nervosa—a comparison of two reinforcement schedules. In *Proceedings of the International Eating Disorder Meeting.* Toronto: Clarke Institute of Psychiatry.

23. Parker, J. B., D. Blazer, and L. Wyrick. 1977. Anorexia nervosa: A combined therapeutic approach. *South. Med. J.* 70:448-56.

24. Garfinkel, P. E., S. A. Kline, and H. C. Stanler. 1973. Treatment of anorexia nervosa using operant conditioning techniques. *J. Nerv. Ment. Dis.* 157:428-33.

25. Agras, W. S., D. H. Barlow, H. N. Chapin, G. G. Abel, and H. Leitenberg. 1974. Behavior modification of anorexia nervosa. *Arch. Gen Psychiatry* 30:279-86.

26. Leitenberg, H ., W. S. Agras, and L. E. Thompson. 1968. A sequential analysis of the

effect of selective positive reinforcement in modifying anorexia nervosa. *Behav. Res. Ther.* 6:211-18.

27. Eckert, E. D., S. C. Goldberg, K. A. Halmi, R. C. Casper, and J. M. Davis. 1979. Behavior therapy in anorexia nervosa. *Br. J. Psychiatry* 134:55-59.
28. Halmi, K. A., P. Powers, and S. Cunningham. 1975. Treatment of anorexia nervosa with behavior modification. *Arch. Gen. Psychiatry* 32:93-96.
29. Agras, W. S., and J. Werne. 1978. Behavior therapy in anorexia nervosa: A data-based approach to the question. In *Controversy in psychiatry,* ed. J. P. Brady, H . Brodie, and H. Keith. Philadelphia: Saunders.
30. Garfinkel, P. E., H. Moldofsky, and D. M. Garner. 1977. The outcome of anorexia nervosa: Significance of clinical features, body image, and behavior modification. In *Proceedings of First International Conference on Anorexia Nervosa.* New York: Raven Press.
31. Bruch, H. 1974. Perils of behavior modification in treatment of anorexia nervosa. *JAMA* 230:1419-22.
32. Beck, A. T., J. A. Rush, B. F. Shaw, and G. Emery. 1979. *Cognitive therapy of depression.* New York: Guilfords Press.
33. Schwartz, D. M., and M. G. Thompson. 1981. Do anorectics get well? Current research and future needs. *Am. J. Psychiatry* 138:319-23.
34. Bemis, K. M. 1978. Current approaches to the etiology and treatment of anorexia nervosa. *Psychol. Bull.* 85:593-617.
35. Sobell, M. R., and L. C. Sobell. 1978. *Behavioral treatment of alcohol problems.* New York: Plenum Press.
36. Miller, P. M. 1976. *Behavioral treatment of alcoholism.* New York: Pergamon Press.
37. Jeffrey, D. B., and R. C. Katz. 1977. *Take it off and keep it off.* Englewood Cliffs , N.J.: Prentice Hall.
38. Ferguson, O. M. 1976. *Habits not diets.* Palo Alto, Calif.: Bull Publishing Company.
39. Stuart, R. B., and B. Davis. 1972. *Slim chance in a fat world.* Champaign, Ill.: Research Press.
40. Pomerleau, O. F., and C. S. Pomerleau. 1977. *Break the smoking habit: A behavioral program for giving up cigarettes.* Champaign, Ill.: Research Press.
41. Loro, A. D., and C. S. Orleans. 1981. Binge eating in obesity: Preliminary findings and guidelines for behavioral analysis and treatment. *Addict. Behav.* 6:155-66.
42. Russell, G. 1979. Bulimia nervosa: An ominous variant of anorexia nervosa. *Psychol. Med.* 9:429-48.
43. Casper, R. C. 1982. Some provisional ideas concerning psychologic structure in anorexia nervosa and bulimia. In *Anorexia nervosa,* ed. P. L. Darby, P. E. Garfinkel, D. M. Garner, and D. V. Coscina. New York: Alan Liss.
44. Rosen, J. C., and H. Leitenberg. 1982. Bulimia nervosa: Treatment with exposure and response prevention. *Behav. Ther.* 13:117-24.
45. Johnson, C., and R. Larson. 1982. Bulimia: An analysis of moods and behavior. *Psychosom. Med.* 44:341-51.
46. Leon, G. R., K. Carroll, B. Chernyk, and S. Finn. In press. Binge-eating and associated habit patterns within college student and identified bulimic populations.
47. Johnson, C. L., M. K. Stuckey, L. D. Lewis, and D. M. Schwartz. 1982. Bulimia: A descriptive survey of 316 cases. *Int. J. Eating Disorders* 2:3-16.
48. Pyle, R. L., J. E. Mitchell, and E. D. Eckert. 1981. Bulimia: A report of 34 cases. *J. Clin. Psychiatry* 42:60-64.
49. Mitchell, J. E., and R. L. Pyle. 1982. The bulimic syndrome in normal weight individuals: A review. *Int. J . Eating Disorders* 2:61-73.

50. Mitchell, J. E., R. L. Pyle, E. D. Eckert, D. Hatsukami, and R. Lentz. In press. Electrolyte and other physiological abnormalities in patients with bulimia.
51. Jackson, J. N., and C. H. Ormiston. 1977. Diet and weight control clinic: A status report. Stanford Heart Disease Prevention Program, Stanford University.
52. Grinc, G. A. 1982. A cognitive-behavioral model for the treatment of chronic vomiting. *J. Behav. Med.* 5:135-41.
53. Mizes, J. S., and S. M. Lohr. 1983. The treatment of bulimia (binge-eating and self-induced vomiting). *Int. J. Eating Disorders* 2:59-65.
54. Long, C. G., and C. J. Cordle. 1982. Psychological treatment of binge-eating and self-induced vomiting. *J. Med. Psychol.* 55:139-45.
55. Fairburn, C. 1981. A cognitive behavioral approach to the treatment of bulimia. *Psychol. Med.* 11:707-11.
56. Johnson, C., M. Conners, and M. Stuckey. 1983. Short-term group treatment of bulimia. *Int. J. Eating Disorders* 2:199-208.
57. Smith, G. R. 1981. Modification of binge-eating in obesity. *J. Behav. Ther. Exp. Psychiatry* 12:333-36.
58. Cautela, J . R. 1967. Covert sensitization. *Psychol. Rep.* 20:459-68.
59. Rimm, D. C., and J. C. Masters. 1979. *Behavioral therapy.* New York: Academic Press.
60. Ellis, A. 1962. *Reason and emotion in psychotherapy.* New York: Lyle Stuart.
61. Beck, A. T. 1976. *Cognitive therapy and the emotional disorders.* New York: International Universities Press.
62. Welch, G. J. 1979. The treatment of compulsive vomiting and obsessive thoughts through graduated response delay, response prevention, and cognitive correction. *J. Behav. Ther. Exp. Psychiatry* 10:77-82.
63. Kennedy, F. T., and L. Solyom. 1971. The treatment of compulsive vomiting through faradic disruption of mental images. *Can. Med. Assoc. J.* 105:1071-1073.

6

Psychopharmacology of Anorexia Nervosa and Bulimia

Craig Johnson Ph.D., Marilyn Stuckey, Ph.D.,

and James E. Mitchell, M.D.

Although psychosocial intervention has dominated the treatment literature about anorexia nervosa and bulimia, a growing literature attests to the benefits of pharmacotherapy in some of these patients. A few studies of the pharmacotherapy of anorexia nervosa appeared more than 20 years ago, but larger control trials are only now finding their way into the medical literature. This chapter critically reviews the published literature on drug treatment of anorexia nervosa and bulimia and offers practical suggestions to the clinician concerning the pharmacotherapy of these disorders.

Much of the published pharmacotherapy treatment literature has focused on therapy with antidepressant agents, reflecting the awareness that these disorders are related to depression. Other treatment approaches have developed from our understanding of the neuroanatomy and neurophysiology of appetite and satiety mechanisms in the brains of animals. In preparation for the discussion of the specific reports and studies involving patients, we will first review some information related to these control mechanisms.

Regulatory Systems

The hypothalamus is an area of the brain that controls a variety of basic processes, including temperature regulation, sexual activity, and eating behavior. The medial hypothalamus is sometimes referred to as the satiety center because stimulation in this area can cause animals to stop eating, even in situations where they should be hungry. Destroying this area by lesioning can cause an animal to overeat to the point of obesity. In contrast, the lateral hypothalamus is sometimes referred to as the eating center. Stimulation of this area frequently leads to eating behavior, even in animals who should be demonstrating a satiety response based on previous food intake. Extensive lesioning in this area can result in starvation. Less extensive lesions will result in decreased food intake and weight loss. The medial and lateral symptoms are believed to be linked to reciprocal inhibition and to exert antagonistic functions.[1]

The neurochemistry of these brain areas has also been studied, with particular interest in the neurotransmitters involved in the regulatory system. Several neurotransmitter systems are involved. The nigrostriatal dopamine pathway that courses from the substantia nigra to the striatum influences the lateral hypothalamus. Lesions off this pathway can lead to hypophagia and eventual weight loss in animals. An intact dopamine system appears to be necessary for adequate feeding in animals. Local injection of dopamine agonists, however, suppresses eating behavior. By analogy, a serotonin pathway appears to innervate the medial hypothalamus and to facilitate satiety. The depletion of serotonin by agents like para-chlorophenylalanine (PCPA) will increase eating behavior in animals.[1] Norepinephrine also appears to be involved in the satiety-feeding regulation. The lateral region contains beta adrenergic receptors that seem to be involved in the induction of satiety through inhibition of the feeding center. Epinephrine or norepinephrine may be the neurotransmitter for these synapses.[2] The medial region, particularly the paraventricular area, contains alpha adrenergic synapses that appear to mediate an inhibitory effect on the satiety center. The neurotransmitter for these synapses appears to be norepinephrine.[2] To summarize this model, an intact dopamine nigrostriatal system is necessary for lateral hypothalamic feeding, serotonin facilitates medial hypothalamic satiety, and adrenergic impulses exert inhibitory effects that vary depending on whether they are mediated by beta or alpha receptors.

Barry and Klawans[3] in a review article discussing the possible role of dopamine in anorexia nervosa speculated that increased dopaminergic activity might be involved in this illness. They argued that dopamine blocking agents might be useful in the treatment of anorexia nervosa, and indeed these agents have been used with some success. One consideration regarding the role of dopamine in eating behavior is the fact that lateral hypothalamic lesioning frequently leads to a variety of other changes in animal behavior not directly related to eating, particularly problems involving motor functioning. Also, the use of dopamine blocking agents such as antipsychotic drugs leads to neurochemical changes in brain areas not directly related to the lateral hypothalamus, producing effects that are far more complex than the simple model presented here.

Is there evidence to support an abnormality of these neurotransmitter systems in patients with anorexia nervosa or bulimia? Studies of biogenic amines in patients with anorexia nervosa have mainly concerned measurement of metabolites.[4] The available literature suggests that 3-methoxy 4-hydroxy phenylglycol (MHPG) (which represents a major central nervous system [CNS] metabolite of norepinephrine) and homovanillic acid (a metabolite of dopamine in the brain) may be decreased in patients with anorexia nervosa when these patients are low in weight. Such values tend to improve with weight gain.[5-7] Halmi et al.[8] have suggested that the low MHPG levels seen in these patients may be related to depressive symptomatology. This group noted that the increase in MHPG levels seen with treatment correlated with improvement of depressive symptoms. Clearly, further work needs to be done regarding neurotransmitters, affective disorders, and eating disorders.

Other systems also appear to be involved in the regulation of eating behavior. For example, much evidence exists that manipulation of the endogenous opiate system can profoundly affect eating behavior. Elevated levels of beta endorphin have been found in pituitary extracts of certain genetically obese mice, and the narcotic antagonist naloxone has been shown to abolish overeating in this species.[9] Considerable research suggests that naloxone may also suppress eating behavior in humans.[10,11] Other neuroregulatory systems are also involved. The complexity of an already confusing picture increases dramatically when one considers peptide neurotransmitter systems. To cite one example, the peptide neurotransmitter cholecystokinin appears to be one of a large family of brain-gut peptides that are involved both in digestive function and in the regulation of eating behavior in infrahuman species and humans.[12,13]

In summary, the component systems involved in the neurophysiological control of eating behavior are complex and not well understood. Several important systems have been identified, but much work needs to be done before a composite picture of these regulatory systems can be drawn.

Pharmacological Treatment of Anorexia Nervosa

Neuroleptics

Shortly after their introduction for the treatment of schizophrenia, neuroleptic medications were tried as treatment for patients with anorexia nervosa. An initial case presentation suggested the possible efficacy of such treatment.[14] Dally and Sargant[15] subsequently reported a controlled trial of the antipsychotic drug chlorpromazine in patients with anorexia nervosa. Twenty patients were treated with active drug in dosages ranging from 150 to 1,000 mg per day. Subjects were also given 40-80 units of insulin in an attempt to stimulate their appetite. They were treated for 23 to 47 days in an open trial, during which they were placed at bed rest. A historical control group of 24 patients that had been treated at the same facility over prior years was used. The drug group gained an average of 2 kg per week compared with an average weight gain of approximately .5 kg a week for the controls. Duration of hospitalization was significantly shorter in the medicated patients, but the duration was at least partly determined by the rapidity of weight gain. Group differences were not apparent at follow-up anywhere from 3 months to 3 years after discharge.

Another large series of patients treated with chlorpromazine was reported by Crisp in 1965,[16] again following an initial successful case report.[17] Crisp treated a series of 21 hospitalized anorexia nervosa patients with chlorpromazine in dosages ranging from 400 to 600 mg a day. Minimum treatment duration was 8 weeks. At follow-up one and a half years after discharge, 15 of 21 patients were of normal weight, although only 11 demonstrated normal eating behavior as defined by the authors. The long-term improvement in this group was approximately equal to the outcome reported by Dally and Sargant.[15]

In examining these two studies, one must remember that the use of a fairly sedative antipsychotic drug, combined with mandatory bed rest, may have facilitated weight gain through decreased caloric expenditure mediated by sedation, as has been discussed by Kuhn.[18]

Plantley[19] reported a case of a patient with anorexia nervosa who was treated with 4 mg of pimozide three times a day. The patient gained 9 kg in 3 weeks. Hoes[20] described the treatment of 8 hospitalized anorectics using a combination of pimozide (1 mg three times a day) and copper sulfate (5 mg three times a day). These were used on the assumption of dopaminergic hyperactivity associated with impaired conversion of dopamine to norepinephrine, the responsible enzyme being dopamine-beta-hydroxylase, which used copper as a cofactor. The results were reported as positive. Vandereycken and Pierloot[21] reported a placebo-controlled, crossover trial of pimozide versus placebo in 18 female inpatients with anorexia nervosa. Following a baseline period, subjects were treated with active drug or placebo for 3 weeks, then crossed over. All patients were also treated with a contingency management program. Although the results suggested that pimozide enhanced weight gain, the advantage did not reach statistical significance. Pimozide had only a marginal influence on attitudes as measured by a nurse-rated instrument that the authors had developed for this study.

Antidepressants

Although there is considerable clinical interest in the use of antidepressants in patients with anorexia nervosa, only two controlled trials have been reported in the literature. Most of what has been published in this area has consisted of case reports and series of cases. The exception to this pattern is the report by Mills,[22] which is difficult to classify and will be discussed first.

Mills treated a group of 80 women exhibiting amenorrhea associated with self-starvation with antidepressant drugs, either amitriptyline or its desmethylated metabolite nortriptyline. Two control groups were used, one with the primary diagnosis of depression and another of Stein-Leventhal patients. Mills reported that 81% of the self-starvers exhibited depression, although the criteria were not stipulated. Patients were treated with amitriptyline or nortriptyline in doses of 50-200 mg a day. Mills suggested that antidepressants might be more useful for these patients than chlorpromazine and insulin, but no actual randomized trial was included in this study.

White and Schnaultz[23] reported the use of imipramine hydrochloride in 2 patients with anorexia nervosa who were also depressed. The 2 patients received a maximum of 150-175 mg a day. The authors noted that both patients improved in mood and weight. Moore[24] reported on the treatment of a patient with anorexia nervosa using amitriptyline at 150 mg a day. Reilly[25] reported on 2 patients treated with antidepressant drugs. One actually received imipramine (100 mg) plus lithium carbonate; the other was treated with amitriptyline (100 mg) plus imipramine (100 mg). The author indicated that both patients seemed to improve. Katz and Walsh[26] reported the case of a patient with anorexia nervosa treated with a combination of chlorimipramine and tryptophan, the amino acid precursor of serotonin. The patient gained a great deal of weight and eventually evidenced hypomanic symptomatology when obese. Kendler[27] presented the case of a depressed anorexia nervosa patient who also experienced improvement in weight and mood on amitriptyline at 100 mg a day. However, the patient continued to gain weight following drug withdrawal and subsequently developed obesity. Needleman and Waber[28] reported the details of the use of amitriptyline in a series of 6 adolescent patients, 5 females and 1 male, who were hospitalized on a pediatric ward and treated with 75-150 mg of amitriptyline a day. The authors reported an improvement in mood in these patients as well as a lessening of food preoccupation. No instruments were used to follow either depression or eating-related behaviors.

A controlled trial was published by Lacey and Crisp in 1980.[29] This study consisted of 16 patients with anorexia nervosa who were hospitalized at bed rest and received concomitant psychotherapy. Patients were randomized to receive either 50 mg of clomipramine at bedtime or a placebo. There were no significant differences between the groups as to duration of illness, age of onset, or body weight at the initiation of the study. The two groups did not differ in terms of weight gain or time needed to reach goal weight. Those taking the active drug demonstrated more stable eating patterns; active drug patients also reported an increased appetite relative to the control group. The two groups did not differ, however, in the time required to reach target weight.

These reports and studies indicate that antidepressants may be beneficial both in terms of eating behavior and mood in some patients with anorexia nervosa, but it is not clear that they help all such patients. Further studies are indicated to determine what characteristics will identify the patients who may respond to antidepressant therapy.

Cyproheptadine

Cyproheptadine is a compound with potent antihistaminic and serotonin-blocking properties. This drug has been reported to promote weight gain in several populations, including underweight adults,[30-33] asthmatic children,[34] and underweight adults with irritable bowel syndrome.[35] Because of this presumed appetite-stimulating effect, the drug has been used experimentally in patients with anorexia nervosa. Following an initial report suggesting the efficacy of this treatment by Benady,[36] Vigersky and Loriaux[37] reported a double-blind, placebo-controlled trial with cyproheptadine in 24 patients with anorexia nervosa. Treatment duration was 8 weeks. There were no significant differences between the two groups in terms of weight gain. Actually, several patients in both groups lost weight during the study. In examining the data, the authors concluded that the active drug group had been composed of patients more resistant to treatment because they were somewhat older, had a longer duration of illness, and were more likely to report self-induced vomiting to maintain weight. The authors suggested that the chronic symptomatology of this group may have made them relatively refractory to drug treatment.

Goldberg, Halmi, Eckert, and their associates[38-40] reported investigations using cyproheptadine in patients with anorexia nervosa. The initial study by this group involved 81 female inpatients treated with cyproheptadine in doses ranging from 12 to 35 mg per day for 35 days. There were four treatment conditions: cyproheptadine plus behavior modification, cyproheptadine alone, placebo plus behavior modification, and placebo alone. There were no significant differences in terms of weight gain between the cyproheptadine and placebo groups. A secondary analysis revealed that there may have been a subgroup of patients responsive to cyproheptadine therapy. These patients were characterized by having a history of birth complications, the greatest percentage of weight loss prior to hospitalization, and failure of outpatient therapy. The authors suggested that this group of more severe cases might be more responsive to the drug.

A subsequent report by this group indicated that the treatment sample had increased to 105 subjects.[40] Data analysis revealed that certain symptoms and attitudes in patients with anorexia nervosa might predict responsiveness to the drug; these included such variables as the attitude "thin ideal or fear of becoming fat" and the variable "being bothered by eating." Halmi, Eckert, and Falk[39] recently reported on a study in progress comparing cyproheptadine at 32 mg a day, amitriptyline at 160 mg per day, and a placebo. Subjects were randomized, and the study design used double-blind conditions. Subjects were treated for up to 3 months and were followed with weight measurement and Hamilton depression ratings. At the time of the report, 57 patients had completed the study. Data analysis revealed a significant drug effect on depression scores and weight gain; the differences were mainly due to the contrast between cyproheptadine and placebo. The authors stressed the relative safety of cyproheptadine in patients with anorexia nervosa, who may be at risk for complications using other drugs such as antidepressants. This work suggested that cyproheptadine may prove a promising treatment in some patients with anorexia nervosa. This project was still in progress, however, and further reports may clarify the usefulness of this medication.

Lithium

Two reports in the literature suggest possible utility for lithium in patients with anorexia nervosa. The first description of this treatment was by Barcai in 1977,[41] who reported on 2 patients treated with lithium carbonate. The author noted the similarities between certain manic-type symptoms and the clinical situation in some patients with anorexia, including unstable mood and hyperactivity. Both patients were given lithium carbonate at 1,500 mg per day and were documented to have lithium levels between .9 and 1.0 meq/1. The author found that both patients improved considerably in weight and mood. Structured instruments were not used. Two additional case reports appeared using lithium therapy in anorexia nervosa. Reilly[25] reported the case of a patient treated with a combination of imipramine hydrochloride at 100 mg per day and lithium at 1,200 mg per day. This patient was also being seen in psychotherapy. Stein et al.[42] reported the case of a patient with mood swings who also had anorexia nervosa. These authors thought that the lithium actually stabilized the patient's affective state without significantly influencing the eating disorder directly.

A double-blind, placebo-controlled trial of lithium carbonate has recently appeared in the medical literature. Gross et al.[43] reported on the use of lithium carbonate versus placebo in 16 hospitalized anorexia nervosa patients. Lithium levels were maintained between .9 and 1.4 meq/1 for 28 days. The study was double blind and randomized. The results indicated a significant benefit for the lithium treatment group, which gained significantly more weight at weeks 3 and 4. The active medication was generally tolerated well, but the authors suggested caution about the use of lithium in patients with anorexia nervosa who may have inadequate fluid intake or electrolyte abnormalities and who may be self-inducing vomiting.

Other Pharmacological Interventions

In 1976, Redmond, Swann, and Heninger[44] reported the case of a patient with anorexia nervosa who was treated with the alpha adrenergic blocking agent phenoxybenzamine. The patient gained weight while on this medication at a dosage of 30 mg per day. When the drug was discontinued because of medical complications, weight loss resumed. When the medicine was reintroduced (20 mg a day), the patient again started to gain weight. The use of the beta adrenergic blocking agent propranolol failed to induce positive weight effect. To our knowledge, no additional studies have been attempted using these medications.

Patients with anorexia nervosa have been demonstrated to have abnormal gastric function including delayed gastric emptying, decreased hydrogen ion output, and decreased gastric fluid output. Saleh and Lebwohl[45] reported on the use of metoclopramide, a dopamine blocker, to enhance gastric functioning in patients with anorexia nervosa. This drug is marketed to improve the symptoms of gastric stasis in patients with diabetes mellitus, the mechanism being increased gastric motility. The drug also can suppress vomiting behavior on a central, antidopaminergic basis. The authors reported that this medication enhanced gastric emptying as measured using a gamma camera technique with technetium-99 labeled meals. The patient also reported an improved tolerance for eating. Dubois et al.[46] attempted to manipulate gastric functioning in anorexia nervosa patients with bethanechol at 0.06 mg/kg given subcutaneously. They were able to demonstrate increased fractional gastric emptying and increased gastric acid output using this medication as a research tool. Because of its route of administration and half-life, this drug would not be practical clinically.

There has been some interest in the relationship between certain trace elements and the eating problems seen in patients with anorexia nervosa. Zinc in particular has been the focus of some attention. Bakan[47] and Horrobin and Cunnane[48] have suggested a possible relationship between hypozincemia and anorexia nervosa. Patients with anorexia have been demonstrated to have impaired taste perception, a problem that has clinically been associated with zinc deficiency. However, hypozincemia and impaired test perception in anorexia nervosa were not associated in research by Casper et al.[49] Zinc therapy has been posed as a possible agent of therapeutic benefit in patients with anorexia nervosa, but to our knowledge it has not been tested.

Moore, Mills, and Forster[50] recently reported on the use of infusions of naloxone hydrochloride in patients with anorexia nervosa. This narcotic antagonist was given by constant intravenous infusion in doses ranging between 3.2 and 6.4 mg per day and was administered for an average of 5 weeks. Weight gain was calculated for periods before, during, and after the use of this medication. Analysis revealed that patients gained more weight during the time of infusion. This was an open trial and controls were not used.

Lastly, Johanson and Knorr[51] reported on the use of levodopa in patients with anorexia nervosa. Six patients were reported originally, and an additional 3 were added in a later publication.[52] The maximum dosage ranged from 1 to 3 grams per day with a duration of therapy of 16 to 27 days. Seven of 9 patients gained some weight, 1 evidenced no change, and 1 lost weight. The medication was tolerated well, and several patients stated that they felt better on the medication.

Pharmacological Treatment of Bulimia

The pharmacological treatment of bulimia has centered on the use of two types of agents: anticonvulsants and antidepressants. The anticonvulsant literature will be reviewed first.

Anticonvulsants

There has been considerable speculation in recent years concerning possible neurophysiological substrates for abnormal eating behavior. Part of the impetus for this hypothesis has been the demonstrated association between abnormal eating behaviors and such neurological conditions as partial complex seizures[53] and other CNS lesions.[54] Certain studies also suggest an increased frequency of EEG abnormalities in patients with eating disorders. Crisp, Fenton, and Scotton[55] reported increased rate of EEG abnormalities in patients with anorexia nervosa compared with controls, but they believed that most of these abnormalities could be accounted for on the basis of metabolic disturbance.

Much of the research in this area has been the work of Rau, Green, and their colleagues.[56-59] This group of researchers originally reported the results of treatment with phenytoin in a series of 10 patients who had what the authors termed compulsive eating disorders. Nine of these patients had abnormal EEGs.[56] Nine of the 10 patients were reported to be treated successfully. In 1977, Green and Rau[57] reported on 31 patients with compulsive eating disorders who were treated with phenytoin. The EEG was abnormal in 14 patients; 6 of these responded well to drug treatment. Three patients with normal EEGs also showed a favorable response to the drug. Medications were administered open label, and the criteria for improvement were not stipulated. These authors also offered a classification of this group of patients into four subgroups: patients who constantly overeat and are overweight; patients who overeat in response to life stress; sneak eaters; and patients who consume enormous amounts of food seemingly against their own will. This last group of patients was believed by the authors to be the "true compulsive eaters." These authors found that 6 of 7 true compulsive eaters responded to phenytoin with decreased binge-eating. In 1978, Rau and Green[58] reported the results of a study involving interviewing "compulsive eating disorder" patients. Twenty-three patients in this series were also treated with phenytoin. The authors concluded that there was a significant correlation between the sum of ten neurological soft signs, the presence of EEG abnormalities, and response to drug.

In 1979, these same authors summarized their experience with the use of phenytoin in the treatment of compulsive eating.[59] A total of 47 patients were reported to have had adequate trials with phenytoin. Operational criteria based on the patient's self-report of progress were stipulated in this article. The analysis revealed a higher percentage of EEG abnormalities among compulsive eaters compared with controls. The authors concluded that patients with abnormal EEGs were more likely to respond to the drug. However, with the exception of 4 patients described in 1977 and 2 in 1979,[57,59] all the subjects reported in these series were treated with open, nonblind protocols. Blood levels of anticonvulsants were not correlated to response.

Subsequent work by Wermuth et al.[60] attempted to solve some of the methodological problems of the earlier work. This group of researchers originally reported EEG abnormalities in 4 of 5 patients with bulimia.[61] A subsequent randomized, placebo-controlled, double-blind trial[60] in 19 bulimic women (one of whom also had anorexia nervosa) was reported. A crossover design with treatment phases lasting 6 weeks was utilized.

Only 3 subjects had definitely abnormal EEGs, and an additional 4 had questionably abnormal EEGs. There was no significant relationship between drug response and EEG abnormality. Phenytoin treatment was found to be associated overall with fewer eating binges, and 8 patients were believed to show "marked" to "moderate" improvement whereas 8 showed "slight" to "no" improvement. In the phenytoin to placebo sequence, the number of binge-eating episodes decreased during drug treatment; however, this improvement continued when the subjects were placed on placebo. This finding confounded the results. There have been additional case reports of phenytoin treatment for bulimia finding success in only a minority of cases.[62-64] The weight histories of some of the patients reported in these studies must also be considered. About 22% of the patients reported by Rau and Green were more than 75% below ideal body weight and may have met research criteria for anorexia nervosa. One of the patients reported in the Wermuth et al. study[60] had active anorexia nervosa.

Available studies suggest that phenytoin may be helpful for some patients with bulimia or compulsive eating disorder, but it is unclear whether the EEG or some clinical parameters can be used to identify this patient group. Rigorous, controlled trials are indicated.

Kaplan et al.[65] recently reported a placebo-controlled, crossover trial of carbamazepine in 6 patients with bulimia. The entire trial lasted 20 weeks, and serum levels were maintained in a therapeutic range. One patient, who had a history suggestive of bipolar affective disorder, had a dramatic response with cessation of binge-eating. Five patients had either an equivocal or no response.

Antidepressants

Several recent reports and investigations indicate that antidepressant therapy may be helpful for patients with the bulimia syndrome. Pope and Hudson[66] first reported on the utility of tricyclic antidepressants in 8 bulimic patients. The patients had received a variety of different antidepressants in usual therapeutic doses, imipramine hydrochloride being the most commonly prescribed drug. Serum levels were monitored. Overall, 6 patients obtained moderate or marked reduction in frequency of eating binges. The reduction persisted for 2 to 7 months. Following this initial encouraging report, Pope et al.[67] completed a placebo-controlled, double-blind study of imipramine hydrochloride versus placebo in 19 chronically bulimic patients. Subjects on active drug demonstrated a 70% reduction in binging after 6 weeks of therapy compared with virtually no change in the placebo group. Of the 9 subjects on imipramine, 4 reported a marked (greater than 75%) and 4 a moderate (greater than 50%) decrease in binging frequency, whereas 1 subject was unchanged. Among the 10 placebo subjects, 1 reported a marked decrease in binging, 8 were unchanged, and 1 was worse. Imipramine was also associated with a significant decrease in the intensity of binges, decreased preoccupation with food, and a greater subjective global improvement, as well as significantly reduced depressive symptomatology. These authors stressed the theoretical point that the results of their study also argued for a relationship between bulimia and an affective disorder.

Sabine et al.[68] reported a randomized, placebo-controlled trial of mianserin in 50 patients with bulimia nervosa. The trial lasted 8 weeks. Subjects initially received mianserin at 30 mg daily or placebo; the dosage was increased to 60 mg after 1 week. The amount of change on the various instruments for rating depression and eating attitudes did not differ significantly between the two groups. Weight did not change during the study, and the number of days per week that the subjects reported binging, vomiting, or purging did not change throughout the 8 weeks of the trial for either group.

Mitchell and Groat[69] recently completed a placebo-controlled, double-blind trial of amitriptyline at 150 mg at bedtime in a series of 32 female outpatients with bulimia. The results indicated that the drug had a significant antidepressant effect. Patients in both the placebo and active drug groups also received what was characterized as a minimal behavioral program, and both groups demonstrated considerable improvement in eating behavior. The magnitude of this improvement was not anticipated. The use of the drug was not associated with weight gain or carbohydrate craving. Hughes et al.[70] recently reported another placebo-controlled, double-blind trial, using desipramine. These authors also found a considerable advantage for the active drug.

Taken together, of the four placebo-controlled, double-blind trials reported to date, three were positive and one showed no significant advantage over placebo.

Pope, Hudson, and Jonas[71] recently summarized their experience using a variety of antidepressant regimens. Data concerning 65 consecutive bulimic patients were presented. The authors concluded that antidepressant therapy appeared very useful for many patients with bulimia.

Additional reports indicate the utility of monoamine oxidase (MAO) inhibitors in patients with bulimia. Walsh et al.[72] described 6 patients with bulimia who were treated with MAO inhibitors, usually phenelzine in dosages of 60-90 mg a day. All 6 patients experienced a prompt improvement in mood and in eating behavior, although 1 patient's remission lasted only 1 month. These authors subsequently reported an open trial in an additional 10 cases[73] and have recently completed a placebo-controlled, double-blind trial.[74] Both strongly support the efficacy of MAO inhibitors in this population. The authors stressed that the use of MAO inhibitors required strict adherence to a diet avoiding thyramine and underscored the problems of dietary compliance in this patient group. It is presently unclear how these drugs work. In summarizing their experience, Brotman, Herzog, and Woods[75] concluded that antidepressant drugs may have separate and unrelated antibinge and antidepressant effects in bulimic patients. Our analysis, however, in examining correlations between changes in depression and eating dysfunction in our subject population indicated that depressed patients as a group show more improvement in depression and less improvement in eating dysfunction than do nondepressed patients but that there is a positive correlation when individual responses are considered between depression improvement and eating improvement.

Ong, Checkley, and Russell[76] recently reported that methylamphetamine infusion reduced self-ratings of hunger and amount of food eaten under laboratory conditions when administered to 8 patients with bulimia nervosa. The use of psychostimulants given orally has not, to our knowledge, been reported.

Discussion

Unfortunately, the available information about pharmacological treatment of anorexia nervosa and bulimia rests mainly on case reports, small series, and a woefully small number of control trials. The problem of diagnosis contributes to the lack of sufficient information. Different criteria for diagnosis have been used by different authors. The lack of objective indices of symptom or weight change in many studies also compromises their worth. Because the literature in this area is in general preliminary, only temporary conclusions can be drawn and tentative suggestions offered.

The current literature about the pharmacological treatment for anorexia nervosa suggests that both antidepressant drugs and cyproheptadine may be useful for at least a subgroup of patients. Whether any depression-related variables would predict antidepressant response is yet to be determined. The available research combined with speculation based on our knowledge of affective disorders suggests that when depression is a prominent part of the clinical picture, and in particular when there is a family history of affective disorder, the use of an antidepressant should be considered in patients with anorexia nervosa. The utility of periactin requires further investigations. Lithium poses a number of hazards in eating-disorder patients, particularly when they are outpatients. The available results to date indicate that lithium may be helpful for some anorexia nervosa patients. Based on the small number of cases reported to date, metoclopramide appears potentially useful in patients with anorexia nervosa who experience gastric distress during the refeeding phase. Again, this requires further work.

Available research about the pharmacological treatment of bulimia suggests that anticonvulsants may be helpful for some patients, but clinical or EEG variables that would identify these patients have not been firmly established. Further controlled trials using anticonvulsant medications are indicated.

There is some evidence that antidepressants may be useful in patients with bulimia. The use of MAO inhibitors pose certain management difficulties but may result in symptomatic improvement. Traditional antidepressant compounds, which require less dietary constraint, also appear promising. Clearly, further studies are indicated in this regard.

In considering the use of pharmacological agents in patients with eating disorders, several other points need to be mentioned. the anticholinergic side effects of some psychotropics may be intolerable to patients with bulimia or anorexia nervosa; such side effects are quite common with certain antidepressant agents. Anticholinergic effects foster gastric retention and a sense of upper gastrointestinal fullness. This should be avoided if possible. Fluid and electrolyte abnormalities, commonly seen in patients with anorexia nervosa and bulimia, may in themselves predispose to cardiac arrhythmias and should be corrected prior to the institution of any potentially cardiotoxic drugs such as lithium or antidepressants. There also appears to be an increased potential for arrhythmias and congestive heart failure in patients with eating disorders (see chap. 3). These factors suggest that careful attention should be given to cardiac functioning when patients are treated with antidepressants or lithium. Finally, pharmacokinetic differences may be seen in patients with anorexia nervosa and bulimia and must be considered in planning therapy. Patients with anorexia, who have very little body fat, will have smaller tissue reservoirs than normals. Also, patients who are vomiting or abusing laxatives may not have adequate absorption of drugs. Whenever possible, blood levels should be monitored.

REFERENCES

1. Hernandez, L., and B. G. Hoebel. 1980. Basic mechanisms of feeding and weight regulation. In *Obesity,* ed. A. Stunkard. Philadelphia: W. B. Saunders.
2. Leibowitz, S. F. 1978. Identification of catecholamine receptor mechanisms in the perifornical lateral hypothalamus and their role in mediating amphetamine and L-Dopa anorexia. In *Central mechanisms of anorectic drugs,* ed. S. Garattini and R. Samanin. New York: Raven Press.

3. Barry, V. C. and H. L. Klawans. 1976. On the role of dopamine in the pathophysiology of anorexia nervosa. *J. Neural Transm.* 38:107-22.
4. Halmi, K. A. 1981. Catecholamine metabolism in anorexia nervosa. *Int. J. Psychiatry Med.* 11:251-54.
5. Abraham, S. F., J. V. Beumont, and D. M. Cobbin. 1981. Catecholamine and body weight in anorexia nervosa. *Br. J. Psychiatry* 138:244-47.
6. Gerner, R. H., and H. E. Gwirtsman. 1981. Abnormalities of dexamethasone suppression test and urinary MHPG in anorexia nervosa. *Am. J. Psychiatry* 138:650-53.
7. Gross, H. A., C. R. Lake, M. H. Ebert, M. G. Ziegler, and I. J. Kopin. 1979. Catecholamine metabolism in primary anorexia nervosa. *J. Clin. Endoctrinol. Metab.* 49:805-9.
8. Halmi, K. A., H . Dekirmenjian, J. M. Davis, R. Casper, and S. Goldberg. 1978. Catecholamine metabolism in anorexia nervosa. *Arch. Gen. Psychiatry* 35:458-50.
9. Margules, D., B. Moisset, M. Lewis, H. Shibuya, and B. Pert. 1978. Beta-endorphin is associated with overeating in genetically obese mice (ob/ob) and rats (fa/fa). *Science* 202:988-91.
10. Atkinson, R. L., W. T. Dohms, G. A. Bray, and M. A. Sperling. 1981. Adrenergic modulation of glucagon and insulin secretion in obese and lean human. *Horm. Metab. Res.* 13:249-53.
11. Kyriakidis, M., and T. Silverstone. 1979. Comparison of the effects of d-amphetamine and fenfluramine on hunger and food intake in man. *Neuropharmacology* 12:1007-8.
12. Morley, J. E. 1980. The neuroendocrine control of appetite: The role of endogenous opiates, cholecystokinin, TRH, gamma-aminobutyric-acid and the diazepam receptor. *Life Sci.* 27:355-68.
13. Smith, G. P., and J. Gibbs. 1981. Brain-gut peptides and the control of food intake. In *Neurosecretion and brain peptides,* ed. J. Martin, S. Reichlin, and K. Bick. New York: Raven Press.
14. Dally, P. J., G. B. Oppenheim, and W. Sargant. 1958. Anorexia nervosa. *Br. Med. J.* 2:633.
15. Dally, P. J., and W. Sargant. 1960. A new treatment of anorexia nervosa. *Br. Med. J.* 1:1770-73.
16. Crisp, A. H. 1965. Some aspects of the evolution, presentation and follow-up of anorexia nervosa. *Proc. R. Soc. Med.* 58:814-20.
17. Crisp, A. H ., and F. J. Roberts. 1962. A case of anorexia nervosa in a male. *Postgrad. Med. J.* 38:350-53.
18. Kuhn, R. 1969. Psychopathology: Pharmacotherapy and psychotherapy of anorexia nervosa. In *Psychotropic drugs in internal medicine,* ed. A. Pletcher and A. Marino. Amsterdam: Excerpta Medica.
19. Plantley, F. 1977. Pimozide in treatment of anorexia nervosa (letter). *Lancet* 1:1105.
20. Hoes, M. J. A. S. M. 1980. Copper sulfate and pimozide for anorexia nervosa. *J. Orthomolecular Psychiatry* 9:48-51.
21. Vandereycken, W., and R. Pierloot. 1982. Pimozide combined with behavior therapy in the short-term treatment of anorexia nervosa. *Acta Psychiatr. Scand.* 66:445-50.
22. Mills, I. H . 1973. Endocrine and social factors in self-starvation amenorrhea. *R. Coll. Physicians Edinburgh Publ.* 42.
23. White, J. H., and N. L. Schnaultz. 1977. Successful treatment of anorexia nervosa with imipramine. *Dis Nerv. Syst.* 38:567-68.
24. Moore, D. C. 1977. Amitriptyline therapy in anorexia nervosa. *Am. J. Psychiatry* 134:11.
25. Reilly, P. P. 1977. Anorexia nervosa. *R. I. Med. J.* 60:419-22.

26. Katz, J. L., and B. T. Walsh. 1978. Depression in anorexia nervosa. *Am. J. Psychiatry* 135:507.
27. Kendler, K. S. 1978. Amitriptyline-induced obesity in anorexia nervosa: A case report. *Am. J. Psychiatry* 135:1107-8.
28. Needleman, H. L., and D. Waber. 1977. The use of amitriptyline in anorexia nervosa. In *Anorexia nervosa,* ed. R. A. Vigersky. New York: Raven Press.
29. Lacey, J. H ., and A. H. Crisp. 1980. Hunger, food intake and weight: The impact of clomipramine on a refeeding anorexia nervosa population. *Postgrad. Med. J.* 56:79-85.
30. Bergen, S. S. 1964. Appetite stimulating properties of cyproheptadine. *Am. J. Dis. Child.* 108:270-73.
31. Noble, R. E. 1969. Effect of cyproheptadine on appetite and weight gain in adults. *JAMA* 209:2054-55.
32. Pawlowski, G. T. 1975. Cyproheptadine: Weight-gain and appetite stimulation in essential anorexia nervosa patients. *Curr. Ther. Res.* 18:673-78.
33. Silverstone, T., and D. Schuyler. 1975. The effect of cyproheptadine on hunger, caloric intake and body weight in man. *Psychopharmacology* 40:335-40.
34. Levenstein, A. F., E. P. Dacaney, L. Lasagna, and T. E. Van Metre. 1962. Effect of cyproheptadine on asthmatic children. *JAMA* 180:912-16.
35. Mainquet, P. 1972. Effects of cyproheptadine on anorexia and loss of weight in adults. *Practitioner* 208:797-800.
36. Benady, D. R. 1970. Cyproheptadine hydrochloride (periactin) and anorexia nervosa: A case report. *Br. J. Psychiatry* 117:681-82.
37. Vigersky, R. A., and D. L. Loriaux. 1977. The effect of cyproheptadine in anorexia nervosa: A double-blind trial. In *Anorexia nervosa,* ed. R. A. Vigersky. New York: Raven Press.
38. Goldberg, S. C., K. A. Halmi, E. D. Eckert, R. C. Casper, and J. M. Davis. 1979. Cyproheptadine in anorexia nervosa. *Br. J. Psychiatry* 134:67-70.
39. Halmi, K. A., E. Eckert, and J. R. Falk. 1983. Cyproheptadine, an antidepressant and weight-inducing drug for anorexia nervosa. *Psychopharmacol. Bull.* 19:103-5.
40. Goldberg, S. C., E. D. Eckert, K. A. Halmi, R. C. Casper, J. M. Davis, and M. Roper. 1980. Effects of cyproheptadine on symptoms and attitudes in anorexia nervosa (letter). *Arch. Gen. Psychiatry* 30:1083.
41. Barcai, A. 1977. Lithium in adult anorexia nervosa: A pilot report on two patients. *Acta Psychiatr. Scand.* 55:97-101.
42. Stein, G. S., S. Hartshorn, J. Jones, and D. Steinberg. 1982. Lithium in a case of severe anorexia nervosa. *Br. J. Psychiatry* 140:526-28.
43. Gross, H . A., M. H. Ebert, V. B. Faden, S. C. Goldberg, L. E. Nee, and W. H. Kaye. 1981. A double-blind controlled trial of lithium carbonate in primary anorexia nervosa. *J. Clin. Psychopharmacol.* 1:376-81.
44. Redmond, D. E., Jr., A. Swann, and G. R. Heniger. 1976. Phenoxybenzamine in anorexia nervosa. *Lancet* 2:307.
45. Saleh, J. W., and P. Lebwohl. 1980. Metoclopramide-induced gastric emptying in patients with anorexia nervosa. *Am. J. Gastroenterol.* 74:127-32.
46. Dubois, A., H. A. Gross, J. E. Ritcher, and M. H. Ebert. 1981. Effects of bethanechol on gastric functions in primary anorexia nervosa. *Dig. Dis. Sci.* 26:7.
47. Bakan, R. 1979. The role of zinc in anorexia nervosa: Etiology and treatment. *Med. Hypotheses* 5:731-36.
48. Horrobin, D. F., and S. C. Cunnane. 1980. Interactions between zinc. Essential fatty acids and prostaglandins: Relevance to acrodermatitis, enteropathica, total parenteral nutrition. The glucagonoma syndrome, diabetes, anorexia nervosa, and sickle cell anemia. *Med. Hypotheses* 6:277-96.

49. Casper, R. C., B. Kirschner, H. H. Sandstead, R. A. Jacob, and J. M. Davis. 1980. An evaluation of trace metals, vitamins, and taste functions in anorexia nervosa. *Am. J. Clin. Nutr.* 33:1801-8.

50. Moore, R., I. H . Mills, and A. Forster. 1981. Naloxone in the treatment of anorexia nervosa: Effect of weight gain and lipolysis. *J. R. Soc. Med.* 74:129-31.

51. Johanson, A. J., and N. J. Knorr. 1974. Treatment of anorexia nervosa by levodopa. *Lancet* 1:591.

52. Johanson, A. J., and N. J. Knorr. 1977. L-Dopa as treatment for anorexia nervosa. In *Anorexia nervosa,* ed. R. A. Vigersky. New York: Raven Press.

53. Remick, R. A., M. W. Jones, and P. E. Compos. 1980. Postictal bulimia (letter). *J. Clin. Psychiatry* 41:26.

54. Kirschbaum, W. R. 1951. Excessive hunger as a symptom of cerebral origin. *J. Nerv. Ment. Dis.* 113:95.

55. Crisp, A. H., G. W. Fenton, and L. Scotton. 1968. A controlled study of the EEG in anorexia nervosa. *Br. J. Psychiatry* 114:1149-60.

56. Green, R. S., and J. H. Rau. 1974. Treatment of compulsive eating disturbances with anticonvulsant medication. *Am. J. Psychiatry* 131:428-32.

57. Green, R. S., and J. H . Rau. 1977. The use of diphenylhydantoin in compulsive eating disorders: Further studies. In *Anorexia nervosa,* ed. R. A. Vigersky. New York: Raven Press.

58. Rau, J. H., and R. S. Green. 1978. Soft neurological correlates of compulsive eating. *J. Nerv. Ment. Dis.* 166:435-37.

59. Rau, J. H., F. A. Struve, and R. S. Green. 1979. Electroencephalographic correlates of compulsive eating. *Clin. Electroencephalogr.* 10:180-88.

60. Wermuth, B. M., K. L. Davis, L. E. Hollister, and A. J. Stunkard. 1977. Phenytoin treatment of the binge-eating syndrome. *Am. J. Psychiatry* 134:1249-53.

61. Davis, K. L., B. Quallis, L. E. Hollister, and A. J. Stunkard. 1974. EEGs of "binge" eaters (letter). *Am. J. Psychiatry* 131:1409.

62. Greenway, F. L., W. T. Dahms, and D. A. Brag. 1977. Phenytoin as a treatment of obesity associated with compulsive eating. *Current Therapeutic Research* 21:338-42.

63. Weiss, T., and L. Levitz. 1976. Diphenylhydantoin treatment of bulimia (letter). *Am. J. Psychiatry* 133:1093.

64. Moore, S. L., and S. M. Rakes. 1982. Binge eating—therapeutic response to diphenylhydantoin: Case report. *J. Clin. Psychiatry* 43:385-86.

65. Kaplan, A. S., P. E. Garfinkel, P. L. Darby, and D. M. Garner. 1983. Carbamazepine in the treatment of bulimia. *Am. J. Psychiatry* 140:1225-26.

66. Pope, H. G., and J. I. Hudson. 1982. Treatment of bulimia with antidepressants. *Psychopharmacology* 78:176-79.

67. Pope, H. G., J. I. Hudson, J. M. Jonas, and D. Yurgelun-Todd. 1983. Bulimia treated with imipramine: A placebo-controlled double-blind study. *Am. J. Psychiatary* 140:554-58.

68. Sabine, E. J., A. Yonace, A. J. Farrington, K. H. Barratt, and A. Wakeling. 1983. Bulimia nervosa: A placebo-controlled double-blind therapeutic trial of mianserin. *Br. J. Clin. Pharmacol.* 15:195S-202S.

69. Mitchell, J. E., and R. Groat. In press. A placebo-controlled double-blind trial of amitriptyline in bulimia.

70. Hughes, P. L., L. A. Wells, C. J. Cunningham, and D. M. Ilstrup. 1984. Treating bulimia with desipramine: A double-blind placebo-controlled study. Presented at the annual meeting of the American Psychiatric Association, Los Angeles, 9 May.

71. Pope, H. G., J. I. Hudson, and J. M. Jonas. 1983. Antidepressant treatment of bulimia:

Preliminary experience and practical recommendations. *J. Clin. Psychopharmacol.* 3:274-81.

72. Walsh, B. T., J. W. Stewart, L. Wright, W. Harrison, S. P. Roose, and A. H. Glassman. 1982. Treatment of bulimia with monoamine oxidase inhibitors. *Am. J. Psychiatry* 139:1629-30.
73. Stewart, J . W., B. T. Walsh, L. Wright, S. P. Roose, and A. H. Glassman. 1984. An open trial of MAO inhibitors in bulimia. *J. Clin. Psychiatry* 45:217-19.
74. Walsh, B. T., J. W. Stewart, S. P. Roose, M. Gladis, and A. H. Glassman. 1984. Treatment of bulimia with phenelzine. A double-blind placebo-controlled study. Presented at the annual meeting of the American Psychiatric Association, Los Angeles, 7 May.
75. Brotman, A. W., D. B. Herzog, and S. W. Woods. 1984. Antidepressant treatment of bulimia: The relationship between binging and depressive symptomatology. *J. Clin. Psychiatry* 45:7-9.
76. Ong, Y. L., S. A. Checkley, and G. F. M. Russell. 1983. Suppression of bulimic symptoms with methylamphetamine. *Br. J. Psychiatry* 143:288-93.

7

Integrated Treatment Program for Anorexia Nervosa

Elke Eckert, M.D., and Leah Labeck, R.N., B.S.N.

Various somatic and psychological treatments have been advocated for anorexia nervosa, including psychoanalysis,[1] a special "fact-finding" psychotherapy,[2] simple supportive therapy,[3] family therapy,[4-6] behavior therapies,[7-15] cognitive therapy,[16] tube feeding,[1] "forced feedings,"[17] bed rest,[18-20] hyperalimentation,[21] pharmacotherapies,[22-29] electroshock,[30] and psychosurgery.[31]

Treatment effects have not been thoroughly assessed. Randomized, controlled studies have evaluated the effectiveness only of behavior and pharmacotherapy. Only one such study has tested the efficacy of behavior therapy when used alone. This study, a large multicenter cooperative effort, found no difference in weight gain between a standard psychiatric ward milieu treatment and the combination of standard milieu treatment and reinforcement for small increments of weight gain.[32] There is evidence, however, that the particular behavioral program used in this study was not maximally effective because it did not use individualized reinforcements and it reinforced weight gain every 5 days rather than daily.[33] The limited study time of 35 days may also have been insufficient to demonstrate a significant treatment difference. Although no clear advantage has been demonstrated for behavior therapy, many empirically based treatment programs have incorporated behavioral techniques into their treatments because it is efficient in producing weight gain and control of eating habits.[34,35] Concern with cost-effectiveness makes it prudent to use treatments that offer rapid results.

Controlled studies have been done using clomipramine, cyproheptadine, lithium, and pimozide. In one study, clomipramine showed no advantage to weight gain over the placebo although the patients receiving it reported an increased appetite and tended toward improved weight maintenance after leaving the drug trial.[36] In another study, cyproheptadine was associated with significant weight gain in a subgroup of more seriously ill anorexia nervosa patients who were more emaciated, had prior treatment failures, and had a history of delivery complications.[37] This study also showed an improvement in some typical anorectic attitudes.[38] In a recent preliminary analysis of another study, cyproheptadine was found to be significantly better than the placebo in both inducing weight gain and reducing depressive symptomatology.[39] Lithium was found in one study to be superior to the placebo in effecting weight gain in weeks 3 and 4 of treatment.[40] In a placebo-controlled, crossover study using pimozide and a placebo, there was a suggestion that pimozide enhanced weight gain although the results were not statistically significant.[41] Pimozide had a marginal effect on anorectic attitudes in the same study. Evidence is thus beginning to emerge that pharmacotherapy may promote weight gain, improve abnormal anorectic attitudes, and improve psychic distress.

No one treatment has been found clearly superior. Hence, no one treatment can currently be viewed as definitive. Anorexia nervosa is best viewed as a heterogeneous disorder with multiple deficits in psychological, social, behavioral, and biological functioning. The most appropriate treatment is therefore an integrated, multifaceted, and flexible one. Although our empirically derived treatment relies heavily on behavioral methods and utilizes a problem-oriented, reeducative therapy approach, it involves elements from various treatment modalities including pharmacotherapy. It is flexible because not all elements of treatment are equally relevant to each patient and to each phase of the illness. Both the physical and psychological aspects of the disorder are addressed: the physical aspects have precedence when the weight is low and the anorectic habits are most dominant, and the psychological aspects have precedence later when weight is more normal and the anorectic behavior and eating habits are under control. This approach makes sense when one realizes that starvation itself produces abnormalities in cognition, emotionality, and physiological changes similar to those present in anorexia nervosa.[42-48] (The effects of starvation are reviewed in chapter 1 of this book.)

Elements of Treatment

The four general treatment goals for an anorectic patient are to gain and maintain weight, to resume normal eating patterns, to assess and treat relevant psychological issues in the patient, and to educate families about the disorder by assessing their impact on maintaining it and assisting them in developing methods to promote normal functioning of the patient. Attention to these goals begins with the initial evaluation.

Initial Evaluation

The first contact with a patient usually comes during an outpatient evaluation. The anorectic patient should first be seen alone to convey the impression that you are interested in her as an individual and in her assessment of her situation, even though (as is often the case), she may have been brought in against her will by desperate family members. A history is obtained that emphasizes her weight and eating history, the circumstances of the onset of her dieting, the psychological and physical changes that have occurred since onset, her own perception of what is wrong, and the possible psychological contributions to her problems. A physical examination includes attention to such vital signs as lying and standing blood pressure, pulse, temperature, and height and weight. Laboratory testing pays special attention to the possibility of electrolyte abnormalities (hypokalemia due to vomiting, diurectics, or laxative abuse), signs of dehydration (elevated blood urea nitrogen and creatinine), possible hematological abnormalities, and liver function abnormalities. The results help in deciding whether hospitalization is necessary.

Parents and other family members are also seen, usually with the patient present. This time is used to clarify the history, give the family a chance to ask questions, and begin the education of all concerned. Parents often harbor unfounded guilt feelings. This first session is also used to educate them about the effects of starvation, the fact that no cause for the illness has been proven, and that no one is to blame—neither the patient nor the family. The general philosophy of treatment, which emphasizes the priority of the need to gain weight and reestablish normal eating patterns, is explained. Treatment must of course include more than attention to food and weight, but other problems can be effectively dealt with only after the patient has gained weight.

Hospitalization is considered if weight is less than 15% below a normal standard and is urged if weight is less than 25% below normal. No firm rule for mandatory hospitalization can be set because the urgency will depend on several indicators, including rapidity of weight loss, medical instability, overriding psychiatric problems (such as depression or thoughts of suicide), or other severe starvation symptoms. Another indication for hospitalization is failure of outpatient treatment, which is defined as 12-16 weeks of ongoing, regular outpatient treatment with no significant improvement or with deterioration. The patient and family are told that the length of hospitalization will usually vary between 2 and 4 months.

Sometimes brief hospitalization is required for anorectics who are not severely malnourished. These reasons include laxative withdrawal and uncontrollable binge-eating and vomiting. Patients who abuse laxatives have a difficult time stopping this pattern as outpatients because withdrawal often causes rebound fluid retention, which is difficult for patients to tolerate. A period of 10 days to 2 weeks in the hospital can provide them with the help needed.

It is desirable to have the patient's consent to hospitalization. In some cases the patient will refuse, however, even if it is urgently needed. Involuntary hospitalization is then required.

Weight Gain, Maintenance, and Normal Eating Patterns

The treatment goals of gaining and maintaining weight and of resuming normal eating patterns are best considered together. Two basic principles of treatment, exposure and response prevention, underlie the attainment of these goals.

Anorexia nervosa can be viewed, in part, as an anxiety-based disorder explainable by learning theory. Regardless of the initial stimulus for dieting, eating or weight gain begin to generate anxiety, whereas not eating and weight loss serve to avoid anxiety. Behaviors like taking laxatives and self-induced vomiting further reduce anxiety by preventing weight gain. Binge-eating, vomiting, and food faddism eventually come to dominate the anorectic's life and usually begin to function autonomously from the original motivation for loss of weight. Therefore, these food-related behaviors must be addressed specifically.

Because of these features, the illness has been compared to obsessive-compulsive[49] or phobic disorders.[50] A helpful treatment for obsessive-compulsive disorder involves exposure to the anxiety-producing stimuli and prevention of the compulsive rituals (response prevention).[51] In phobic disorders, the essential therapeutic requirement is thought to be exposure to the phobic object.[52] However, there is controversy about how precisely anorexia nervosa can be regarded as a phobic illness. Salkind, Fincham, and Silverstone have argued against a precise association because they found minimal skin conductance chances in anorectic patients to the presentation of a series of stimuli related to food and weight.[53]

Rosen and Leitenberg have described, in a single-case study of a normal-weight bulimic patient, that exposure and response prevention were effective in eliminating binge-eating and vomiting, reducing anxiety after eating, and increasing food intake without vomiting.[54]

Application of these treatment principles to anorexia nervosa requires exposure to the twin fears of eating and weight gain. We observe clinically that exposure to weight gain and normal eating is associated with gradual reduction of these fears. Preliminary reports have shown that psychological improvement does occur with weight gain.[21,55,56] Further systematic studies specifying the extent of these changes are necessary. If this principle of treatment is accepted, several different approaches to treatment may be effective provided the patient eats and gains weight. In practice these treatments may include "forced feedings," operant contingencies for eating or weight gain, or the presentation of structured diets where the patient is persuaded to eat.

As an extension of these principles, response prevention can be used to treat anorectic "rituals" that have an anxiety-reducing function. These rituals include vomiting after meals, food faddism, use of laxatives, compulsive exercising, and frequent weighing. Response prevention entails forced avoidance of these rituals: for example, not allowing access to laxatives and monitoring after meals to stop vomiting.

The precise approach to each patient is based on clinical judgment. In general, patients should retain as much control as possible as long as the desired result is achieved. Patients who cannot or will not cooperate with the necessary "exposure," however, require external controls. This is obviously more easily done in the hospital than in the outpatient clinic. If external controls are applied, especially in the hospital, it is imperative that gradual transfer of control back to the patient be accomplished before discharge. This means that if external controls such as structured diets, tube feeding, or operant contingency programs for weight gain are initially used, a patient should not be discharged before she resumes control over eating and weight. This resumption of control is usually done by a graded stepwise procedure. To discharge a patient before she has been able to accomplish this is an open invitation for relapse.

Outpatient Treatment

Some patients, usually those better motivated to change, may benefit from outpatient treatment. Education about the effects of starvation and application of the principles of exposure and response prevention, coupled with simple support, may suffice to produce weight gain. Further means include the development of external structure through use of behavioral techniques that the patient can apply herself: keeping a record of food intake, using structured meal plans, practicing "nonanorectic" eating, and self-reinforcement for more appropriate behavior. A dietician can help design a diet consisting initially of 1,200-1,500 calories in three meals (later the amount of calories is increased to perhaps 2,500-3,000). Although a balanced diet with all types of food is recommended, patients at first may be unable to follow such a diet because they fear certain foods. In this situation, a diet utilizing foods that cause little anxiety is helpful. Feared foodstuffs can be introduced later into the diet.

Patients are advised not to weigh themselves at home; normal minor variations of weight may trigger intolerable anxiety and interfere with the normalization of weight and eating patterns. They are weighed weekly in the clinic to assess progress.

Binge-eating, vomiting, and laxative abuse are features of anorexia nervosa that, if present, must be stopped. To promote this, we provide patients with monitoring sheets on which to self-monitor their meals and problem behaviors. Although they may at first resist keeping records, such labeling and feedback devices can help them feel better able to control their behavior.

These behavioral methods can be utilized in either individual or group treatment. We have found groups helpful to anorectics who are not severely malnourished and who are motivated. It is useful to have patients at varying stages of improvement in the group. The role modeling done by recovering anorectics, as well as the support and appropriate confrontation by the entire group, can be powerful. Patients often remark later in treatment how important it was for them to have observed the improvement of others. The group can often break through the denial or failure to acknowledge illness that interferes with treatment in some patients more effectively than can an individual therapist.

Some patients begin to improve rapidly; however, it is not unusual for patients to begin to change their anorectic behavior and gain weight only after 2 or 3 months of therapy. Taking risks and exposing themselves to their fears is often a slow process.

Hospital Treatment

Medical Stabilization Phase. The first few days of hospitalization serve several purposes: complete medical evaluation, medical stabilization, and assessment of the external controls needed. Immediately on admission, a complete search is done of the patient's person and belongings; any food and medication—such as diuretics, diet pills, and laxatives—are confiscated. Patients do not always admit their medication use and may try to sneak such products onto the ward. The only medications prescribed during these days are supplemental vitamins and supplemental potassium if hypokalemia is present. Laxatives are rarely necessary; patients are told that constipation will correct itself with weight gain.

The medically unstable patient remains at bed rest. Otherwise, the patient is up and about but confined to the ward. The expectation is that she will at least maintain her weight during these first few days. Further weight loss is not tolerated, leading to consequences that will be described.

The anorectic behaviors needing correction are defined through observation and discussion with the patient, after which judgments are made about the external controls that will be necessary. Hospitalization alone sometimes provides enough structure for patients to establish control, which includes stopping abnormal behaviors like binge-eating and vomiting. If these behaviors continue, they are addressed through such response prevention techniques as mealtime monitoring by nursing staff to prevent binge-eating, hoarding of foods, or vomiting. This monitoring may require constant attendance for 1 hour after meals, including accompanying patients to the bathroom to prevent vomiting.

Because it is expected that no further weight loss will occur, and because the patient has probably already demonstrated that she needs external control by failing at outpatient therapy, strict control of the diet is maintained by the staff during the stabilization phase. She is begun on a balanced diet of 1,500 calories per day in divided meals that she is required to finish. This may include feared foods that she has systematically deleted from her diet, only foods not associated with extreme anxiety, or a nutritionally balanced liquid diet. A liquid diet is useful because some patients feel less anxious drinking their calories than eating them. It also allows them to avoid making decisions about which foods to eat. It is imperative, though, that feared foods are soon systematically added because exposure to them is important. Not to do so would be to condone maintenance of anorectic behavior.

If the patient does not finish the food provided within a prescribed length of time, specific contingencies follow. For example, the next meal may be liquid. If that meal is not finished in the specified time, tube feeding takes place. Given clear guidelines and strict application of the treatment plan, tube feeding is rarely needed. If tube-fed once, most patients do not require it again. Intravenous feeding is rarely necessary, and the necessity for hyperalimentation is exceedingly rare.

Patients are usually weighed every morning in a hospital gown after voiding, and they are told what they weigh. The weight scales are never available for patients during the day. Anorectic patients become anxious and may decrease food intake with each upward movement of their weight. Teaching them to control this anxiety is made easier by keeping a daily weight graph. Some patients should be weighed less frequently because they are then more likely to maintain a steady dietary intake.

Weight Gain Phase. A goal weight (or goal weight range, as will be described later) is decided upon that is not lower than the weight that will assure regaining menses.[57] This is often taken to be the lowest normal standard weight for age and height (Metropolitan Life Insurance Company weight-height scale; pediatric growth chart).[58,59] No negotiation is allowed on this goal. the patient is expected to gain an average of one-half pound per day, which is realistic and safe for most patients. In actual practice, we make a weight graph for the patient indicating the expected weight gain with a diagonal line.

Operant contingencies for weight gain are used; these consist of a combination of individualized daily reinforcers plus a gradual expansion of off-ward privileges. The reinforcers are earned on any day that the patient's weight achieves or exceeds the expected minimum. If this fails, we sometimes change to an operant plan that requires the patient to remain isolated in her room for 24 hours if her weight falls below the expected weight for the day. This isolation is very effective in promoting weight gain in most patients.[33] There are occasional patients who are socially withdrawn and prefer to isolate themselves in their rooms. For these patients, it is better to make access to their rooms contingent on weight gain.

If a controlled diet is utilized, the guidelines mentioned earlier apply. Calorie content of provided food gradually increases to approximately 3,500 kcal per day, which should be enough to ensure the required weight gain. Meals are given at prescribed times only, and the kitchen is otherwise locked. Measures to prevent vomiting and binge-eating may be used.

Weight Maintenance Phase. As patients approach their goal weight, their anxiety may again increase at the prospect of being unable to either regulate or maintain weight. A period of weight maintenance lasting 2-4 weeks at "normal weight" prior to discharge may reassure the patient that she will not keep gaining and get "fat." We think that this period also helps to correct body image distortion, to solidify psychiatric gains, and to allow time for the physiological changes to stabilize. We find it best to change the goal to a range of weights—usually within 5 pounds—once the goal weight has been attained. There are two main reasons for this. Anorectics tend to be perfectionistic and to think rigidly. Any deviation of the scale, especially in an upward directon, may create anxiety. For example, we have seen anorectics whose goal weight was 100 pounds become anxious if the scales read 100.5 or 99.5 pounds. Since some weight fluctuation is inevitable, keeping weight within a range is a more realistic goal that helps protect against anxiety. Second, the upper limit on weight conveys the message to patients that the staff is equally concerned with the evidence of their becoming overweight as underweight.

During weight maintenance, external control of the diet varies depending on individual needs. If external control is needed, a simple discussion by the patient with the dietician to clarify the amount of food necessary for weight maintenance may suffice. Maximum control may entail a prepared diet sufficient for maintenance that may still require close monitoring. The important point is normal eating during this time; if external controls are still applied, they must be removed before discharge. If eating in various situations such as restaurants is a potential problem, the patient may benefit from practice sessions. For example, staff may accompany the patient the first time she goes for an outing to a restaurant. Later she can practice eating in situations alone, with family members, and with others.

We normally continue using operant behavioral contingencies for maintaining weight during the maintenance phase. This involves daily off-ward privileges for the patient who remains within the goal range. These contingencies are removed before discharge to test her capacity to maintain weight on her own.

This maintenance period is intended to provide gradual transition to outpatient status. We therefore encourage normal physical activity, including normal "noncompulsive" exercising. Exercise increases the patient's sense of control. When it is clear that she is maintaining her weight, we encourage passes home for increasingly long intervals. This is useful because problems involved with the transition to the home environment can be identified and addressed before discharge. In our experience, one can often predict which patients will relapse on the basis of how well the patient does during the maintenance period. Patients who continue to need external controls are at high risk of relapse soon after discharge and may require more extended therapy.

Assessment and Treatment of Psychological Issues

Supportive Treatment During Weight Gain

While weight is low and eating behaviors are very disordered, psychotherapy should mainly support efforts to modify eating behavior and gain weight.

First, patients are repeatedly educated about the effects of starvation and the physiological changes that can be expected as weight is regained. The anorectic's illogical thinking concerning weight and food issues is usually very ingrained. A typical example of illogical thinking is the belief that within just a few days of eating normal meals, the required weight will be gained. This belief leads to unrealistic expectations. To counter this illogical idea, the actual process of what is involved in weight gain is conveyed. Patients are instructed that the starvation process slows the digestive system, increases the time necessary for gastric emptying, and causes constipation. The result is that they feel full despite eating very little. Less often, patients feel hungry despite a large meal. This unnatural hunger may reinforce the anorectic's fears of "losing control." They are taught that this is an effect of starvation that diminishes with weight gain.

Abnormal eating behavior is explicitly identified as abnormal. Such behaviors can be used as examples illustrating how the anorectic behavior controls the patient and not, as the patient thinks, that she has perfect control of her behavior. To clarify this, the patient may be challenged to demonstrate her imagined control by eating normally.

Weight gain is associated with physiological and anatomical changes that may be distressing. A straightforward approach to this is best. Patients are warned that as rapid weight gain occurs, the added weight may not be properly distributed. Redistribution may take a month of maintenance at normal weight. The weight gained appears first on the trunk and face areas; this distribution produces an enlarged "tummy" and waist and a round face. This faulty distribution reinforces "feeling fat." Patients need to ignore these feelings temporarily. Also, a program of moderate, noncompulsive exercise may more effectively redistribute the weight gained and often gives useful reassurance to patients.

Use of Medications

Because no drug has been proven to be efficacious in most or all patients with anorexia nervosa, medications are used as adjunctive treatment based on the problems seen in each individual case. During the low-weight period, several drugs may be useful.

Cyproheptadine[37-39] in fairly high doses (32 mg per day) may be helpful in facilitating weight gain and in reducing depressive symptoms;[39] it also appears to be very safe even considering the unstable physical condition of many acute anorectics. Further research is needed, however, to clarify which anorectic patients are best suited for treatment with this drug. Chlorpromazine,[18,20,24] which has been used for years in anorectics, especially in England, may be useful for severely obsessional or highly anxious anorectics. It should be started in small doses of 10-40 mg a day because phenothiazines may aggravate the hypotension and other cardiovascular problems seen in anorectics. The dose can be slowly increased depending on the response obtained.

Although depressive symptoms usually improve as weight is gained,[56] amitriptyline and other antidepressants may be useful for significantly depressed anorectics.[26,29] These medications should also be started at small doses because of the possible aggravation of already existing cardiovascular instability. Treating depression at this phase may allow greater energy and motivation to be applied to strictly anorectic problems. Another class of problems that may be treated with medication during this time are gastrointestinal symptoms. Metoclopramide was recently found to enhance gastric emptying and improve subjective gastrointestinal symptoms such as bloating in anorexia nervosa patients.[60] Drugs of this type may be useful adjunctive treatment.

After the patient has regained weight, the treatment team can complete a thorough reassessment of psychiatric status, especially with respect to the possibility of a primary affective disorder. It has been suggested that anorexia nervosa is a variant of affective disorder. This hypothesis reflects the finding that depressive signs and symptoms are often present during the course of the illness and because a family history of affective disorder is frequent.[61-63] Low self-esteem, lack of motivation, and passivity may suggest depression even though all diagnostic criteria for major depression may not be met.

The presence or absence of a personality disorder should be decided only after weight gain because starvation may obscure correct evaluation. For example, starvation increases obsessive-compulsive thinking and behavior.[42,43] After weight gain, these characteristics should be improved. The remains of these characteristics may be an evident reflection of personality or an expression of depression requiring antidepressant medication. Anorectics frequently possess borderline personality traits during the starvation state. Our clinical experience indicates that these traits improve somewhat after weight gain. Reassessment of patients having these traits after weight gain should consider the possibility of an affective disorder like cyclothymia or a bipolar II disorder that may respond to medication. Akiskal has recently suggested that such personality disorders as borderline, cyclothymic, or even severe obsessive may be subclinical, "subsyndromic," or "subaffective" manifestations of affective disorders that may respond to antidepressants or lithium.[64-66] (Lithium is contraindicated in patients who vomit or abuse laxatives or diuretics because of the possibility of rapid lithium toxicity.)[67]

Common Psychological Themes

When starvation is no longer a factor, weight gain has occured, eating problems are under control, and fears of weight gain have diminished, significant psychotherapeutic issues rekindled by the return of overt signs of biological maturity become evident. Each patient has a unique set of problems, but there are common and recurring themes. These are failure to acknowledge illness, disturbance in cognition, problems with separation and autonomy, poor psychosocial skills, a negative self-concept, and defective recognition and expression of certain affective states. Through a problem-oriented reeducative therapy, we focus on each specific problem and teach patients the skills to facilitate normal thinking and functioning.

Failure to Acknowledge Illness. The failure of some anorectic patients to acknowledge illness—or their denial of illness—is a frustrating and difficult problem. They may fail to acknowledge their thinness or their hunger and fatigue. This failure is made more difficult by the pleasure they derive from being thin. In addition, they interpret the attention given their thinness as acknowledgement that being thin is desirable. No sure way to break through this impediment to treatment is available, but various techniques involving confrontation, at times gentle and at times forceful, are helpful.

Straightforward confrontation about the patient's thinness is not the most effective approach. They respond more positively to a discussion of the associated symptoms of the illness, which the anorectic can agree are problems and which she may want to correct. These include the symptoms that starvation has produced: sleep disturbance, irritability, depression, preoccupation with food, and social withdrawal with resulting alienation. Physicians often think that pointing out a dangerously low level of serum potassium to a patient, resulting from vomiting, or diuretic or laxative abuse, should shock her into acknowledging the illness and cooperating with treatment. Sometimes this approach is effective, but very often it fails. The reasons are probably multiple; one is that the patient does not feel the effect of the low level of serum potassium in her body, and hence she disbelieves the doctor's pronouncement. The best approach is to find something that the patient can agree is a problem and then relate it to other anorectic symptoms.

Another effective technique involves use of objective instruments. Several patient-related and observer-related scales have been developed that assess the symptoms and psychophysiological features of anorexia nervosa: the Slade Anorectic Behavior Scale,[68] Anorectic Attitude Scale,[69] Eating Attitudes Test,[70] and an unpublished Situational Discomfort Scale. Patients are told that the higher the scores, the more likely they are to have abnormal concerns about eating and weight. We have found these scales useful in helping anorectic patients to acknowledge that they do have significant problems. Another instrument that is sometimes useful is a body size estimation apparatus that compares the patient's estimation of sizes of her various body parts with their actual sizes, resulting in a composite body image distortion score.[71] The effect of the pronouncement of the score reflecting the distortion is sometimes dramatic; the single number strikes patients as more objective than many words.

The anorectic illness may be thought of as an avoidance or escape from the problems of life. Failure to acknowledge illness sometimes extends beyond the strictly anorectic issues to include even psychological changes. Denial may serve a purpose: it may be the glue that holds a shattered self-esteem system together. Hence high levels of support must be available if the patient is to begin to acknowledge illness. Psychotherapy must focus painstakingly on the appeal for the patient to remain anorectic versus the fear and drawbacks of being at a normal weight. The anorectic illness, with its associated behaviors and its past, present, and future consequences, must receive firm emphasis in treatment. Other anorectics, especially in groups, can often confront these issues more effectively than an individual therapist. Even other anorectics who have only partially shed their own denial systems are in a good position to help new patients because we often see another's problems more clearly than our own. Other anorectics are also good at providing the necessary understanding and support to help patients accept their illness. Family meetings that include the patient can often provide pertinent information about the patient's illness, personal life, and psychopathology that the patient cannot well deny. We have sometimes found that meeting with only one trusted family member and with the patient is helpful. This person may be able to indicate problems that the patient has not considered, information that is more acceptable coming from this trusted person alone.

Disturbance in Cognition. Disturbed cognition involves distortion of body image as well as the already described distortion about food and weight. Disturbed cognition may extend to other areas as well. For example, anorectic patients often exaggerate self-reference. They not only feel that other people watch every bite that they put into their mouths and notice every ounce of weight gain, but also that they are the focal point of everyone's attention. These distortions are repeatedly "labeled" and corrected with cognitive confrontation.[16] Body distortion is brought to the patient's attention early in treatment. The patient is told that during weight gain, she will probably continue to misperceive her body size because this misperception will constantly be reinforced by the physiological changes that are occurring. She is told that she cannot trust her own perceptions in this area and must temporarily ignore these feelings. Some patients, but not all, benefit from seeing themselves on videotape or in pictures taken while wearing underwear or tights.

Problems with Separation and Autonomy. Anorectic illness has been said to begin when the individual fails to proceed normally toward independence. The illness may exaggerate dependent, immature, or regressed traits, often reinforced by family members. It is instructive to look at an anorectic's hospital room. Not only is it often impeccably neat and orderly, but there are often posters of children or young animals; stuffed animals are frequently a feature of their exquisitely neat beds. We have treated a 15-year-old girl who used a coloring book depicting young farm animals. Patients often behave as if they were much younger, manifesting clinging behaviors and exaggerated crying when parents leave. Their activities expose their immaturity.

Independence is encouraged. One element in this is to teach the patient to distinguish her motivations from the expectations of others. This ability is an integral part of normal adolescent maturation.

Poor Psychosocial Skills. Many anorectic patients have major interpersonal problems, and follow-up studies have shown that they have high levels of social anxiety.[55] They are often described as shy and nonassertive. These difficulties are often present before the onset of illness, but they are certainly compounded by the disruption of normal social development associated with this illness. For example, many anorectics come for treatment when they are well beyond the age when dating normally begins. Many would like to begin dating, but they are subject to many misperceptions and lack elemental skills in dating. Assertiveness and social skills training can be invaluable.

Negative Self-Concept. Anorectic patients often have a negative self-concept. Starvation reinforces this self-concept because of the associated depression and increasing withdrawal and alienation. Also, the perfectionism and high expectations of anorectics are difficult standards to maintain that increase the likelihood of failure. They are overachievers striving to get A's, and they see themselves as failures if they do not. Interpersonal problems like being shy and nonassertive and hence not the most popular girls in school add to low self-esteem. Cognitive correction plus assertiveness and social skills training can help. Again, low self-esteem may be an aspect of depression that responds to drug treatment.

Defective Recognition and Expression of Affective States. Certain affective expressions, especially anger, may not be recognized by anorectics; if recognized, they are inappropriately expressed (perhaps by not eating). Patients often think it inappropriate to feel and especially to express anger. They need to be taught to recognize, accept, and appropriately express feelings. Keeping a written journal about difficult interactions coupled with assertiveness training is helpful.

Teaching these skills can be accomplished in part in groups, but each patient has problems needing individual attention, at least initially. Patients differ as to the intensity and length of individual attention needed. Some, especially those with a good premorbid adjustment, may require little; whereas others have much greater difficulty facing the problems of adolescence and life in general. An ongoing, open relationship with a therapist they can respect and trust, who can share experiences and be a role model, may be extremely important.

Education of Families

If the patient is young or living at home, education of the family is important to the patient's recovery. Family members should be interviewed early to assess their concerns and to teach them about the course, prognosis, and treatment of anorexia nervosa. This often relieves guilt feelings and anxiety. Early contact with family is also important to obtain their help in engaging the patient in treatment and to establish an alliance between family members and the therapeutic team so that treatment efforts are not sabotaged.

If a patient is hospitalized, the family should be seen or at least contacted weekly. Anorectic patients are notorious for their manipulations. This behavior springs from their anorectic fears as well as their poor interpersonal skills. For example, patients when first admitted to the hospital often complain about the therapeutic program, the food, the staff, or almost anything else. However, they may direct their complaints not to the staff but instead to family members. The family should be warned and instructed not to collude with patients by getting involved in these issues. They should instead refer the patient back to the treatment team. Family members are requested not to talk about weight and food issues with patients; they should leave those to the patient and the treatment team.

In outpatient treatment, the family and patient should attempt to agree on an approach to food and weight. Although the family should have little direct involvement in these matters except to support constructive efforts, there are exceptions. For example, after failing to gain weight on her own, one 14-year-old patient agreed to eat a specified diet only if her mother would serve it. She could or would not serve herself; she could not decide on portions, played and fussed with food, became increasingly anxious, and eventually did not eat. Having the mother serve was an acceptable initial step because weight gain was the first priority. It also accomplished the necessary exposure to normal eating that we have described. Later, of course, the patient had to manage her own meals. Consistency, not rigidity, is emphasized to help relieve the confusion and anxiety surrounding eating. Limits on anorectic behavior within the family are warranted. Families must not let the anorectic illness dictate dietary habits or otherwise dominate the family life. For example, special low-calorie diets offered in an attempt to stimulate food intake seldom get the anorectic to eat; such measures only reinforce the illness. Other limits may be placed on binge-eating and vomiting by requiring payment for missing food and requiring that the bathroom be cleaned after vomiting. If laxatives are found, they should be thrown out and the patient should be confronted.

The treatment team should also understand the interrelationships within the family system. If necessary, this can wait until starvation is no longer a factor because it is difficult to focus on the interrelationships and problems within the family while the illness itself demands attention. Relationships within the family are also likely to have changed in the emergency presented by the starving child. Faced with this, the family often reinforces the illness and the patient's dependency. It is vitally important that the family understand this and is helped to overcome it by promoting more autonomous functioning of the patient. The amount of help needed varies from case to case. Some families require only a few sessions, whereas others require prolonged therapy.

Despite hospitalization and other intensive attempts to help the family, some anorectic patients do better in a long-term placement away from their home. Some more seriously ill patients may need a carefully chosen residential treatment center, day-care center, or halfway house that can continue to give appropriate attention to weight and food and otherwise encourage psychological development.

Conclusion

Anorectic patients are often very difficult to treat even by an experienced treatment team. It can be a very complex illness—variable and chronic. Much research is needed to determine efficacious treatments. The treatment approach described in this chapter, which has been developed over the last 10 years, is basically empirical. Flexibility and an open mind are necessary prerequisites; adaptation to specific challenges may be required at any time. We do think, however, that this approach in the hands of an experienced treatment team can help most patients to control their illness and eventually to reverse it.

REFERENCES

1. Silverman, J. 1974. Anorexia nervosa: Clinical observations in a successful treatment program. *J. Pediatr.* 84:68-73.
2. Bruch, H . 1973. *Eating disorders.* New York: Basic Books.
3. Farquharson, R. F., and H. H. Hyland. 1966. Anorexia nervosa: The course of 15 patients treated from 20 to 30 years previously. *Can. Med. Assoc. J.* 94:411-19.
4. Minuchin, S., L. Baker, B. Rosman, R. Liebman, L. Milman, and T. Todd. 1975. A conceptual model of psychosocial illness in children: Family organization and family therapy. *Arch. Gen. Psychiatry* 32:1031-38.
5. Minuchin, S., B. L. Rosman, and L. Baker. 1978. *Psychosomatic families: Anorexia nervosa in context.* Cambridge, Mass.: Harvard University Press.
6. Palazolli, M. S. 1978. *Self-starvation.* New York: Jason Aronson.
7. Hallsten, E. A. Jr. 1965. Adolescent anorexia nervosa treated by desensitization. *Behav. Res. Ther.* 3:87-91.
8. Lang, P. 1965. Behavior therapy with a case of anorexia nervosa. In *Case studies in behavior modification,* ed. L. P. Ullman and L. Krasner. New York: Holt, Rinehart and Winston.
9. Agras, W. S., D. H. Barlow, N. H. Chaplin, G. G. Able, and H. Leitenberg. 1974. Behavioral modification of anorexia nervosa. *Arch. Gen. Psychiatry* 30:279-86.
10. Azerrad, J., and R. L. Stafford. 1969. Restoration of eating behavior in anorexia nervosa through operant conditioning and environmental manipulation. *Behav. Res. Ther.* 7:165-71.

11. Bachrach, A. J., W. J. Erwin, and J. P. Mohr. 1965. The control of eating behavior in an anorexic by operant conditioning techniques. In *Case studies in behavior modification,* ed. L. P. Ullman and I. Krasner. New York: Holt, Rinehart and Winston.
12. Halmi, K. A., P. Powers, and S. Cunningham. 1975. Treatment of anorexia nervosa with behavior modification. *Arch. Gen. Psychiatry* 32:93-96.
13. Garfinkel, P. E., S. A. Kline, and H. C. Stancer. 1973. Treatment of anorexia nervosa using operant conditioning techniques. *J. Nerv. Ment. Dis.* 157:428-33.
14. Kenny, F. T., and L. Solyom. 1971. The treatment of compulsive vomiting through faradic disruption of mental images. *Can. Med. Assoc. J.* 105:1071.
15. Wulliemier, F., F. Russel, and K. Sinclair. 1975. La therapie comportementale de l'anorxie nerveuse. *J. Psychosom. Res.* 19:967-72.
16. Garner, D. M., and K. Bemis. 1982. A cognitive-behavioral approach to anorexia nervosa. *Cognitive Ther. Res.* 6:1-27.
17. Janet, P. 1926. *Psychological healing.* New York: Allen and Unwin.
18. Crisp, A. H . 1965. Clinical and therapeutic aspects of anorexia nervosa—a study of 30 cases. *J. Psychosom. Res.* 9:67-78.
19. Russell, G. F. M. 1977. General management of anorexia nervosa and difficulties in assessing the efficacy of treatment. In *Anorexia nervosa,* ed. R. A. Vigersky. New York: Raven Press.
20. Dally, P. J., and W. Sargant. 1966. Treatment and outcome of anorexia nervosa. *Br. Med. J.* 2:793-95.
21. Maloney, M. J., and M. K. Farrell. 1980. Treatment of severe weight loss in anorexia nervosa with hyperalimentation and psychotherapy. *Am. J. Psychiatry* 137:310-14.
22. Benady, D. R. 1970. Cyproheptadine hydrochloride (Periactin) and anorexia nervosa: A case report. *Br. J. Psychiatry* 117:681-82.
23. Barcai, A. 1977. Lithium in anorexia nervosa: A pilot report on two patients. *Acta Psychiat. Scand.* 55:97-101.
24. Dally, P. J., and W. Sargant. 1960. A new treatment of anorexia nervosa. *Br. Med. J.* 1:1770-73.
25. Green, R. S., and J. H. Rau. 1974. Treatment of compulsive eating disturbances with anticonvulsant medication. *Am. J. Psychiatry* 131:428-32.
26. Johanson, A. J., and N. J. Knorr. 1977. L-Dopa as treatment for anorexia nervosa. In *Anorexia nervosa,* ed. R. A. Vigersky. New York: Raven Press.
27. Needleman, H. L., and D. Waber. 1977. The use of amitriptyline in anorexia nervosa. In *Anorexia nervsa,* ed. R. A. Vigersky. New York: Raven Press.
28. Moore, R., I. H. Mills, and A. Forster. 1981. Naloxone in the treatment of anorexia nervosa: Effect on weight gain and lipolysis. *J. R. Soc. Med.* 74:129.
29. Mills, I. 1976. Amitriptyline therapy in anorexia nervosa. *Lancet* 2:687.
30. Bernstein, I. C. 1964. Anorexia nervosa treated successfully with elecroshock therapy and subsequently followed by pregnancy. *Am. J. Psychiatry* 120:1023-25.
31. Crisp, A. H ., and R. S. Kalucy. 1973. The effect of leucotomy in intractable adolescent weight phobia (primary anorexia nervosa). *Postgrad. Med. J.* 49:833-93.
32. Eckert, E. D., S. C. Goldberg, K. A. Halmi, R. C. Casper, and J. M. Davis. 1979. Behavior therapy in anorexia nervosa. *Br. J . Psychiatry* 134:55-59.
33. Eckert, E. D. 1983. Behavior modification in anorexia nervosa: A comparison of two reinforcement schedules. In *Anorexia nervosa: Recent developments in research,* ed. P. L. Darby, P. E. Garfinkel, D. M. Garner, and D. V. Coscina. New York: Allan R. Liss.
34. Agras, W. S., and J. Werne. 1978. Behavior therapy in anorexia nervosa: A data-based approach to the question. In *Controversy in psychiatry,* ed. J. P. Brady and H. K. H. Brodie. New York: W. B. Saunders.

35. Agras, W. S., and H. C. Kraemer. 1983. The treatment of anorexia nervosa: Do different treatments have different outcomes? *Psychiatric Ann.* 13:928-35.
36. Lacey, J. H., and A. H. Crisp. 1980. Hunger, food intake and weight: The impact of clomipramine on a refeeding anorexia nervosa population. *Postgrad. Med. J.* 56:79-85.
37. Goldberg, S. C., K. A. Halmi, D. E. Eckert, R. Casper, and J. M. Davis. 1979. Cyproheptadine in anorexia nervosa. *Br. J. Psychiatry* 134:67-70.
38. Goldberg, S. C., E. D. Eckert, K. A. Halmi, R. C. Casper, J. M. Davis, and M. Roper. 1980. Effects of cyproheptadine on symptoms and attitudes in anorexia nervosa (letter). *Arch. Gen. Psychiatry* 31:1083.
39. Halmi, K. A., E. D. Eckert, and J. R. Falk 1982. Cyproheptadine for anorexia nervosa (letter). *Lancet* 1:1357-58.
40. Gross, H. A., M. H. Ebert, V. B. Faden, S. C. Goldberg, L. E. Nee, and W. H. Kaye. 1981. A double-blind controlled trial of lithium carbonate in primary anorexia nervosa. *J. Clin. Psychopharmacol.* 1:376-81.
41. Vandereycken, W., and R. Pierloot. 1982. Pimozide combined with behavior therapy in the short-term treatment of anorexia nervosa. *Acta Psychiatr. Scand.* 66:445-50.
42. Keys, A., J. Brozek, A. Henschel, O. Mickelsen, and H. L. Taylor. 1950. *The biology of human starvation.* Minneapolis: University of Minnesota Press.
43. Schiele, B. C., and J. Brozek. 1948. "Experimental neurosis" resulting from semistarvation in man. *Psychosom. Med.* 10:31-50.
44. Casper, R. C., and J. M. Davis. 1977. On the course of anorexia nervosa. *Am. J. Psychiatry* 134:974-78.
45. Halmi, K. A., and J. R. Falk. 1981. Common physiological changes in anorexia nervosa. *Int. J. Eating Disorders* 1:16-27.
46. Halmi, K. A. 1978. Anorexia nervosa: Recent investigations. *Annu. Rev. Med.* 29:137-48.
47. Boyar, R. M., J. Katz, and J. W. Finkelstein. 1974. Anorexia nervosa: Immaturity of the 24-hour luteinizing hormone secretory pattern. *N. Engl. J. Med.* 291:861.
48. Holt, S., M. J. Ford, S. Grant, and R. C. Heading. 1981. Abnormal gastric emptying in primary anorexia nervosa. *Br. J. Psychiatry* 139:550-52.
49. Solyom, L., R. J. Freeman, and J. E. Miles. 1982. A comparative psychometric study of anorexia nervosa and obsessive neurosis. *Can. J. Psychiatry* 27:282-86.
50. Crisp, A. H. 1979. Anorexia nervosa: 'feeding disorder', 'nervous malnutrition', or 'weight phobia'? *World Rev. Nutr. Diet.* 12:452-504.
51. Steketee, G., E. B. Foa, and J. B. Grayson. 1982. Recent advances in the behavioral treatment of obsessive-compulsive disorder. *Arch. Gen. Psychiatry* 39:1365-71.
52. Klein, D. F., C. M. Zitrin, M. G. Woerner, and D. C. Ross. 1983. Treatment of phobias. II. Behavior therapy and supportive psychotherapy: Are there any specific ingredients? *Arch. Gen. Psychiatry* 40:139-45.
53. Salkind, M. R., J. Fincham, and T. Silverstone. 1980. Is anorexia nervosa a phobic disorder? A psychophysiological enquiry. *Biol. Psychiatry* 15:803-8.
54. Rosen, J. C., and H. L. Leitenberg. 1982. Bulimia nervosa: Treatment with exposure and response prevention. *Behav. Ther.* 13:117-24.
55. Stonehill, E., and A. H. Crisp. 1977. Psychoneurotic characteristics of patients with anorexia nervosa before and after treatment and at follow-up 4-7 years later. *J. Psychosom. Res.* 21:189-93.
56. Eckert, E. D., S. C. Goldberg, K. A. Halmi, R. C. Casper, and J. M. Davis. 1982. Depression in anorexia nervosa. *Psychol. Med.* 12:115-22.
57. Frisch, R. E. 1977. Food intake, fatness, and reproductive ability. In *Anorexia nervosa,* ed. R. A. Vigersky. New York: Raven Press.

58. Metropolitan Life Insurance Company Weight-Height Scale. 1959. Height and weight tables. Statistical Bulletin of the Metropolitan Life Insurance Company 40:1-4.
59. Jackson, R. L., and A. G. Kelly. 1945. Growth charts for use in pediatric practice. *J. Pediatr.* 27:215-29.
60. Saleh, J. W., and P. Lebwohl. 1980. Metoclopramide-induced gastric emptying in patients with anorexia nervosa. *Am. J. Gastroenterol.* 74:127.
61. Cantwell, P. D., S. D. Sturzenberger, and J. Burroughs. 1977. Anorexia nervosa—an affective disorder? *Arch. Gen. Psychiatry* 34:1087-93.
62. Winokur, A., V. March, and J. Mendels. 1980. Primary affective disorder in relatives of patients with anorexia nervosa. *Am. J. Psychiatry* 130:695-98.
63. Gershon, E. S., J. R. Hamovit, J. L. Schreiber, E. D. Dibble, W. Kaye, J. I. Nurnberger, Jr., A. Anderson, and M. Ebert. 1983. Anorexia nervosa and major affective disorders associated in families: A preliminary report. In *Childhood psychopathology and development,* ed. S. B. Guze, F. J. Earls, and J. E. Barrett. New York: Raven Press.
64. Akiskal, H. S. 1981. Subaffective disorder: Dysthymic, cyclothymic, and bipolar II disorders in the 'borderline' realm. *Psychiatr. Clin. North Am.* 4:25-36.
65. Akiskal, H. S., M. K. Khani, and A. Scott-Strauss. 1979. Cyclothymic temperamental disorders. *Psychiatric Clin. North Am.* 2:527-54.
66. Carroll, B. J., J. F. Greden, M. Feinberg, N. Lohr, N. James, M. Steiner, R. F. Haskett, A. A. Albala, J. deVigne, and I. Tarika. 1981. Neuroendocrine evaluation of depression in borderline patients. *Psychiatric Clin. North Am.* 4:89-100.
67. Spring, G. K. 1974. Hazards of lithium prophylaxis. *Dis. Nerv. Syst.* 35:351-54.
68. Slade, P. D. 1973. A short anorexic behaviour scale. *Br. J. Psychiatry* 122:83-85.
69. Goldberg, S. C., K. A. Halmi, E. D. Eckert, R. Casper, and J. M. Davis. 1980. Attitudinal dimensions in anorexia nervosa. *J. Psychiat. Res.* 15:239-51.
70. Garner, D. M., and P. E. Garfinkel. 1979. The Eating Attitudes Test: An index of the symptoms of anorexia nervosa. *Psychol. Med.* 9:273-79.
71. Slade, P. D., and G. F. M. Russell. 1973. Awareness of body dimensions in anorexia nervosa: Cross-sectional and longitudinal studies. *Psychol. Med.* 3:118-99.

8

Integrated Treatment Program for Bulimia

James E. Mitchell, M.D., and Gretchen M. Goff, M.P.H.

Much of the published treatment research on bulimia has concerned drug therapy, as was reviewed in chapter 6. Only a few articles have been published on the nonpharmacological treatment of patients with bulimia who do not meet weight criteria for anorexia nervosa. Before the last few years, most of these treatment papers assumed a psychodynamic orientation. Behavioral therapies have dominated more recent published reports. Much of this material has been reviewed in the previous chapters on psychodynamics (chap. 4) and behavioral treatment (chap. 5). In this chapter, we will discuss the practical aspects of bulimia treatment.

General Considerations

Let us begin by discussing the most appropriate setting for treating patients with bulimia. Assuming that a patient is found to have nonanorectic bulimia by careful diagnosis and has been physically screened to make sure that she or he is medically stable, what type of treatment approach is the most likely to prove safe and effective?

Both inpatient and outpatient treatment programs have been developed for bulimia; although both treatments have their proponents, it is unclear whether either approach has any particular advantage. One obvious advantage of hospitalization if the proper environment is provided is the interruption of the binge-eating cycle.[1] However, taking the control of eating behavior away from patients with bulimia is at best a mixed blessing because it is only temporary. These patients eventually need to learn control over their eating. Many recent reports have proposed outpatient treatment programs for bulimia,[2-5] which keeps the responsibility for eating behavior with the patient. But the problem of interrupting the binge-eating/purging cycle remains. Various authors have used different approaches to accomplish this, including meeting with patients several times a week[2] or even daily[3] early in treatment.

Another important question concerns group versus individual therapy. Is one type of therapy superior? Again, the question is presently unanswerable. Both group[5] and individual[2] approaches have been developed and appear promising. Clear advantages of one or the other have not been found, and no comparison studies have appeared.

A third important consideration, and many might say the most important one, is the nature of the therapeutic process once the place (inpatient vs. outpatient) and format (group vs. individual) have been decided. Although several strategies have been suggested, much of the recent published literature focuses on behavioral treatment approaches that attempt to employ specific behavioral paradigms to address specifically defined parts of the syndrome. Although various authors have introduced psychodynamic techniques (as suggested in chap. 4), most clinicians writing in this area seem to use behavioral techniques, particularly early in the course of therapy.

Treatment Reports

Group Therapy Techniques

Several reports have described the use of group strategies to treat women with bulimia (or bulimarexia as defined by Boskind-Lodahl and White).[4,6] The first treatment report of these researchers concerned 12 women with bulimarexia who were treated for 11 weeks using 2-hour sessions.[4] In addition, a 6-hour marathon session was held during the middle part of the treatment. Individuals with bulimarexia, according to these authors, are trying desperately to fit themselves into a stereotyped female role in terms of both thinness and passivity. The therapy was directed to the exploration and development of the patient's strengths, with emphasis on an examination of the cultural bias that leads women to be "passive, dependent and accommodating, and to value their bodies principally for physical attractiveness." The authors termed their approach "experiential-behavioral." By this they apparently meant that the therapy used both Gestalt and behavioral techniques. Specific elements of the therapy included discussion of the problem of personal isolation and of shame resulting from the behavior; an examination of relationship problems; and the use of specific behavioral strategies, such as daily journals to record feelings and factors that precede binges, short-term goal contracting, role-playing of feared situations, and assertiveness training.

Psychological test results were compared with those from a control group of 13 women who were assigned nonrandomly to a waiting list. No attempt was made to compare the eating behaviors of the treated patients with those of controls. Frequency of various eating behaviors before and after therapy was not documented, and several patients required subsequent therapy. The authors concluded that the syndrome was difficult to treat.

These same authors subsequently reported a new group strategy based on the same observations and theoretical formulations regarding bulimarexia women. The subject population consisted of 14 women who responded to an article in a national magazine. The group met daily for 5 hours, Monday through Friday. On the first day the focus was on goal setting. For the remaining 4 days, the sessions were divided into two parts using a female therapist in the morning and a male-female therapist team in the afternoon. This was done to allow the women to work independently of men in the morning and to keep from attributing passive change solely to male involvement. Subsequent sessions focused on such issues as the need to take responsibility for one's behavior, fear and hatred of men, the use of role playing "to help participants identify attitudes and projections that often interfered with realistic perceptions of the self and others . . . ," group confrontation of members who continued to binge, and an examination of one's sense of self-worth particularly as it relates to men. Six months after the group sessions, 3 of the women had stopped binge-eating completely and 7 reported that the frequency of this behavior had decreased. None of these women was engaging in purging behaviors. The 4 remaining women reported little change in their binge-eating behavior, and each of them had continued in some kind of therapy.

In 1981, Dixon and Kiecolt-Glaser[7] presented data concerning 36 women diagnosed by DSM-III criteria as bulimic. The women were seen for weekly group therapy, which was described as using both behavioral techniques and insight-oriented psychotherapy. Only 11 of these subjects attended for a full 10 weeks, although 4 were still enrolled in the group at the end of the research period. The group met weekly for 1½-hour sessions. Specific behavioral techniques included the use of daily food diaries for self-monitoring, an examination of behavioral chains associated with binge-eating, goal and priority setting, and the development of "specific behavioral interventions" that were not described in detail. Insight-oriented discussion centered on self-awareness and the acceptance of responsibility of one's behavior, the need for approval, the use of food as an irresponsible escape, and conflictual relationships with others. Within 10 weeks, the 11 patients all reported improvement in their bulimic symptoms, although only 3 were binge-free. In follow-up at 9 months to 1 year, 7 patients rated themselves as improved since terminating the group. At that time, 5 patients were no longer binge-eating.

Responses on a battery of psychological instruments obtained before and after treatment were compared with the responses of two control groups, one consisting of bulimic women who received no treatment and one of individual bulimic patients in psychotherapy. The authors concluded that group therapy appeared to be superior to individual psychotherapy alone; however, patients were not randomized between groups, and the high dropout rate makes interpretation of the data difficult.

Lacey[5,8] recently reported a short-term outpatient treatment program for patients with bulimia nervosa, a diagnostic group described by Russell[1] that has much clinical overlap with the DSM-III category of bulimia. The program sessions involved one-half day per week for 10 consecutive weeks, each session being conducted by two therapists. Patients in each group attended half-hour individual sessions with one therapist before meeting together as a group with both therapists for 1.5 hours. Subjects kept dietary diaries. Lacey stressed that the cardinal features of the program were contracting to maintain a stable weight, the prescription of a proper diet, and use of supportive yet insight-oriented psychotherapy, which was not described in detail. Of the 30 women who started the treatment program, all had improved eating behavior and 24 had stopped binge-eating and vomiting by the end of treatment. At follow-up, 20 patients had no bulimic or vomiting symptoms, 8 had occasional bulimic episodes, 1 refused follow-up clinic, and 1 was hospitalized shortly after treatment ended. The author stressed that the program was brief, effective, and cost-effective and that it offered the advantage that it could be conducted by paramedical staff under medical supervision.

Johnson, Connors, and Stuckey[9] have also described a short-term outpatient group program for the treatment of bulimia. The group program consisted of 12 two-hour sessions over a 9-week period. The program was held twice a week during the first 3 weeks to intensify the experience. The program was divided into three phases: the first focused on self-monitoring and presentation of information; the second on goal contracting; and the third on assertiveness, relaxation techniques, and alternative coping strategies. Preliminary results indicated that the program was effective in improving attitudes and changing eating behavior in a series of 10 patients.

Our group at the University of Minnesota has also developed an outpatient group treatment program for bulimia that will be described in detail later in this chapter.

Individual Psychotherapy Techniques

Most of the reports of individual psychotherapy with bulimic patients have centered on individual case reports or on a small series of cases. An exception has been the work reported by Fairburn concerning his use of a cognitive behavioral approach to the treatment of bulimia.[2] In 1981, he described an outpatient approach in which he worked with 11 women. This group represented fairly impaired patients who had been binge-eating and self-inducing vomiting for a mean duration of 3.9 years. The mean frequency of vomiting behavior in this group was 3 times daily with a range of 1 to 20 times per day.

The treatment was conducted on an outpatient basis and was divided into two parts. During the first part, the patients were seen frequently, usually 2 or 3 times a week, to interrupt the habitual nature of the overeating and vomiting. During this part of treatment, education about bulimia, self-monitoring of eating behavior, the development of alternative behaviors, and goal-setting were all employed. Once patients mastered self-monitoring, the patients were instructed to eat only at conventional mealtimes and to engage in behaviors incompatible with binge-eating at other times. An attempt was also made to involve the patient's friends and relatives. Fairburn suggested that interviewing family and friends at this point in treatment served to bring the problem into the open and to help establish an optimal environment for the patient by explaining the treatment to others. This phase rarely continued beyond 8 weeks. In the second part of therapy, the therapist attempted to help the patient to develop better coping skills, to use problem-solving techniques, and to examine irrational concerns. The strategy of exposure was used to teach patients not to fear certain foods or situations that previously had been associated with binge-eating.

Of the 11 patients, 9 reduced their frequency of overeating and vomiting to less than once a month. At 12-month follow-up, data were available on only 6 patients. One patient had failed to benefit at follow-up, 1 was abstinent, and 4 binge-ate and vomited very infrequently.

Other recent published literature has focused on descriptions of individualized treatment for individual cases. Long and Cordle[10] described in detail the treatment of 2 patients with binge-eating and self-induced vomiting episodes. One subject was treated with a total of 48 one-hour sessions over a 10-month period and the other for 12 one-hour sessions over 3 months. Both patients were taught behavioral self-control measures that included self-monitoring of eating behavior, weekly goal-setting, relaxation training, and response delay. Dietary education was also used, as was cognitive restructuring. Both patients did quite well with the treatment.

Rosen and Leitenberg[11] described the case of a 21-year-old patient with bulimia nervosa who had been actively ill for 6 years. The patient was originally treated with supervised exposure and response prevention. This paradigm involved instructing her to eat an amount of food that would cause her to feel a strong urge to vomit; she was, however, not permitted to do so. During this initial phase, she was not instructed to avoid binge-eating and vomiting but was later instructed to schedule a gradual decrease in vomiting frequency. Only one episode of vomiting had occurred in 10 months of follow-up.

Grinc[12] treated a 26-year-old female who had been self-inducing vomiting for the previous 10 years. She was seen for a total of 20 visits over a 7-month period. She was taught self-monitoring and stimulus control (avoiding or limiting situations related to vomiting) techniques. The cognitive component of this treatment followed rational emotive therapy guidelines and attempted to examine her irrational beliefs about vomiting and eating behavior. At 1-year follow-up, the patient had not vomited in 5 months.

Mizes and Lohr[13] reported the treatment of a 26-year-old female bulimic who had a 3-year history of binge-eating and self-induced vomiting. She was treated for a total of 22 sessions. The authors initially used stimulus narrowing to establish appropriate stimulus control over proper nutritional habits; she was taught to momentarily reenforce herself for eating only during prescribed times. This did not seem to reduce the frequency of the bulimic symptoms. Self-controlled relaxation was then added, using an audiotape to induce relaxation as a coping response to the urge to binge, and was followed by an apparent reduction in the frequency of the binge-eating episodes. The authors suggested that the use of this combined therapy—stimulus narrowing, self-reinforcement, and self-control relaxation—might be useful in the treatment of bulimia.

Additional individual psychotherapeutic approaches have also followed psychodynamic lines, as examined in chapter 4.

Overview of Techniques

This section summarizes some of the specific strategies that have been used to treat bulimia. Many have been referred to in the literature review above, and most have been used by more than one author. Many of the behavioral techniques that have been used represent modifications of techniques designed for the treatment of other types of eating problems, such as obesity.[14-17] Specific techniques include the following:

1) Patient education. Several authors have commented on the need to educate patients about the nature and possible complications of the

disorder.[3,5,9,11] When explicitly mentioned as a technique, this is suggested as an early component in the treatment. Education about bulimia gives the patient a sense that something is known about their problem, that is not uncommon, and that treatment methods exist. Although patients need to be made aware of the medical consequences of the behavior, fear of such complications rarely forces patients to quit.

2) Self-monitoring techniques. Several authors have suggested the utility of self-monitoring as a way to increase the patient's awareness of their eating behavior, as well as to gather baseline data to evaluate subsequent change.[2-4,6,9-12] A variety of techniques have been used, ranging from food diaries to special instruments designed to measure abnormal eating-related behaviors.[18]

3) Contracting and goal-setting. Several authors use these techniques as part of therapy.[2,5,6,9,10] This can involve group or individual contracting to meet certain target changes, such as reduction of frequency of binge-eating or vomiting or maintenance of weight within a certain range.

4) Examination of behavioral antecedents. Binge-eating and vomiting episodes clearly become associated with certain cues. The types of behavioral antecedents include situational factors (coming home from work, driving by a grocery store), social factors (not having a date, argument with mother), emotional factors (anger, boredom), cognitive factors (feeling fat), and physiological factors (hunger, feeling tired). Several authors[2,3,12] have found it quite useful to examine these behavioral antecedents in depth so that patients realize which cues serve to trigger binge-eating or vomiting and can learn to avoid those situations or foods.

5) Manipulation of behavioral antecedents. These techniques follow logically from those discussed under item 4. In addition to restructuring one's environment to avoid certain antecedents, response delay[10,19] has been suggested as a management technique. For example, patients may be allowed or encouraged to binge-eat to a point where they would normally vomit and then to suppress this urge and not to vomit.

6) Use of alternative or competing behaviors. It has been well-recognized clinically that patients with bulimia can often avoid a binge-eating episode if they have competing activities scheduled or if they can shift to an alternative behavior when they feel the desire to binge-eat. For some patients, the urge to binge-eat will pass if they walk around the block or straighten the living room. Many find that they can prevent the development of the urge if they plan to be busy with friends rather than stay home alone. This approach is specifically incorporated into some treatment approaches.[2,3]

7) Manipulation of the consequences of behavior. Patients can learn to reinforce adaptive eating behavior in a variety of ways, including the

use of cognitive, monetary, or social rewards.[3] They can learn to praise themselves for not binge-eating and to plan special activities that are particularly reenforcing as a reward.

8) Adaptive skills. Many therapists have noted that teaching patients more adaptive life skills seems to improve their bulimia. Specific skills or techniques includes assertiveness training,[4,6,7,9] behavioral problem solving,[2] relaxation training,[7,9,13] role playing,[6] and guided fantasy.[4]

9) Cognitive restructuring. In many treatment programs, considerable effort is devoted to examining the ideas and beliefs of patients about their body, their sense of self-worth, and their relationships with others. Also important is the meaning of food in their life. Do they use food to avoid unpleasant or anxiety-provoking situations? Do they binge-eat to deal with strong emotions? Different authors may focus on different techniques or theoretical models; however, most workers in the field agree that some kind of attempt at cognitive restructuring is necessary for therapy to be successful.[2,3,7,10,12]

Intensive Treatment Program

We turn now to a discussion of the Intensive Treatment Program at the University of Minnesota. This program, which has been in operation for about 3 years, will serve as an example of programs specifically designed to treat patients with bulimia on an outpatient basis. The design of the program reflects certain biases as to treatment approach, and these biases naturally reflect the backgrounds of the staff members involved—psychiatrists, a psychologist, a social worker, a chemical dependency counselor, and a psychiatric nurse. Although all of these disciplines have been influential in the program, two major influences can be discerned.

The first is the drug abuse treatment model that is widely used in our region and that is based on an Alcoholics Anonymous mode.[20] In this model, bulimia is seen as an addictive behavior that is analogous in some ways to drug abuse. The insistence upon abstinence from bulimic behavior while in treatment, the time-intensive structure of the program, the focus on the behavior, and the use of group pressure to reinforce abstinence from bulimia are all compatible with this model, underscoring the similarities between chemical abuse problems and bulimia.[21] The other major theoretical influence has been behavioral psychology, both operant and cognitive. It has been our experience that bulimic behavior can be very conveniently viewed from such a perspective, and many of the behavioral techniques that were described previously in this chapter have been incorporated in the intensive program.

General Structure of the Program

The program is 2 months long, with about 10 patients in each treatment group. All sessions are held in the evening between 5:00 and 8:00 p.m. Patients are thus occupied in clinic activities during the time when they are most likely to binge-eat and self-induce vomiting.[22]

The structure of the program is outlined in figure 8. During the first week, patients are seen Monday through Friday for a period of 3 hours each night. As the program progresses, the duration and frequency of each clinic visit decreases; during the entire second month, patients are seen twice a week for 1.5 hours during each visit. Patients are also seen for individual sessions before beginning the treatment, at the end of the first month, and at the end of treatment. During the individual sessions, an

---

First Week: Monday-Friday—five sessions

Monday-Thursday	Lecture and discussion
	Dinner and informal discussion
	Group therapy and assignments
Friday	Dinner
	Support group
	Group therapy and assignments

Second Week: Monday, Tuesday, Thursday, Friday—four sessions

Monday, Tuesday, Thursday	Lecture and discussion
	Dinner and informal discussion
	Group therapy and assignments
Friday	Dinner
	Support groups
	Group therapy and assignments

Third Week: Monday, Wednesday, Friday—three sessions

Monday, Wednesday	Lecture and discussion
	Dinner and informal discussion
	Group therapy and assignments
Friday	Support group

Fourth Week: Monday, Wednesday, Friday—three sessions

Monday	Group therapy
Wednesday	Group therapy
Friday	Support group

Fifth to Eighth Weeks: Tuesdays and Fridays—two sessions

| Tuesdays | Group therapy |
| Fridays | Support group |

Figure 8. Schedule for Bulimia Intensive Program

effort is made to evaluate the progress of the patient in the program and to determine what aftercare needs will exist.

There are three parts to each evening's activities. During the first segment, the patients spend 45 minutes listening to a lecture on a topic related to bulimia and then discuss the lecture. The group then eats together with one of the staff members in a separate hospital dining room. The last segment of the evening is devoted to 1.5 hours of group psychotherapy. The group discusses the lecture material and reviews homework assignments, if any. The staff for the program, which consists of nine members representing a variety of disciplines, meets weekly as a group. At these meetings, the program is discussed in general and the progress of each intensive group is reviewed.

Specific Components of the Program

Focus on Eating Behavior

Abstinence from binge-eating, self-induced vomiting, and laxative abuse is expected from the time of the initial session. The patients are informed of this expectation before beginning the program.

The program focuses on eating behavior throughout. Patients are informed early in the program that they will need to maintain a stable weight if they plan to stabilize their eating pattern. If they desire weight change, they are instructed to wait until after their eating pattern has stabilized, at least until after the end of the intensive program. There is a strong emphasis on eating three balanced meals a day that are planned in advance using specified meal-planning techniques. Patients are told that they should eat the foods on their meal plan rather than responding to either internal or external cues.

Beginning the first night of the program, patients are instructed in meal planning and a simple dietary exchange system such as those used by many nutritionists for patients with diabetes mellitus. Adequate caloric intake is stressed. The patients are given a caloric level that is calculated for ideal body weight maintenance. They are also informed that any significant fluctuations in their weight, particularly any significant weight loss, may be grounds for termination from the group. The patients are weighed twice monthly while in the program. They are instructed to avoid foods that have triggered binge-eating episodes in the past. However, they are strongly encouraged to eat foods from all food groups and to have a balanced menu despite their fears of certain foods.

As part of each evening's activities, the group eats in a cafeteria setting with one of the therapists. At this time the discussion from the lecture may be continued, and the foods selected by each patient may be reviewed and discussed. This is also used as a time for socialization.

As the program progresses, the focus on eating behavior continues. There is a shift, however, away from the more concrete aspects of eating (meal planning, dietary exchange) to a discussion about attitudes concerning weight, healthy eating habits, and body image.

Most patients who begin the program are very concerned about their weight and insist that they will gain weight if they start to eat regular meals; most have been eating irregularly when not binge-eating. The usual approach to the program is to insist that patients eat three meals per day. In our experience, patients are usually quite successful in doing this.

Lecture and Discussion Topics

A series of eleven topics are covered by lecture and group discussion over the course of the program. These are coordinated with homework assignments.

a) Introduction. The first night's lecture is devoted to a review of the literature on the bulimia syndrome and an outline of the treatment program. Patients are instructed on meal-planning techniques, rules for participation in the group are reviewed, and the need for regular prompt attendance is strongly reinforced.

b) Behavioral cues and chains. Behavioral antecedents associated with binge-eating and vomiting are reviewed. The discussion centers around awareness of these cues and the necessity for manipulating antecedents and finding substitute behaviors. The homework includes completion of printed forms that allow an examination of behavioral chains.[14] These forms, which patients use to diagram their activities during the day and their feelings associated with what transpires, allow patients to examine the antecedents that trigger binge-eating episodes. For example, patients may discover that they binge-eat in response to stressful situations or boredom. A cue may be an argument with one's spouse or the fear of being too heavy. Understanding such cues prepares patients to develop alternative responses.

c) Nutrition. The program nutritionist discusses good nutritional habits and reinforces meal-planning techniques and the use of the simple exchange system. The patients practice making meal plans as part of the session and continue these as a homework assignment.

d) Medical complications, depression, and other problems. During this lecture, the medical complications of bulimia—including gastric dilatation, dental problems, fluid and electrolyte abnormalities, and salivary gland problems—are reviewed. As outlined in chapter 2, depression is a common and frequently disabling associated finding in bulimic patients.

Drug abuse is also common in this group of patients, as might be predicted considering the similarity between bulimia and drug abuse. Patients with bulimia also frequently develop problems with stealing and lying. It is impossible to be bulimic and to be secretive about it unless you lie to friends and family about where you have been, why you can't go places, and why food is missing. Bulimia also becomes an expensive habit, similar to drug abuse, and many patients resort to stealing food.

e) Designing a plan of action. This lecture falls on the evening before the first weekend. Patients make detailed plans for the weekend that include meal plans, relaxation, exercise, and time to contact other group members.

f) Stress management. The role of stress in bulimic behaviors is discussed, a stress inventory is completed, and stress management techniques using relaxation and regular exercise are reviewed. Homework involves the assignment to develop a plan of stress management and exercise.

g) Assertiveness training. Patients with bulimia frequently have problems with assertiveness. A simple assertiveness model and definition of terms associated with assertiveness are reviewed. Specific problems covered include the ability to accept apologies, give and accept compliments, give and receive criticisms, and say "no" rather than feel that they have to do what others want. Patients are given a book on assertiveness as homework.[23]

h) Family systems. Group members discuss specific problems in their families that have tended to perpetuate their eating disorder. This frequently involves issues of responsibility. Are the patient or the parents responsible for the patient's eating behavior? Are problems discussed in the family? Are family members given support? Are family members allowed enough autonomy?

i) Self-help groups. Available support groups in the community are discussed. As homework, each patient sets up a plan for follow-up in the community after discharge from the group. Patients are encouraged to begin such groups prior to completing the intensive program.

j) Cognitive restructuring. Patients are given a basic introduction to rational emotive theory and cognitive behavioral techniques. Cognitions concerning eating behavior and body weight are examined as possible examples of irrational ideas. Do they see themselves as too heavy? Can they eat regular meals and still not get fat? Homework involves the completion of work sheets that encourage patients to examine their own beliefs about food and weight.

k) Relapse prevention. Available information about the longitudinal course of bulimia is reviewed. Each patient is asked to compose a written plan for avoiding relapse after completing the program, as well as a plan to handle "slips." What techniques will they continue to use after leaving the program, and for how long? Will they continue to make meal plans and to avoid binge foods? Who will they call if they have a "slip"?

Group Therapy

The last 1.5 hours of each evening's activities are devoted to group therapy, where the focus on eating behavior is maintained. The therapist attempts to direct attention to patients who are doing well in the program, not to reinforce bulimic behaviors by spending a large amount of group time on members who are having more difficulty. Lengthy discussions of breaches of abstinence are discouraged. The last 20 minutes of each group session is devoted to meal planning.

Family and Friends

Two evening sessions for family or interested friends are conducted by clinic staff during the 2 months of the program. During the first session, family members and friends are provided with information about bulimia and the treatment program and are encouraged to ask questions; patients themselves are not present. The second meeting includes families, friends, and patients in a large group. Discussion centers around relationship issues. Are there patterns in the family that prevent the patient from taking responsibility? Are parents overprotective? Has the identified patient been irresponsible? The usual outcome of these sessions is that family and friends leave with the understanding that the responsibility for change must remain with the patient.

Other Aspects of the Program

In addition to the group experience, patients are encouraged to contact each other outside of the group and to see each other socially, particularly when grocery shopping and eating. We require members to contact at least two other group members during any 24-hour period. This fosters a sense of cohesiveness in the groups, and by completion of the program some of the groups are quite socially active as a unit.

There is a significant risk of chemical abuse problems in patients with bulimia.[24,25] Patients who have active problems with alcohol or other drug abuse are not accepted in the intensive program unless they have been abstinent from those problems for several months and are continuing in aftercare. As a general rule, patients are instructed that they should not drink alcohol or use other drugs of abuse while they are in the intensive program. In our experience, some patients increased their drug usage when they became abstinent from bulimia. Other patients seemed to binge-eat in response to the disinhibition of alcohol.

Patients are informed at the onset of the program that their course will be reviewed on a weekly basis by the treatment staff. Those who remain uncooperative—failing to complete homework assignments, consistently late or missing sessions—or failing to achieve any kind of control over their bulimic behavior may be asked to leave the program. About 1 out of every 20 patients who enters the program is asked to leave before finishing. Patients who are terminated prior to completion are usually offered hospitalization as an alternative.

Patients who have been abstinent for a period of at least 3 months can serve as volunteers for the program. By utilizing recovering bulimics as volunteers, we are able to expose patients to good role models for recovery. One or two volunteers are permitted to attend the groups in the intensive program, to participate in family groups, and to serve as speakers at a general outpatient support group held on Friday evenings in the clinic. If questions come up as to the value of certain parts of the program, such as the making of meal plans or the eating of three meals a day, volunteer's endorsement can be a very powerful influence in getting other patients to accept such tasks. Volunteers may also serve as "food sponsors." Outpatients assigned to sponsors may call them during the evening to review their meal plans. At that time, the volunteer will offer suggestions and encouragement to the patient.

Outcome

Although long-term follow-up results of this program are not yet available, we have some information about the success of the program on a short-term basis. A survey of 104 patients who completed the intensive program in its present form revealed that 47% were completely abstinent throughout the program, 25% reported between one and three "slips" of vomiting during the program, and 11% reported four or more slips. Overall, these patients represented 83% of those who started the program, and most were regarded as successful completers. Eleven percent dropped out before the end of the second month of treatment. Most of these were assumed to be actively bulimic at termination; however a few left early for unrelated reasons. Six percent were asked to leave for reasons of noncompliance. Though the short-term outcome results are encouraging, long-term data are not yet available.

The focus of the program remains on eating behavior, but patients who have completed this program frequently demonstrated marked decrease in depressive symptomatology, improved relationships, and improved self-esteem. Studies are under way to evaluate these changes objectively.

Conclusions

As this review has demonstrated, the literature on the treatment of bulimia is quite limited; however, a few basic principles can be extracted. The first and perhaps the most important principle is that the bulimic behavior must be addressed as a specific problem. The second principle is that a healthy eating pattern must be established. Third, the responsibility for change and control of eating must at some point reside with the patient, even if this responsibility is temporarily taken away during hospitalization. The fourth principle, not often cited in the literature but nonetheless important, concerns the possibility of relapse. In our experience, many patients are able to control bulimia temporarily but later may slip back into the behavior. It would seem logical that any treatment program for bulimia should address the possibility of relapse.

Addressing the Behavior

The primary goal of all the treatments reviewed has been to interrupt the binge-eating, vomiting, laxative abuse, and fasting pattern, and the behavioral approaches described seem to be the most popular methods to achieve this goal. Many patients have been demoralized by their failure to stop the bulimic behavior. By attempting to build a period of successful abstinence into the treatment plan, the therapist encourages a sense of hope and personal power in the patient.

Although focusing on either psychodynamic or relationship issues may in some cases lead to an attenuation of or abstinence from bulimic behaviors, experience has shown that such an outcome is the exception rather than the rule. In most patients, the behavior must be considered a problem to be directly addressed.

Establishment of Healthy Eating Patterns

Patients with bulimia eat abnormally when they are not binge-eating as well as when they are binge-eating. Many fast for protracted periods or demonstrate other abnormal eating habits, such as having odd food preferences and never eating with others. It cannot be assumed that patients with bulimia will return to or develop healthy eating patterns simply by interrupting the binge-eating, vomiting, and laxative abuse cycle. For example, many patients fast when they are first abstinent in an effort to avoid triggering a binge-eating episode. Fasting, of course, may predispose to further binge-eating. For this reason, it is of utmost importance that patients understand and develop appropriate eating behaviors. The avoidance of foods that are known to trigger binge-eating episodes, particularly early in the treatment, may also prove a useful tool.

Responsibility for Change

The third important principle is the concept that at some point, either throughout treatment or by the end of treatment, patients must assume responsibility for their own eating behavior. "Enhance the patient's self-control" is a phrase used by Fairburn in his discussion of bulimic treatment. Patients feel loss of control over their eating as the principal problem, and they are eager to increase their sense of self-control. It is the therapist's role to assist patients in uncovering their own abilities and resources in this area.

Relapse Prevention

Very little data is available regarding the longitudinal course of bulimia or the outcome of bulimia treatment, but our impression has been that relapse is a major problem among bulimics following treatment. For this reason, some training in relapse prevention should be implemented as part of any treatment plan. Behavioral techniques that have been useful in achieving abstinence may be assumed to be useful in preventing relapse. Maintaining contact with support groups, continuing to make meal plans, and continuing to eat regularly planned meals may all be quite helpful in this regard.

Role of Medication and Psychotherapy

Antidepressant drugs have been shown to be quite effective in improving the eating behavior and mood of bulimic patients (see chap. 6); however, the long-term outcome of drug treatment has not been assessed. Investigators have also not determined whether the efficacy of the drugs is improved when used in combination with psychotherapy. These are important questions for future research.

The outlook for bulimia treatment appears to be quite positive at this time, with many vigorous and innovative researchers focusing their attention on the problem. Behavioral techniques seem to be of considerable value. Patients with bulimia are usually eager to cooperate with treatment and to enhance their own sense of self-control. Antidepressants also are of benefit for many patients. Further research is needed to evaluate and compare the various treatment techniques suggested and to correlate subtypes of bulimia with particular treatment responses.

REFERENCES

1. Russell, G. 1979. Bulimia nervosa: An ominous variant of anorexia nervosa. *Psychol. Med.* 9:429.
2. Fairburn, C. 1981. A cognitive behavioral approach to the treatment of bulimia. *Psychol. Med.* 11:707.
3. Mitchell, J. E., D. Hatsukami, G. Goff, R. L. Pyle, E. D. Eckert, and L. E. Davis. In press. An intensive outpatient group treatment program for patients with bulimia. In *Treatment of anorexia nervosa and bulimia,* ed. D. Garner and P. Garfinkel.
4. Boskind-Lodahl, M., and W. C. White. 1978. The definition and treatment of bulimarexia in college women—a pilot study. *J. Am. Coll. Health Assoc.* 27:84.
5. Lacey, J. H. 1983. Bulimia nervosa, binge-eating, and psychogenic vomiting: A controlled treatment study and long-term outcome. *Br. Med. J.* 286:1609.
6. White, W. C., and M. Boskind-White. 1981. An experiential-behavioral approach to the treatment of bulimarexia. *Psychother. Theory Res. Practice* 18:501-7.
7. Dixon, K. N., and J. Kiecolt-Glaser. 1981. Group therapy for bulimia. Presented at the annual meeting of the American Psychiatric Association, New Orleans, 15 May.
8. Lacey, J. H. 1983. An outpatient treatment program for bulimia nervosa. *Int. J. Eating Disorders* 2:209-14.
9. Johnson, C., M. Connors, and M. Stuckey. 1983. Short-term group treatment of bulimia: A preliminary report. *Int. J. Eating Disorders* 2:199-208.
10. Long, C. G., and C. J. Cordle. 1982. Psychological treatment of binge-eating and self-induced vomiting. *J. Med. Psychol.* 55:139.
11. Rosen, J. C., and H. Leitenberg. 1982. Bulimia nervosa: Treatment with exposure and response prevention. *Behav. Ther.* 13:117-24.
12. Grinc, G. A. 1982. A cognitive-behavioral model for the treatment of chronic vomiting. *J. Behav. Med.* 5:135.
13. Mizes, J. S., and S. M. Lohr. 1983. The treatment of bulimia (binge-eating and self-induced vomiting). *Int. J. Eating Disorders* 2:59.
14. Ferguson, O. M. 1976. *Habits not diets.* Palo Alto, Calif.: Bull Publishing Company.
15. Jeffrey, D. B., and R. C. Katz. 1977. *Take it off and keep it off.* Englewood Cliffs, N.J.: Prentice Hall.
16. Smith, G. R. 1981. Modification of binge-eating and obesity. *J. Behav. Ther. Exp. Psychiatry* 12:333-36.
17. Stuart, R. B., and B. Davis. 1972. *Slim chance in a fat world.* Champaign, Ill.: Research Press.
18. Mitchell, J. E., R. L. Pyle, and E. D. Eckert. 1981. Frequency and duration of binge-eating episodes in patients with bulimia. *Am. J. Psychiatry* 138:835.
19. Welsh, G. J. 1979. Treatment of compulsive vomiting and obsessive thoughts through graduated response delay, response prevention and cognitive correction. *J. Behav. Ther. Exp. Psychiatry* 10:77.
20. Johnson, V. E. 1973. *I'll quit tomorrow.* New York: Harper and Row.
21. Hatsukami, D., P. Owen, R. Pyle, and J. Mitchell. 1982. Similarities and differences on the MMPI between women with bulimia and with alcohol or drug abuse problems. *Addictive Behav.* 7:435.
22. Johnson, C. L., M. K. Stuckey, L. D. Lewis, and D. M. Schwartz. 1982. Bulimia: A descriptive survey of 316 cases. *Int. J. Eating Disorders* 2:3.
23. Alberti, R., and M. Emmans. 1978. *Your perfect right.* San Luis Obispo, Calif.: Impact Publishers.
24. Pyle, R. L., J. E. Mitchell, and E. D. Eckert. 1981. Bulimia: A report of 34 cases. *J. Clin. Psychiatry* 42:60.

25. Mitchell, J. E., and R. L. Pyle. 1982. The bulimic syndrome in normal weight individuals: A review. *Int. J. Eating Disorders* 2:61.

Part 3

Research Report

9

Adolescent Behaviors and Attitudes toward Weight and Eating

John T. Kelly, M.D., M.P.H. and Sonia E. Patten, M.S.

Americans have created a society that is not only food sufficient but has a greater array of food choices than ever existed before. Problems of undernourishment result largely from unequal distribution of income and from inadequate or inappropriate information about nutritional needs, rather than from problems of production or distribution of food. In the midst of this bounty there exists a cultural ideal for body shape that emphasizes extreme slenderness, especially for females. This contradiction between our society's capacity to produce an overabundance of food and our cultural ideal of slimness, which requires adolescents and adults to strictly control food intake, is manifested by cultural and personal preoccupations with weight gain and loss. Self-control is exhibited by "keeping one's weight down," with the accompanying fear of loss of control over one's eating behavior. The cultural ideal is more stringently defined for females than for males, and thus the ensuing preoccupations seem to be more characteristic of females.

Several studies have examined these issues, Hueneman et al.[1,2] reported on a 4-year longitudinal and cross-sectional study conducted in the early 1960s of body size, shape, and composition of about 1,000 California teenagers. In a subsample of 200, a questionnaire was used to gather information regarding food preferences, conceptions and knowledge about food and eating, activity level, and feelings about the individual's own body conformation. Fifty percent of females identified themselves as obese, whereas only 25% were anthropometrically identified as obese. The male population, in contrast, did not overestimate its fatness. The main priority of females with regard to their body conformation was, at all ages, to lose weight through dieting rather than through a change in physical activity.

Dwyer et al.[3,4] examined attitudes toward weight and appearance in an adolescent population of 446 females and 145 males. They found high levels of dissatisfaction with weight, body contours, and appearance in the group as a whole. The nature of the dissatisfaction was, however, quite different for females than for males. Fully 80% of the females wanted to weigh less, although only 43% could be categorized as above average in fatness based on triceps measurements. Only males who were actually obese indicated that they wanted to lose weight. The majority of males expressed a preference for increases in height, weight, shoulder breadth, and upper arm and chest cage girth. Males and females both expressed a desire for smaller waists, hips, and buttocks. Examining dieting behavior in the females of the group, the authors concluded that by the time they reached 12th grade, a much higher number had tried reducing diets than could be objectively classified as needing weight reduction. Dieting behavior, then, was related to perception of being overweight as well as actually being overweight in females.

The impression of being overweight is apparently a pervasive one for female adolescents. It was identified by Nylander[5] as a predeterminant of a syndrome similar to, if not identical to, anorexia nervosa. In a study of 2,370 Swedish adolescents aged 14 through 19, most of the females reported that they had, at one time or another, felt themselves to be fat. A high proportion of these girls had attempted to diet, whereas the males rarely reported dieting. Five percent of the entire sample (107 females and 12 males) reported experiencing at least three of the following symptoms while dieting: anxiety, depression, chilling, constipation, amenorrhea, mental lassitude, and a drop in school performance. Fifteen of the females had lost 10 kg or more, and 8 had been treated at a child psychiatry clinic for anorexia nervosa.

Shontz[6] has concluded that males and females arrive at an assessment of their own bodies in different ways, with females assessing their bodies on a part-by-part basis and males making whole-body assessments. Schilder[7] has suggested that distorted assessments of body conformation are associated with the areas of focused attention. Wingate and Christie[8] reported that nonpatient schoolgirls (mean age of 17.4 years) with low ego strength as measured by the Es scale of the MMPI consistently overestimated the width of their shoulders, waist, and hips when compared with a control group consisting of schoolgirls similar in age and body conformation but with normal Es. There were no significant differences in the overestimations of shoulder and hips given by the low Es schoolgirls and a group of hospitalized females with diagnosed anorexia nervosa (mean age of 20.8 years). However, the overestimation by the anorectics of waist width was significantly greater than that of the schoolgirls with low Es.

The positive value placed on thinness is internalized at an early age in American society.[9-11] This has implications for the health of both adolescent and adult females because the health of adolescent females correlates highly with their health in adulthood.[12] Early teenage personality traits are related to adult health; those teenagers who have good feelings about themselves are under less stress than their peers who have a negative self-image, and this is correlated with good health in adulthood. If adolescent females have learned that they can feel good about themselves only when they are thin, and if a high proportion feel they are not thin enough— with 10-15% developing serious eating disorders as a consequence of distorted efforts to achieve the societal goal—then this places at risk the adolescent and adult health of a substantial proportion of the population.

The research project reported in this chapter was undertaken with the following objectives: to assess the magnitude of adolescent involvement in the high cultural value assigned to slenderness; to discern differences in this involvement that may exist between male and female adolescents; and to collect and analyze date on weight-associated behaviors, attitudes toward food, food preparation and eating, social circumstances under which eating occurs, and attitudes toward one's own physical appearance. There was also an underlying research interest in the behaviors and attitudes of adolescents that might predispose them to the disorders of anorexia nervosa and bulimia.

Methods

The present research consisted of a survey by questionnaire of adolescents attending surburban high schools in a single metropolitan area. This was the most effective way, in terms of cost, of securing a large amount of pertinent information from a large number of individuals.

A 78-item questionnaire was developed to collect information about behaviors and attitudes associated with weight, eating, and food, as well as the individual's attitudes toward his or her own physical appearance. The items were developed from a survey of the clinical and epidemiological literature, personal clinical experience, and from the diagnostic criteria for anorexia nervosa and bulimia that appear in DSM-III.[13] The questionnaire was pretested and required an average time for completion of about 30 minutes.

The questionnaire was administered in 12 surburban high schools. Health and physical education classes with the highest enrollments of 15- and 16-year-olds were chosen for administration of the questionnaire. Because these courses were required, they approximated a representative sample of this age group. Subjects were concentrated in the 15- and 16-year age bracket because it appears to be the lower limit of heightened risk for anorexia nervosa.[14]

The total sample size was 2,276 surburban students between the ages of 13 and 18, including 1,298 females and 968 males. Breakdown by age is presented in table 16. The surburban population represented in the study has low minority representation. Property values in the surburbs where their schools are located, when compared with other parts of the metropolitan area, indicate that the socioeconomic status of the population is middle to upper middle class. The results, therefore, cannot be generalized beyond a white, relatively affluent, surburban population concentrated in the 15- to 16-year age group.

Table 16. Age of Subjects

Age	Number	Percentage of Total
13	11	.5%
14	350	16.0
15	1,089	48.0
16	667	30.0
17	102	4.5
18	31	1.0

Results

Students were asked to indicate their height, weight, and what they considered their ideal weight. A standard weight table for height and age[15] was used to convert these weights to percentages of standard. Differences betweeen percentage of standared for indicated weight and percentage of standard for ideal weight were used to ascertain the dissatisfaction or satisfaction with indicated body weight.

A total of 1,929 students responded to all questions about weight, height, age, and ideal weight. Of these, 85.2% fell between the 85th and 114th percent of standard weight for height and age, 9.8 percent were above 114, and 4.8 were below 85% of standard. With the exception of 4 males and 3 females who were satisfied with their weight, all others who fell below 85% of standard wanted to gain weight. Of those who weighed over 114 percent of standard, 1 male and 2 females wanted to weigh still more, 1 male was satisfied with his weight, and all others wanted to lose.

Concern about Weight

Table 17 sumarizes the weight preferences of that 85.2% of students whose indicated weights were between the 85th and 114th percent of standard. Table 18 displays the weight preference categories of each sex by percentage. These data indicate that American adolescents, both male and fe-

Table 17. Weight Preference Categories by Weight Categories and Sex

Weight as Percentage of Standard	Want to Weigh Less		Satisfied with Weight		Want to Weigh More	
	Females	Males	Females	Males	Females	Males
85-94%	4.7%	3.3%	38.1%	32.6%	57.2%	64.1%
95-104	43.0	38.5	37.2	41.7	19.8	19.8
105-114	79.3	75.0	15.7	17.6	5.0	7.4

male, continue to experience a high level of dissatisfaction with their weight. Representation of males and females with each weight preference category is not markedly different. When the categories "want to weigh more" and "want to weigh less" are added together, it is apparent that 71% of young women and young men believe that their ideal weight is something other than their indicated weight. It is rather surprising that a higher percentage of males than females (44.4% and 38.6% respectively) would like to weigh less. Males, too, appear to be caught up in the cultural preoccupation with slenderness in the United States. The context in which the preoccupation is expressed differs for males and females, however. A factor analysis of these data[16] reveals something of the contexual difference. A .001 correlation emerged between female study participants and a concern about being or becoming overweight in the absence of indicated overweight. The young women in the sample diet to lose weight, like to lose weight, and like to be thin. They feel an increased need for exercise after eating and anger after overeating. Individuals in this group weighed themselves once or more daily and ate at the end of the day. They viewed themselves as less attractive than most other people.

The second most important factor was a correlation, at the .001 level, between being male and having a high level of participation in sports and exercise and a view of oneself as more active than one's associates. This high activity level was not correlated with an expressed need for exercise after eating. For adolescent males, then, a desire to weigh less than one's indicated weight seems to exist in the absence of drastic measures to modify weight. Behaviors such as exercising or controlling food intake do not seem to represent the more generalized preoccupation with weight or eating that characterizes adolescent females.

Table 18. Weight Preference Categories by Sex

	Females	Males
Want to weigh less	38.6%	44.4%
Satisfied with weight	29.0	29.0
Want to weigh more	32.4	26.6

Figure 9 displays the difference that exists between adolescent males and females in the sample as to level of concern about being or becoming overweight. It illustrates the magnitude of adolescent female emotional involvement with the issue of weight. Although about 40% of the entire sample believed that, for them, thinner would be better, 69.3% of females and 20.7 of males experienced frequent or constant concern about overweight.

A forced-choice question dealing with self-assessment of overall physical attractiveness reinforced this picture of a preoccupation with weight on the part of adolescent females. For females, there was an inverse relationship at the .001 level between feeling attractive and percent weight according to standard. No female who fell above the category of 85 to 94% of standard reported that she felt more attractive than most other people. All such responses were concentrated in the category of 85 to 94% or below. For males, responses indicating that they felt more attractive than most other people were concentrated in the category of 95 to 114% of standard.

In sum, a high level of dissatisfaction with indicated body weight among both adolescent females and males was identified. Comparable percentages of each sex wanted to gain or lose; only about 30% of the sample expressed satisfaction with body weight. Females were much more likely than males to experience worry or concern about overweight and to relate self-attractiveness to slenderness.

Behaviors, Attitudes, and Context

Since this adolescent population displayed such a high level of discontent with body weight, we will also present data that describe a number of behaviors, attitudes, and situations involving food and eating. Within each of these general categories we will report the differences between male and female responses on each variable. Finally, a number of variables will be discussed that are significantly related to weight and height as percentages of standard.

Behaviors Related to Food Intake and Modification of Weight

The students were asked to indicate if they were either dieting to gain weight or dieting to lose weight at the time they filled out the questionnaire. A significant difference between sexes emerged in the responses to both questions about attempts to modify and control food intake in order to change body weight.

Changing or attempting to change food intake as a strategy for losing weight was significantly related to being female. Male adolescents, on the other hand, were significantly more likely to attempt such changes in order

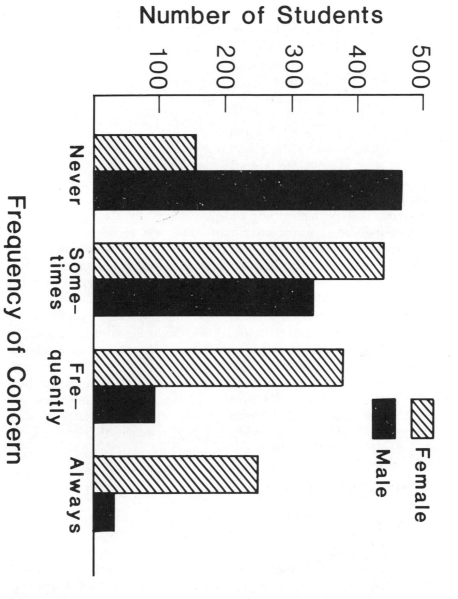

Figure 9. Concern about being or becoming overweight

to gain weight (see table 19). This is a particularly impressive difference in view of the finding, previously mentioned, that 44.4% of the males wanted to lose weight. They were obviously not trying to decrease body weight through controlling intake, nor did they relate physical exercise to an expressed desire to weigh less. This would seem to indicate that a substantially larger proportion of adolescent females than males respond behaviorally to an expressed desire to decrease body weight.

Females were much more likely than males to acknowledge engaging in what might be called cognitive behavioral attempts to monitor their own efforts to modify body weight; they weighed themselves more frequently, were more likely to keep count of the calories they consumed, and more often reviewed the day's food intake at the end of the day or before going to sleep at night (see tables 19 and 20).

A certain percentage of adolescents acknowledged engaging in behaviors aimed at weight control or modification that are potentially more damaging, both physiologically and psychologically, than sporadic dieting. Self-induced vomiting and use of laxatives in response to what was self-defined as "overeating" characterized under 5% of both males and females. There was no significant differences between the sexes in involvement in either of these extreme approaches to dealing with problematic food intake (table 19).

Most students who vomited after overeating induced the vomiting. We know only that the immediate stimulus for inducing vomiting and using laxatives was a feeling of having overeaten. We can speculate that for some males, attempting to make a weight category for competitive wrestling or gymnastics may function as a more general stimulus for these behaviors. For some females, involvement in ballet or gymnastics may function in a similar manner. However, since adolescent females are more heavily involved than males in dieting to lose weight, they may also be more likely than males to induce vomiting or use laxatives to lose weight in the absence of any motive other than the weight loss itself.

Attitudes Related to Food Intake and Modification of Weight

Adolescent males and females invested significantly different levels of feeling or emotion in eating and weight. We have displayed the magnitude of the differences between the sexes in their expressed concern about being or becoming overweight (fig. 9). There were similar differences in endorsements of the items "I enjoy losing weight" and "I would like to be very thin"; females were also much more likely to experience anger as a result of overeating and to direct that anger toward themselves (table 21).

Table 19. Questions and Responses about Efforts to Control Weight

Question	Yes	No
Are you now dieting to lose weight?		
Female	48.1%	51.9%
Male	8.4	91.6
(phi = .42413; df = 1; $p < .0000$)		
Are you now dieting to gain weight?		
Female	3.0	97.0
Male	30.4	69.6
(phi = .38209; df = 1; $p < .0000$)		
Do you know how many calories you eat in a day?		
Female	10.2	89.8
Male	1.0	99.9
(phi = .23090; df = 1; $p < .0000$)		
Do you mentally review food intake at the end of the day?		
Female	31.5	68.5
Male	9.2	90.8
(phi = .26360; df = 1; $p < .0000$)		
Do you often vomit after eating too much?		
Female	4.0	96.0
Male	3.1	96.9
(phi = .02342; df = 1; $p < .05$)		
Do you often induce vomiting after eating too much?		
Female	2.8	97.2
Male	2.2	97.8
(phi = .01856; df = 1; $p < .05$)		
Do you often take laxatives after eating too much?		
Female	2.6	97.4
Male	2.1	97.9
(phi = .01862; df = 1; $p < .05$)		

Table 20. Frequency of Weighing Oneself

	Once Every Few Months	Once a Month	More than Once a Month /Less than Once a Week	Once a Week	Every Day	More than Once a Day
Female	5.0%	13.0%	10.0%	41.4%	24.2%	6.4%
Male	10.1	40.2	26.9	15.8	6.0	1.0

Note: Cramer's V = .29542; df = 5; $p < .0000$.

Table 21. Questions and Responses about Weight and Self-Image

Questions	Yes	No
Do you enjoy losing weight?		
Female	67.8%	32.2%
Male	26.1	73.9
(phi = .41130; df = 1; p < .000)		
Would you like to be very thin?		
Female	59.2	40.8
Male	15.9	84.1
(phi = .43267; df = 1; p < .0000)		
Do you get angry with yourself after eating too much?		
Female	68.9	31.1
Male	21.4	78.6
(phi = .40432; df = 1; p < .0000)		

Context in Which Eating Takes Place

The social and psychological context is one of the most intriguing parts of our data. A series of questions was asked about mealtime in the family setting and whether family members ever attempt to exert power over one another by giving or holding back food. The results are summarized in table 22.

Table 22. Questions and Responses about Family Meals

Questions	Yes	No	Never	Sometimes	Often
Is food used in the context of power within the family?					
Female	32.8%	67.2%			
Male	23.9	71.1			
(phi = .04106; df = 1; p < .0580)					
Do your parents urge you to eat more?					
Female			53.5%	38.3%	8.2%
Male			60.0	33.0	7.0
(C = .06483; df = 2; p < .009)					

About three-quarters of the students indicated that they usually ate with members of their families, 13.7% regularly ate with friends, and 12.2% ate alone. When asked which of these social settings they preferred, 64.6% indicated a preference for eating with family members, 35.4% preferred to eat with friends, and no one preferred to eat alone. When asked to rate meals with family as generally pleasant, sometimes pleasant, or generally unpleasant, 28.1 endorsed the last two categories. These responses may explain in large part why fully 35.4% of the students would prefer to eat with friends rather than family.

The dynamics of family mealtimes were explored in a question about family members exerting power over one another by giving or refusing to give food. Surprisingly, almost one-third of the students indicated that food is used in this kind of power context in their families (table 22). No significant relationship was found between gender of the student and response to the question. However, when students were asked whether parents try to make them eat more than they feel they can, a relationship significant at the .01 level was found to exist between female gender and the frequent experience of being prodded to eat larger quantities of food (table 22). This relationship is a complex one, and varies depending on the weight for height of the female adolescent. A cross tabulation of gender, ratio of weight for height and age according to standard, and endorsements of possible responses to the question of parents urging the student to eat more indicated that the lower the weight ratio of an adolescent female, the more likely she was to be urged to consume more food ($C = .18866$; df $= 16$; p$<$ .0001). No such relationship pertains for males. Such urging is apparently a common response on the part of parents who see their daughters try to become or remain very thin. If their families use food to exercise power over family members, daughters, in turn, respond to such prodding by hiding food to make it appear as if they had eaten more (Cramer's V $= .23713$; df $= 5$; p$<$ .0000). From these data emerges the picture of a substantial proportion of females in which sharing a meal is unpleasant and includes power plays revolving around food, pressure tactics to modify food intake of family members, and efforts to obscure knowledge about food intake.

Developmental Concomitants of Weight for Height and Age

We have discussed the differing characteristics of adolescent male and female dissatisfaction with indicated body weight, the behaviors and attitudes that may be adopted, as well as the social context within which eating occurs. One's weight and associated feelings about appearance may relate to other significant areas in the adolescent years in ways that are very different for males and females.

When a standard weight table for height and age was used to convert indicated weights to percentage of standard, nine weight-ratio categories were created. These categories were then cross tabulated with a number of other variables. Responses to four of these variables are clearly related to both weight ratio and gender: marks in school, number of friends, participation in sports or exercise, and interest in dating. Relationships among weight ratio, gender, and each of the four variables are summarized in table 23.

Table 23. Developmental Concomitants of Weight for Height and Age

	Weight Ratio (Low to High)	
	Females	Males
Marks in school (A's to D's and F's)	C = .19498 df = 24 p < .0025	C = .13765 df = 24 Not significant
Number of friends (several to none)	C = .33543 df = 24 p < .0000	C = .16558 df = 24 Not significant
Participation in sports or exercise (less than to more than my companions)	C = .10960 df = 8 Not significant	C = .18194 df = 8 p < .0005
Interested in dating (yes, no)	C = .11407 df = 8 p < .0438	C = .06306 df = 8 Not significant

For females, there was a significant relationship between relatively low weight for height and age and the achievement of A's and B's rather than C's and below. For males, no such significant relationship between marks and weight ratio was found to exist.

Not only did females who had low weights for height and age achieve higher marks, but they also had more friends during the school year and were more interested in dating than girls in the higher weight categories. Thus, in three vital developmental areas—intellectual achievement, interpersonal relationships, and gender relationships—females in lower weight categories had more positive experiences than those in higher weight categories. No such correlations existed for males; their positive experiences in these areas were not related to weight.

A weight-related association did emerge for males with regard to participation in sports and exercise. Males in the higher weight categories were more likely to indicate participation at the same level or above the level of their companions.

Conclusion

The adolescents who participated in the research project described in this chapter exhibited a high level of concern, if not preoccupation, with body weight in relation to physical appearance. A large proportion (71%) of both males and females were not satisfied with their present body weight. Overwhelmingly, females indicated a level of concern or worry about the possibility of becoming overweight and an emotional involvement with this issue that could appropriately be characterized as a preoccupation. They responded behaviorally to this concern by dieting even in the absense of an objectively defined problem with weight. A small but significant proportion of both males and females resorted to drastic measures, such as self-induced vomiting and the use of laxatives, as a response to concern about overeating and overweight.

Clearly, slenderness of body, especially for adolescent females is associated with a complex of cultural meanings that move it out of the realm of health and well-being and into a much broader arena of self-concept, participation in developmentally significant activities, and the establishment of a sound psychological base from which to enter adult life. The enormous significance with which American society imbues physical appearance and slenderness form a cultural backdrop for the serious eating disorders that are increasing in incidence among adolescents and young adults.

REFERENCES

1. Hueneman, R. L., M. C. Hamptòn, A. R. Behnke, L. R. Shapiro, and B. W. Mitchell. 1974. *Teenage nutrition and physique.* Springfield, Ill.: Charles C Thomas.
2. Hueneman, R. L., L. R. Shapiro, M. C. Hampton, and B. W. Mitchell. 1966. A longitudinal study of gross body composition and body conformation and their association with food and activity in a teen-age population. *Am. J. Clin. Nutr.* 18:325-38.
3. Dwyer, J. T., J. J. Feldman, C. C. Seltzer, and J. Mayer. 1969. Adolescent attitudes toward weight and appearance. *J. Nutr. Ed.* 1:14-29.
4. Dwyer, J. T., J. J. Feldman, and J. Mayer. 1967. Adolescent dieters: Who are they? *Am. J. Clin. Nutr.* 20:1045-56.
5. Nylander, I. 1971. The feeling of being fat and dieting in a school population: Epidemiology interview investigation. *Acta Sociomed. Scand.* 3:17-26.
6. Shontz, F. C. 1963. Reanalysis of data from 'Some characteristics of body size estimation.' *Perc. Mot. Skills* 17:438-48.
7. Schilder, P. 1935. *The image and appearance of the human body.* London: Kegan-Paul.
8. Wingate, B. A., and M. J. Christie. 1978. Ego strength and body image in anorexia nervosa. *J. Psychosom. Res.* 22:201-4.
9. Richardson, S. A., A. H. Hastorf, N. Goodman, and S. M. Dornbusch. 1961. Cultural uniformity in reaction to physical disabilities. *Am. Soc. Rev.* 26:241-47.
10. Staffieri, J. R. 1967. A study of social stereotype of body image in children. *J. Pers. Soc. Psych.* 7:101-4.
11. Felker, D. W. 1972. Social stereotyping of male and female body types with differing facial expressions by elementary age boys and girls. *J. Psychol.* 82:151-54.
12. Bayer, L. M., D. Whissell-Buechy, and M. P. Honzik. 1980. Adolescent health and personality: Significance for adult health. *J. Adol. Health Care* 1:101-7.
13. American Psychiatric Association. 1980. *Diagnostic and statistical manual of mental disorders.* 3rd ed. Washington, D.C.
14. Jones, D. J., M. M. Fox, H, M. Babigian, and H. E. Hutton. 1980. Epidemiology of anorexia nervosa in Monroe County, New York: 1960-76. *Psychosom. Med.* 42:551-57.

15. Rosenthal, H ., P. C. Baker, W. A. McVey, eds. 1949. *Stein's applied dietetics.* 3rd ed. Baltimore: Williams and Wilkins.
16. Kelly, J. T., S. E. Patten, and A. Johannes. 1982. Analysis of self-reported eating and related behaviors in an adolescent populations. *Nutr. Res.* 2:417-32.

Contributors

Elke D. Eckert, M.D.
Associate Professor
Department of Psychiatry
University of Minnesota Medical
  School
Minneapolis, Minnesota

Gretchen M. Goff, M.P.H.
Coordinator
Bulimia Intensive Treatment
  Program
Department of Psychiatry
University of Minnesota Medical
  School
Minneapolis, Minnesota

Dorothy Hatsukami, Ph.D.
Assistant Professor
Department of Psychiatry
University of Minnesota Medical
  School
Minneapolis, Minnesota

Craig Johnson, Ph.D.
Associate Professor
Department of Psychiatry
Northwestern University Medical
  School
Chicago, Illinois

Allan M. Josephson, M.D.
Clinical Assistant Professor
Department of Psychiatry
Division of Child and Adolescent
  Psychiatry

University of Minnesota Medical
  School
Minneapolis, Minnesota
Medical Director
Kiel Clinics

John T. Kelly, M.D., M.P.H.
Professor and Associate Head
Department of Family Practice
  and Community Health
Professor of Psychiatry
Professor, School of Public Health
University of Minnesota
Minneapolis, Minnesota

Leah Labeck, R.N., B.S.N.
Psychiatric Specialist
Department of Psychiatry
University of Minnesota
  Hospitals and Clinics
Minneapolis, Minnesota

James E. Mitchell, M.D.
Associate Professor
Department of Psychiatry
University of Minnesota Medical
  School
Minneapolis, Minnesota

Sonia E. Patten, M.S.
Research Fellow
Department of Family Practice
  and Community Health
University of Minnesota Medical
  School
Minneapolis, Minnesota

Richard L. Pyle, M.D.
Assistant Professor
Department of Psychiatry
University of Minnesota Medical
  School
Minneapolis, Minnesota

Marilyn Stuckey, Ph.D.
Research Associate
Northwestern University Medical
  School
Chicago, Illinois

Index

Index

ANOREXIA NERVOSA AND BULIMIA
JAMES E. MITCHELL, M.D., editor

James E. Mitchell earned his M.D. at Northwestern University, Chicago, in 1972. He
served an internship in internal medicine at
Indiana University Hospitals, Indianapolis,
and a residency in psychiatry at the University
of Minnesota. Mitchell is now associate professor in the department of psychiatry and co-
director (with Elke Eckert) of the eating
disorders program at the University of Minnesota Medical School.